C000071453

The National Concert Hall

at Earlsfort Terrace, Dublin

the
NATIONAL
CONCERT
HALL

an
CEOLÁRAS
NÁISIÚNTA

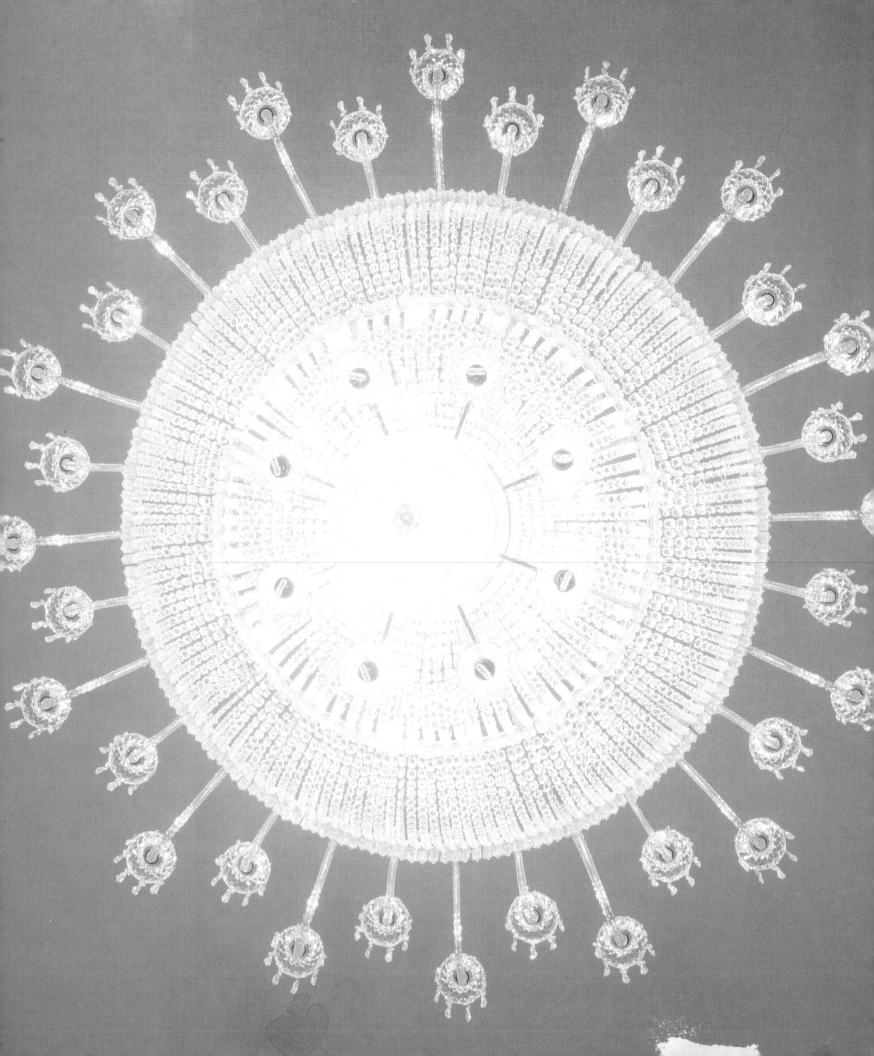

The National Concert Hall

at Earlsfort Terrace, Dublin

A HISTORY

Patricia Butler & Pat O'Kelly

WOLFHOUND PRESS

Throughout its long history, G&T Crampton Ltd has earned a reputation for high-quality construction and development work. Founded in 1879, G&T Crampton is associated with some of Dublin's most celebrated buildings, including the National Concert Hall. G&T Crampton Ltd built the new university buildings at Earlsfort Terrace in 1914, and in 1981 undertook the restoration work for the National Concert Hall.

The National Concert Hall and the Publishers acknowledge, with gratitude, the financial support of G&T Crampton for this publication.

First published in 2000 by
Wolfhound Press Ltd
68 Mountjoy Square
Dublin 1, Ireland
Tel: (353-1) 874 0354
Fax: (353-1) 872 0207

© Text: Patricia Butler and Pat O'Kelly

British Library Cataloguing in Publication Data

A catalogue record for this book is available from the British Library.

ISBN 0-86327-825-6

5 4 3 2 1

Front Cover Photo: Façade of the National Concert Hall
(Photo: Eugene Langan)
Back Cover Photo: Detail of the Kenneth Jones organ at the NCH
(Photo: Eugene Langan)
Editorial Consultant: Roberta Reeners
Design: Red Dog
Printed and bound in Spain by Estudios Gráficos Zure

All rights reserved. No part of this book may be reproduced or utilised in any form or by any means digital, electronic or mechanical including photography, filming, video recording, photocopying, or by any information storage and retrieval system or shall not, by way of trade or otherwise, be lent, resold or otherwise circulated in any form of binding or cover other than that in which it is published without prior permission in writing from the publisher.

The publishers have made every reasonable effort to contact the copyright holders of photographs and other images reproduced in this book. If any involuntary infringement of copyright has occurred, sincere apologies are offered and the owners of such copyright are requested to contact the publishers.

Contents

march

Brendan Kennelly

'Take me down to the house in the glen' she said.
'I want to listen to the March sea
where the voices of all my living and dead
come home to me.
Fourteen families lived in the glen,
they made their way
through good times and bad times,
living the best they could. What more can I say?

The Piper McCarthy fed wife and children,
playing his pipes all over North Kerry
in hungry times. His music was gold.

Gold was the music played in the glen
when the mad Atlantic danced in the dark.
Is it any wonder I never feel old?'

This poem was commissioned by the National Concert Hall for its Millennium 2000 Calendar, sponsored by ACC Bank and TSB Bank.

Foreword

'When an attendant lays out a paper in Latin

As a fervid concentration descends,

A tuned-in orchestra hushed under the baton.'

It is difficult for me to enter the auditorium of the National Concert Hall without the image of some of its earlier existence being present to the inner eye. My most predominant recollection of this impressive space is as the Great Hall when the main home of University College Dublin was in Earlsfort Terrace. It is probably the fact that it served as an examination hall that imprints it so firmly on the mind. The serried rows of lonely desks, the silent distribution of examination papers and the seemingly immediate 'time is up now' as manuscripts were collected – rich material for Kafkaesque recollection or for poetic reflection such as Micheal O'Siadhail's 'Rite of Passage' quoted below. But the Hall holds other memories from those times – canvassing, successfully, on my own behalf for votes on polling day in the elections to the Students' Representative Council; being involved in a group which organised a concert in the hall by Seán Ó Riada and Ceoltóirí Chualann, a series of events which represented something of an alternative to the more official marking of the anniversary of the founding of the NUI; the daring presence in, I think, 1967, of the first small group of women to wear trousers in the Terrace – hitherto firmly banned; conferring, with the Mammy journeying from Adare to be in attendance.

Then, as now, the hall was the centre of a wonderful complex. Where Paddy Keogh presided over the Porters' Desk is now the restaurant under the management of The Commons, appropriate too, since their main restaurant is located in the basement of Newman House, better remembered by my generation as a student canteen where one-third pint bottles of milk and fern cakes from Kylemore were staple fare.

The gradual exodus of the university to the new campus in Belfield opened up the possibility of a new life for Earlsfort Terrace and its Great Hall. Music-lovers had long-awaited the Concert Hall promised as the State's tribute and memorial to the late John Fitzgerald Kennedy. However, the resources and self-confidence which Ireland enjoys today were not the defining characteristics of our community in the 1960s and 70s. Ultimately, it was something of a compromise that the choice was made to locate the new National Concert Hall in Earlsfort Terrace. It may not have been a perfect location but, as we know to our cost, the perfect can often be the enemy of the good. The years since have breathed new life into a fine building, have laid down a new store of memories, have created something new for a new generation and enriched the musical life of the capital city and of the country as a whole.

I have many fond recollections over the past twenty years – from the opening Gala concert, the premiere of my late friend and colleague Gerry Victory's Ultima Rerum (I remember in the noisy enthusiasm after the performance his hearing me describe his work as 'a rouser' when, speaking in Irish as we often did, I had described it as being *ar fheabhas ar fad*, ie brilliant), the inauguration by Gerard Gillen of the new Kenneth Jones organ, the RTÉ Young Musician of the Future, the Dublin International Piano Competition and countless other evenings of musical wonder.

One of the National Concert Hall's principal functions was to provide a home for the RTÉ National Symphony Orchestra. They have distinguished themselves on so many occasions since in the annual series of subscription concerts. It was entirely fitting that the celebration of the fiftieth anniversary of the founding of the Symphony Orchestra should take place in this hall and it was a particular pleasure for me to be the Director-General of RTÉ to whom fell the duty to pay public and well-deserved tribute to all the players over that half century of service to music in Ireland. Music-making has long been a central part of RTÉ's purpose and it continues to be a mainstay of the contribution which RTÉ makes to its audience as a public service broadcaster. The performing groups in their public performance, in their broadcast work and in their reaching out to communities and events throughout Ireland have made themselves an indispensable part of the expression of the cultural life of Ireland. Each of them has graced the platform of this hall with distinction.

It is good to take advantage of occasions such as this to reflect on what has been achieved, to look back on the efforts of visionaries and the fruits of fortune which have given us the architectural inheritance which we enjoy today and, more importantly, to look to the future with expectation and confidence, knowing that the place of music in the life of Ireland is secure.

Tá stair iontach ag baint leis an Áras seo. Is iomaí feidhm a baineadh as agus bhí tionchar nach beag aige ar shaol na nglúnta. Fiche bliain ag fás atá sé mar Cheoláras Náisiúnta agus is fiú comóradh a dhéanamh air sin. Ghlac buíonta ceoil RTÉ páirt lárnach san obair le linn na tréimhse sin. Rath buan bisiúil go raibh ar an gCeoláras, agus ar an gceol in Éirinn, sa ré atá le teacht.

Bob Collins

Director General, RTÉ

streetscape

Micheal O'Siadhail

A street in which our days and bricks conspire
And walls have ears to hear and make their own
Whole symphonies of remembrance and desire.

Stella Maris vanished as a city began to grow
And boom but still on this honking boulevard
Pillars of what was our exam chamber's portico

That now canopy the doors to a concert hall's
Vestibule. As listeners hush to the raised baton
A silence of nervous memory echoes in its walls.

Lives cast in the light and tenor of a streetscape
That gathers up our musics in stick and stone.
Our shells and selves shaped by what we shape.

Earlsfort Suite is a set of three songs for mezzo and orchestra, commissioned by Dúchas, The Heritage Service, to celebrate the National Concert Hall. It is the final piece in Ceol Reoite (Frozen Music), a series of fifteen musical commissions celebrating important buildings and historic properties in Ireland. The poems for this set of songs were specially written by the poet Micheal O'Siadhail, to music by Seóirse Bodley.

Introduction

An Ceoláras Náisiúnta is one of the nation's finest cultural assets, occupying a landmark building in the centre of Dublin. Over the twenty years of its existence, it has initiated and developed a diversity of music-making. In the classical repertoire, it has placed Ireland on the world stage for international performers and orchestras. The musical activities at the National Concert Hall reflect a sense of pride in the achievement of Irish musicians and composers, and display our cultural identity within the European community.

Prior to the foundation of the National Concert Hall, many dedicated people shared the dream and aspiration that a concert hall and home for the National Symphony Orchestra would be realised some day. We are delighted that their wonderful commitment and persistence is recognised and recorded in this history of the NCH. We owe them all a great debt of gratitude. The work and achievement of Boards of Management and staff members over the years are also highlighted and we feel privileged and fortunate to have the opportunity of building on those developments. During the tenure of the fourth Board, we have had the wholehearted support of Ministers Michael D. Higgins and Síle de Valera (Department of Arts, Heritage, Gaeltacht and the Islands). Due to their commitment past and present, we hope to achieve our next major goal of a Second Recital Hall in Earlsfort Terrace. We have been working closely with the OPW on this and other projects and we would like to record their continued professional and enthusiastic help in the development of the National Concert Hall. G&T Crampton Ltd provided the financial support for this book, which seemed particularly appropriate to us as they were the chosen builders for the restoration of the NCH in 1981, as well as being the builder of new university buildings in 1914. We thank them for their generous sponsorship.

Finally, we would like to warmly thank our authors, Pat O'Kelly and Patricia Butler. We think they have added something very special to the history of cultural and musical life in Ireland. We hope music and history lovers everywhere will enjoy it.

Dermot Egan, Chairman, National Concert Hall

Judith Woodworth, Director, National Concert Hall

CHAPTER 1
THE SETTING

The history of the National Concert Hall on Dublin's Earlsfort Terrace is a long and fascinating one. It is, in a way, the story of Dublin from the seventeenth century to this day. To put the National Concert Hall into perspective, it is first necessary to go back to the 1600s and view the development of St Stephen's Green and Earlsfort Terrace in the context of the time – along with those who shaped those times.

St Stephen's Green

In order to understand the history and importance of the site of the National Concert Hall and its immediate surroundings, one must begin with St Stephen's Green, and in particular the buildings on the south side.

St Stephen's Green may have taken its name from the Leper Hospital of St Stephen which had been sited at the north-western end of this common pasture.[1] The Green itself is first shown on Sir William Petty's 1655 *Down Survey of Dublin and its Environs* as an area of unenclosed, marshy, common ground. Consisting of around sixty acres, it was the property of Dublin Corporation.

In the earliest days of its known history, the Green area of St Stephen was used mainly as a common for pasturing livestock. This right was confined to the free citizens of Dublin as laid down in an Act of the City Council (1577)[2] which stated: 'that none shall with their cattle pasture the commons but free citezens...'. In the second half of the seventeenth century, as a result of the battles of the Confederation and the ravages of Cromwell, the treasury of the city was in a state of exhaustion and suffering from an acute shortage of funds. The Dublin City Assembly of Easter 1663 met to consider

how that by reason of the late rebellion and long continud troubles of this kingdome the threasury of this cittie is cleerly exhausted and the yearly revenue thereof is reduced to little or nothing.[3]

It was agreed, in order to raise money, to augment their yearly revenue: 'the outskerts of Saint Stephen's Greene and other wast lands about this cittie, that now addeth nothing att all to pleasure or profitt...' should be let for a term of ninety-nine years.

The committee appointed for this purpose reported to the Michaelmas Assembly of 1663[4] that seventeen acres had been surveyed by a Captain Robert Newcomen and could be set for a yearly rent.[5] The land in question was divided into eighty-nine plots which were distributed by ballot to a wide cross-section of Dublin's citizens – including nineteen committee members who had been engaged in the original transaction. Brewers, maltsters, masons, bakers, vintners, butchers, gentlemen, alderman, tallow-chandlers, cutlers, tanners and three knights all became owners of plots which measured approximately sixty feet in width, each one varying in depth but each one possessing frontage onto the Green.[6] Each new holder had to pay a ground rent of one penny per square foot on the north, east and west sides, and one halfpenny for those on the south side. Lessees were not required to build, but if they did, any houses built on the plots were to be of brick, stone and timber, with at least two floors or lofts, and covered with tiles or slates. They were not to be built of the perishable mud or wattle 'cage-work' prevalent in Dublin at that time. (This would appear to be Dublin's first venture upon the stormy sea of town-planning.)

Thus, in the 1660s, the central part of the Green consisted of around thirty acres and was considered to be one of the largest 'squares' in Europe. This area was marked out by Dublin Corporation to be preserved as an open space to be used for the pasturage of citizens' cattle and horses. Improvements were paid for by the ground rents. The area

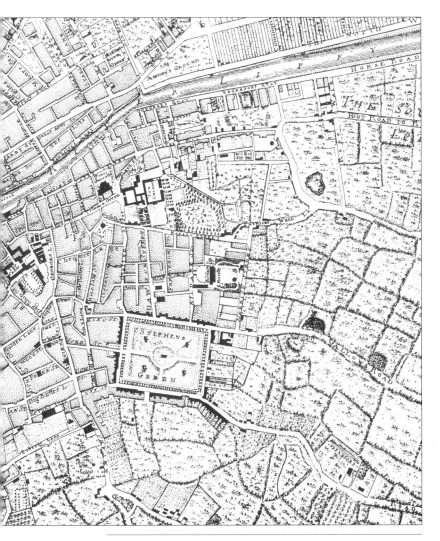

St Stephen's Green and the surrounding area of Dublin, from John Rogue's map of 1756. (Gilbert Collection)

was planted with trees, and further enhanced by a condition which required plot-holders to plant six sycamore trees along the edge of the Green.

In 1669, the area was surrounded by a 4½ foot stone wall, inside of which a ditch was dug to drain the swampy ground. On either side of the ditch, a thirty-five foot wide walk was laid out. Later on, in the eighteenth century, these walks were extended to include the famous Beaux Walk on the north, Monk's Walk on the east, Leeson's Walk on the south and French Walk on the west. The inner grass walks were planted with hawthorn hedges, while the outer walk was made of gravel and lined with lime trees. Outside these walks was the public roadway; just inside this was a ha-ha, the purpose of which was to protect the Corporation's grazing.

Bernard de Gomme's map of Dublin reveals that, by 1673, a sprinkling of townhouses had already begun to surround the Green which would, in time, transform it into one of the most elegant squares in Europe.

As a fashionable promenading area, the heyday of the Green was from the middle to the end of the eighteenth century. Described as 'a place of public resort especially on Sundays when the nobility and gentry take the air and parade in their carriages', the walk along the north side – Beaux Walk – became a fashionable promenade. This 'scene of elegance and taste'[7] was well captured in James Malton's (c.1760-1803) view of 1796. It also shows the equestrian statue of George II by John Van Nost, the Younger, elevated on an extraordinarily high pedestal and unveiled in 1758.[8]

Writing to Stella from London as early as 1711, Dean Jonathan Swift enquired:

Why don't you walk in the Green of St Stephen's, the walks are finer gravelled than the mall?

Mrs Pendarves (1700-1788), later the wife of Dr Patrick Delany[9] who was a friend of Dean Swift, had nothing but praise:

I think it may be preferred justly to any square in London on the north side of St Stephen's Green which resembles that in St James's Park, London.

Military displays, concerts, exercising of troops and political gatherings made the Green a focal point for mass entertainment in the city in the eighteenth century. James Malton's view of 1796 shows St Stephen's Green at its most fashionable. However, by 1814, decay had set in and

the hedge was ragged and gapped, and the ditch covered in green duckweed... the double row of elm and lime trees mostly gone.

The principal entrance to the Green, a gateway of four piers of black stone, was on the west side and faced York Street. It too had fallen into disrepair, along with the road leading to it. As a result of agitation by many of Dublin's citizens who held the Green in great affection, an Act was put through parliament in 1814 for the improvement of the square. Under this Act, commissioners were appointed who proceeded to level and drain the central area, plant trees and shrubs, remove decaying trees and plant new ones, form walks, fill in the ditch and remove the wall erected in 1669, and surround the entire area with iron railings. The total cost exceeded £8,000. The old formal avenues were replaced by gardens designed according to the basic principles of the 'Picturesque' style, with serpentine walks, clumps and spinneys of shrubs and evergreens. The gardens of the Green were enclosed with high cast-iron railings and locked gates which could only be opened by house-owners (provided they paid a fee) who lived in houses around the square. As a result, the

St Stephen's Green, Dublin. The 'Beaux Walk' with, in the mid-distance, a view of Van Nost's statue of George II. James Malton (c.1760-1803). Aquatint and etching. Published London 1796. (Courtesy of the National Gallery of Ireland)

Green effectively became private property, a private park which was closed off to the citizens of Dublin. This provoked strong resentment and agitation by Dubliners who sought to have the area opened once again to the public. Their efforts, however, were opposed by the commissioners and by Dublin Corporation.

In 1876, Sir Arthur Guinness (1840-1915), MP for the city, made a cash offer to the commissioners, which was accepted, for reopening the park. The following year, the St Stephen's Green (Dublin) Act was passed which resulted in the Green being freely available to the citizens of Dublin once again. Responsibility for its upkeep was placed in the hands of the Board of Works (now the Office of Public Works), and in whose care it remains to this day.

Guinness undertook the conversion of the park with verve and enthusiasm, transforming it into the elegant, beautiful Green that we know and enjoy today. Assisted by the civil engineer, A.L. Cousins, Guinness designed much of the layout himself. An ornamental lake with a rockery cascade was created, the water coming from the Grand Canal at Portobello and drained at Huband bridge. J.F. Fuller (1835-1924) designed a keeper's lodge and 'Swiss' shelters. To commemorate the generosity of Sir Arthur Guinness (created Baron Ardilaun in May 1880), the citizens of Dublin erected a statue to him in 1892. On the west side of St Stephen's Green, it is still there today.

Leeson's Fields

During the latter part of the seventeenth century, many of the plots leased from Dublin Corporation and situated on the south side of the Green were to have a direct influence on the National Concert Hall site and adjoining areas. By 1664, Hugh Leeson (1620-1700), founder of the 'Milltown Leeson' dynasty and described as 'of Culworth, Northamptonshire',[10] had become the owner of a number of sites around the square, including No. 5 South, later to become known as 82 St Stephen's Green.[11]

It was on this site that Hugh Leeson built his fashionable townhouse with its extensive gardens at the rear. Here, too, he erected his large and 'great brewery'. This land was known as 'Leeson's Fields' and through it ran the city boundary. Hugh's only son, Joseph (1660-1741), continued in the family business and demonstrated an extraordinary ability to increase his family's wealth, particularly in the area of real estate. The Dean of St Patrick's Cathedral, Jonathan Swift, disapproved, and described him as a 'fanatic brewer, reported to have some hundreds of houses in this town'.[12] Joseph died in 1741, leaving his only surviving son, also called Joseph (1711-1783) and later to become 1st Earl of Milltown, a vast fortune, part of which he used to build Russborough House in Co. Wicklow.[13] However, before his death, the elder Joseph Leeson had succeeded in letting the 'brew-house, malt-house, kilns, store-house, granaries, mill, and ponds in the rear thereof'[14] to a Patrick Sweetman, brewer, for thirty-one years.[15]

In 1777, Harcourt Street[16] was built southwards from the south-west corner of St Stephen's Green. With its graceful, gentle curve laid out partly for beauty and partly for geological reasons,[17] the first house to be built there was Clonmell House, now 17 Harcourt Street, in 1778. Clonmell House was built for 'Copper-faced' Jack Scott (John Scott, 1st Earl of Clonmell 1739-1798),[18] whose 'somewhat precarious dignity it was designed to support', according to Dr Maurice Craig.[19] As a lawyer, Scott had risen through the ranks with alarming speed and in just ten years had become Lord Chief Justice of Ireland. His

Joseph Leeson, later 1st Earl of Milltown, 1744 (1711-1783). Pompeo Batoni (1708-1787). Oil on canvas. (Courtesy of the National Gallery of Ireland)

friend, collaborator and fellow-scoundrel was the infamous 'Buck' Whaley, whose house on the south side of St Stephen's Green (No. 85) backed on to 'Leeson's Fields'. Scott's wealth stemmed largely from lands which he held in trust for Catholics who, until 1778, were not legally allowed to hold land. Dishonouring these agreem... was noted for 'swearing, sloth, gross eating, exc... drinking and indolence, [and] needed a couple of ab... bodied lackies to carry him home nightly to bed'.[20]

Scott was anxious to acquire a garden as a suitable appendage for his fine Harcourt Street townhouse.[21] In 1782, he approached Richard, Archbishop of Dublin, to see if it might be possible to lease part of the farm of St Sepulchre. This land eventually become known as the Coburg – or Cobourg – Gardens. Today, it is referred to as the Iveagh Gardens and is situated directly behind the National Concert Hall.

The archbishop agreed, and Scott was given permission to lease some 9¾ acres for forty years at an annual rent of £22/4/9d.[22] Scott also purchased eleven acres of 'Leeson's Fields' from the Leeson family. Both tracts of land lay on the east side of Harcourt Street, so in order to reach it, Scott built a subterranean passage (no longer in existence) from one of the (now) demolished wings of Clonmell House, with two entrances into the 'Fields'. A Dublin city map dated 1797 names the area as 'Lord Earlsfort's Lawn', after Scott's first title, Baron Earlsfort.[23]

The Coburg Gardens

In 1817, 'Lord Earlsfort's Lawn' was opened to the public and renamed the Coburg (or Cobourg) Gardens. The name was possibly suggested by the marriage in 1816 between Princess Charlotte, daughter of George, Prince of Wales (later King George IV), and Prince Leopold of Saxe-

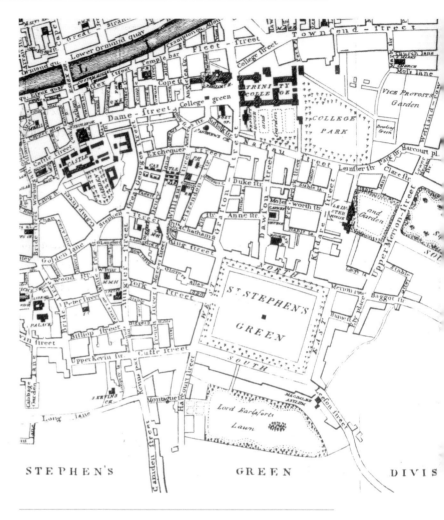

A map of Dublin city, dated 1789, showing 'Lord Earlsfort's Lawn'.

Coburg.[24] The gardens soon began to occupy a fashionable position among Dublin's upper-class citizens. There were two entrances – one from Harcourt Street, the other through the Royal Horse Bazaar at 94 St Stephen's Green in the approximate location of Stokes' Place today.

The gardens continued to prosper and on 20 June 1828, a grand evening show was held to commemorate the Battle of Waterloo. Another event in the summer of 1830 celebrated the coronation of King William IV. On this occasion:

...some splendid 'set pieces', then, no doubt a great novelty were announced for the conclusion of the fireworks display – one of which was to represent the Battle of Navarino, and the destruction of the Turkish fleet, with the burning and exploding of five ships, with usual accompaniment of bombarding, cannonading, and other great noises, which might fairly have alarmed the inhabitants of the district... A fine stage was erected... in the Cobourg Gardens on this night for spectators to see the fireworks from, and part of the green was mowed and boarded likewise for their comfort. [Parties were also informed that] a strong force of military, horse and foot, will be stationed round the gardens, and ladies need not apprehend the least inconvenience from the presence of the crowd.

Some of the fireworks seen on that summer night were:

...blue Turkey lights, rattlesnakes, a grand fountain of Palestine fire, fiery pigeons, a beautiful Chinese pyramid, a Prussian mill, a superb yew tree, a grand Malta piece with changing coloured fire, a spiral wheel representing fiery serpents in chase with a Salamander... The finale exceeded all expectations with a correct representation of a volcanic eruption of Mount Vesuvius.[25]

Later, the gardens were the setting for political gatherings. In his 1865 guide book to Dublin, W.F. Wakeman commented that:

This tract had long lain waste, and years ago was used as the scene of more than one of those celebrated open-air demonstrations which characterised the O'Connell agitation.[26]

By the 1830s, however, the popularity of the Coburg Gardens was in decline and on 4 August 1836, these extensive pleasure grounds reverted to Thomas, 2nd Earl of Clonmell.[27] Clonmell appears to have been in favour of encouraging plans to build a new street, to be called Clonmell Street, which would cut across the gardens. However, other developments were underway which would have a considerable influence on the area. These were set in motion by the Wide Streets Commission, a committee of powerful and influential gentlemen and peers who displayed a scale and consistency of vision remarkable in the late nineteenth century.

Among the projects of the Commission was 'the making of wide and convenient streets', i.e. developing new thoroughfares through the fabric of the city of Dublin. In 1839, they removed a row of gabled houses, numbers 62-65 inclusive,[28] at the meeting point of Leeson Street and St Stephen's Green South. A Commission map dated 1837 shows the 'Intended New Street' extending from the corners of St Stephen's Green South and Leeson Street to the proposed Clonmell Street. Upon its completion in 1839, the 'Intended New Street' was named Earlsfort Terrace, after a title in the Earl of Clonmell's family. This succeeded in opening up the terrace.[29]

By 1841, two houses had been completed at Earlsfort Terrace. A year later, Lord Clonmell sold part of the land adjoining the terrace to Thomas Lefroy, a barrister who in turn erected three more houses. Part of their agreement was that Clonmell should build a road from Harcourt Street to Earlsfort Terrace which would cross the Coburg Gardens. However, Clonmell Street never materialised beyond its present form, i.e. extending a few hundred metres east of Harcourt Street.[30]

Iveagh House

A 'key' building in relation to the site of the National Concert Hall at Earlsfort Terrace is 80 St Stephen's Green, now known as Iveagh House. Situated on the south side of the Green, it was built for antiquarian, philosopher and Protestant bishop, Doctor Robert Clayton.[31] A man who succeeded in 'uniting the dignity of the ecclesiastic with the ease of the fine gentleman',[32] Clayton was an ambitious cleric who eagerly sought the limelight within Dublin's influential society. He fell rapidly from favour, however, when he publicly disputed various aspects of the doctrine of the Holy Trinity.[33]

Bishop Clayton's townhouse is believed to be the work of the German-born architect-engineer, Richard Castle (c.1690-1751), and was his first such commission. Begun in the latter half of 1736, it was probably not completed until the spring of 1737. A handsome house which was three bays wide, it consisted of three storeys over a basement. To the left of the house, a carriageway led to the stables and coach-house at the rear. To the right was a two-storeyed projection containing the end portions of rooms which overlooked the garden. The basement and ground floor were of cut stone; above the first-floor level, the façade was of brick dressed with stone. A four-columned entrance portico was spread across the width of the front façade. This may have been influenced by architect Inigo Jones' work, as seen in his design for St Paul's Church, Covent Garden, London, a building admired by Castle.

On a visit to the Claytons in September 1731, Mrs Mary Delany (in a letter to her sister in England) compared the façade of the bishop's house in Dublin to Devonshire House, saying it was '...very magnificent but more for show than comfortable living ...'.[34]

The bishop's wife was one of the most fashionable members of eighteenth-century Dublin society and gave splendid entertainments in her house on the Green. Fond of show, her coach was drawn by six powerful Flanders mares, surpassing all her neighbours, including the Lord

Iveagh House, St Stephen's Green, Dublin, former home of the Guinness family and now the Department of Foreign Affairs. Pat Liddy. Pencil on paper. (Courtesy of the National Library of Ireland)

Lieutenant himself. When her husband died in 1758, the house was purchased from his widow by Stephen, 2nd Earl of Mountcashel. He remained there only a few years,

Dr Robert Clayton, Bishop of Cork and Ross, and his wife, Catherine, the first occupants of Iveagh House. James Latham (1696-1747). Oil on canvas. (Courtesy of the National Gallery of Ireland)

selling it in 1807. In 1809, it was bought for £3,000 by John Philpot Curran, noted wit, parliamentarian, barrister and orator. On his resignation as Master of the Rolls in 1814, Curran sold the house to his successor, the Rt Hon. Sir William McMahon, after which it passed into the hands of another barrister and eventual Justice of the King's Bench, Charles Burton. The latter died in 1847, and Burton's son-in-law, a barrister named Robert Beatty West, owned the house for a few years. West's debts were numerous, so on his death, the property passed to the Commissioners of Encumbered Estates.

Alterations and additions to Bishop Clayton's original eighteenth-century house began when Benjamin Lee Guinness purchased it from the Commissioners at the bargain price of £2,500 in May 1856. The process was well underway in 1862 when Guinness acquired the leasehold of the house next door, 81 St Stephen's Green. This was dismantled, and its site eventually used to enlarge the original house, in effect doubling its size. In order to unify the original house and the addition, a façade of Portland stone was added.

The second stage of alterations began in 1880 and lasted until 1884, with additions on the other side of the building being carried out for Edward Guinness. A complete remodelling of 79, under the guidance of architect J.F. Fuller, led to the complete rebuilding of the house. The next phase took place in 1884 when 78 was purchased, rebuilt and made to form a symmetrical pair with 79.

The end result was one large townhouse suitable for Guinness to entertain on a lavish scale. A vast ballroom, built in the most ostentatious classical style, was added in 1896. Designed by the Glasgow-born architect, William Young (1843-1900), its execution was supervised by the Irish architect, Sir Thomas Drew (1838-1910).

Three generations of the Guinness family continued to use Iveagh House on the Green, as well as Farmleigh, Castleknock, as their Dublin residences until the late 1930s. In 1939, the 2nd Earl of Iveagh (1874-1967) generously offered Iveagh House and its gardens to the Irish nation,[35] a gift which the Taoiseach, Éamon de Valera, formally accepted on 19 May 1939. In December of that year, it was allocated to the Department of External Affairs (renamed the Department of Foreign Affairs in 1969). A number of small alterations were added, including an office wing, in 1949. A scheme of refurbishing was carried out in the early 1950s under the direction of the principal architect at the Office of Public Works, Raymond McGrath (1903-1977). Today, Iveagh House carries on the tradition of entertaining, with receptions, political gatherings and heads of state enjoying the magnificent surroundings of this great house on the Green.

The Changing Face of Coburg Gardens

Through the years, the Coburg Gardens fell into neglect until the field at the rear of 80 St Stephen's Green was purchased by Benjamin Lee Guinness. As early as 1860, Guinness had been keen to acquire a rear garden for his house. In a letter from the Earl of Clonmell's agent dated 17 August 1860, Guinness was asked to decide if he preferred a lease of the Coburg Gardens in perpetuity or an assignment of the property. After lengthy negotiations, an indenture was drawn up on 4 April 1862, stating that part of the land of St Sepulchre (Coburg Gardens) was to be sold for £18,896 by Henry, Earl of Clonmell, to Benjamin Lee Guinness with no restriction on the agreement with regard to future buildings on the site.[36] The arrangement was ultimately successful and as a result,

Benjamin Lee Guinness acquired a garden which not only protected his privacy but also prevented the proposed Clonmell Street from being opened up from Harcourt Street.

When Guinness purchased the Coburg Gardens,[37] they had deteriorated to such an extent that they were no more than a large field divided by a high stone wall where:

> ... *sheep were allowed to graze. Heaps of rubbish were thrown in several parts of it, and nothing remained to show that it had ever been at one time a thickly-wooded pleasure ground, save the projecting roots of large trees, and one venerable elm, which now stands as the only remnant of the once famous Cobourg Gardens.*[38]

By April 1863, a complete remodelling of the gardens at Earlsfort Terrace was well underway. The task was undertaken by Scotsman, Ninian Niven (*c.*1799-1879), landscape architect and curator of the (Royal) Botanic Gardens at Glasnevin between 1834-38. Born at Kelvin Grove near Glasgow, Niven came from a family preoccupied with gardening; his father had been gardener at Keir House near Stirling. Niven served his apprenticeship at Bothwell Castle and Belladrum House, Inverness-shire, before coming to Ireland in 1827 as head gardener at the Chief Secretary's Lodge in Phoenix Park. After practising as 'Professor of Landscape Gardening' and designing gardens which included Baronscourt, Santry Court, Templeogue House, the People's Park in Phoenix Park and Monkstown Public Park, he was invited to join the team engaged in designing and laying out the gardens for the Dublin International Exhibition which was scheduled to open at Earlsfort Terrace in May 1865.

Also working with Ninian Niven was Julius Wilhelm Keit (1841-1916) who had trained in horticulture in Dresden and worked as a gardener at Wessenstein, Nurenberg and

Linden's nursery in Brussels in the early 1860s. Arriving in Ireland in 1865,[39] Keit acted as supervisor and Niven as designer.

The challenge for Niven was the complete remodelling of what was almost a derelict site. Niven's objective was to demonstrate the art of the Victorian landscape architect, with the gardens being asked to serve many purposes – recreational, sporting, exhibition, botanical and landscaping. As early as 1863, Niven's intended design for the grounds, the 'Palace Park', had been published in a supplement to *The Irish Farmer's Gazette*. With minor adaptations, this was to be the blueprint.

Niven began by surrounding the site with 'moundings', an unusual approach for this landscape architect as it was the only garden designed by him which did not act as the foreground to a distant view. Large amounts of earth were thrown up which had been excavated from the sunken gardens.[40] These were used to break up the flat surface of the site, conceal walled boundaries of adjoining gardens, and screen ugly buildings from view. Numerous tall pines were planted on these high banks at the western end to 'conceal the gables and the unromantic stables of the houses in Harcourt Street'.[41]

A formal French layout was chosen for the central portion of the garden because of its capacity to facilitate the great crowds which would undoubtedly throng to the Great Dublin International Exhibition of 1865. (While on a visit to Paris at the end of the 1830s, Niven had been impressed by this formal style of gardening popular in France.) Avenues, statues and fountains with a cataract on the main axis were some of the principal features which have largely remained unchanged to this day.

From the apse at the rear (west) of the Exhibition's proposed glass and iron building, to be known as   the

Winter Garden, a spacious, raised terrace traversed the garden. On either side were sunken panels resplendent with flowers around raised circular basins. At the centre of this, the Goddesses of Arts and Industry held torches aloft from which *jets d'eau* reached skyward, falling in droplets at the spectators' feet.[42] At the end of the broad avenue which led towards the western boundary of the gardens, the vista terminated in a spectacular cascade which sprang from a grotto or *rocher* (rock-work). (This has recently been restored and is functioning once again.) The inspiration for both the cascade and the *rocher* probably derived from Hubert Robert's *Bains d'Apollo* at the Chateau de Versailles where river gods disported themselves in a series of rocky niches sited at various levels, while shimmering water descended from the upper levels into the pool below. The scheme to illuminate the water

'The Cascade', Ninian Niven's dominating feature in the Coburg Gardens (the Iveagh Gardens) for the 1865 Exhibition. This has been restored by the OPW and is functioning once again today. (Illustrated Record)

using a variety of coloured lights would appear to have been adapted from Le Notre's unexecuted plan for the *parterre d'eau*, also designed for Versailles.

Niven's cascade, with the capacity to pump 1,400 gallons of water per minute, was supplied from the shallow boating lake constructed at the rear of Benjamin Lee Guinness' Iveagh House. It was described in the *Dublin Builder* on 15 June 1863.

As a terminus to the central broad walk of terraced promenade, a capacious basin is being made some 80 feet across to be constructed in rustic or rockwork fashion, so that, from a second basin of minor dimensions, elevated about 14 feet to 16 feet, an overfall cascade of water will be projected, and so constructed, that it may at pleasure, with facility, be illuminated, possibly in various colours.

A further description in the *Dublin Builder* of November 1863 states:

The grotto is flanked at either side by two exquisitely constructed rustic arches, leading to flights of spiral steps by which the top of the grotto is reached. The arched entrances are more effective than those of a similar kind which are in the Bois de Boulogne.

This small lake behind Iveagh House provided the water for the fountains of the pleasure gardens and also acted as a boundary behind and between Benjamin Lee Guinness'

land and the pleasure gardens. A small pavilion built of Bath stone was erected as a boat-house (in the private garden of Iveagh House) and dates from this period. It was designed as a centrepiece for the small lake, possibly by Benjamin Lee Guinness himself, and is a miniature of the oratory found on the island of Innisfallen, Co. Kerry.

Adjacent to the lake, and on the north side of the gardens close to St Stephen's Green, there was – and still is – a three-acre archery ground which, when flooded in winter, was to act as a skating rink.[43] The original intention may have been to waterproof the base and sides before adding water and allowing it to freeze. Given its quick-draining capacity and the uncertainty of the weather, it is doubtful whether the area ever fulfilled this function.[44]

The Pavilion, built of Bath stone, Coburg Gardens (the Iveagh Gardens). It was erected c.1863, probably to the design of Benjamin Lee Guinness. This area now forms part of the rear garden of Iveagh House (the Department of Foreign Affairs). (Illustrated London News, May 1865)

The Grand National Archery Fete held in the Exhibition Gardens at Earlsfort Terrace. (Illustrated London New, 6 May 1865)

In Victorian times, archery enjoyed a new lease of life and two major competitions were held here in 1865. In May/June, the Irish Grand National Archery Club held its fourth annual meeting at the grounds, and in September, the Leinster Archery Society also met. The star of the former event was the formidable Miss Betham who had been declared 'Championess of England', having earned the title by winning every competition she entered in both 1864 and 1865.

Along the southern boundary, the 'American grounds' were laid out with North American species and 'planted with rhododendrons and other natives of the western Continent'.[45] Adjoining this was a miniature maze, inspired by the Tudor maze at Hampton Court, London. An attractive rose garden with a geometrical arrangement of alternating circular and chimney-stack beds was also included in this area, together with rockeries of polished granite from Dalkey, Co. Dublin – and an elm tree, which survives to this day as the only reminder of the Earl of Clonmell's Lawn.

Advancing northwards, and parallel to the glass and iron building built for the 1865 Exhibition, a long, curved terrace united the buildings with the grounds and was bordered and decorated at intervals by 'classical' statues on plinths. These statues (many of which have disappeared) were in locations throughout the gardens and came, it is thought, from various English country estates. It is possible that the two fountain statues representing Industry and Arts may not have been in place for the duration of the 1865 Exhibition, as their locations seem to have been used for displays, one of which possessed the intriguing title: 'Barbezat's Fountain in the Exhibition Garden'.

One of the more curious landscape features of the gardens was the rootery, a concept much beloved by Victorians. The roots were inverted and bedded into embankments which, in turn, would have been thickly planted with an abundance of suitable plant material.

The Harcourt Street entrance to the gardens was via Clonmell Street. An imposing columned portico was built, of which there is no remaining evidence. It is very likely that it was only intended to remain *in situ* for the duration of the exhibition.

Within the confines of this relatively small site, Ninian Niven also managed to include an arboretum, an area for the erection of Turkish tents and a perimeter woodland walk. By the spring of 1865, a remarkable and adventurous Victorian landscape had been created which would provide a splendid setting for the opening of the Great Dublin International Exhibition due to take place on 9 May.

More than seven decades would pass before the 'modern' story of Earlsfort Terrace could be told. It begins in 1937 when Lord Rupert Iveagh, continuing the generosity of the Guinness family, presented the Iveagh Gardens to the Irish nation.

Barbezat's Fountain, a much-admired feature of the 1865 Exhibition.
(Illustrated Record, 1866)

A Gift to the Nation

Once the Earlsfort Terrace site had been transferred to the Royal University of Ireland and then to University College, Dublin,[46] the pressure for space had a direct effect on the Iveagh Gardens and their future. In May 1937,[47] Dr Denis J. Coffey, President of UCD, wrote to Éamon de Valera regarding a rumour that Iveagh House and its grounds were about to be put up for sale. Dr Coffey urged the government to consider the acquisition of the grounds as they 'would form the most perfect situation for acquisition by the college...'. Two years later, on 18 March 1939, Lord Rupert Iveagh wrote this private letter to his secretary, Christopher H. Bland.

Dear Bland,[48]

I have given very careful thought to the suggestion in regard to 80 St Stephen's Green. I appreciate that my use of the house is never likely to be very great... On the whole I have come to the conclusion that if it is to pass out of the possession of my family I would prefer to make a gift of it to the Government on certain conditions: – That the grounds except in so far as they may desire to develop the frontage furthest from the house, for the purpose of adding to the National University, should be left an open space in perpetuity. That those institutions which for many years have been allowed to use the Gardens should continue to have a similar privilege and the frontage of the house on St Stephen's Green as constructed by Sir Benjamin Guinness should be left as it is. The last I understand would be unlikely to stand in the way as I gather that it would not be the intention to demolish the house, but to use at any rate the principal rooms for the purpose of a dwelling house...

It would therefore be my proposition to hand over the house unfurnished, and the land (subject to existing head rents) without payment, my only firm condition being that the Garden should never be built on except as regards the frontage.

Yours very sincerely, IVEAGH [49]

Lord Iveagh's generosity was made official two months later in a letter to de Valera[50] in which he offered both Iveagh House and the grounds to the Irish nation, his only firm condition:

being that the open space should be left as such except in so far as the frontage on Hatch Street may be required for the enlargement of the National University.

Iveagh was also keen to see that institutions such as the Fencing Club and other societies which had used the Iveagh Gardens down through the years should be allowed to hold their annual functions there.[51] His offer generated a rapid response, with de Valera promising to bring his generous gift before the government 'without delay'.[52] On 17 May 1939, the cabinet met and accepted Lord Iveagh's

The Iveagh Gardens today. showing the surrounding developments in recent years. The National Concert Hall is shown bottom right. Inset: the original layout of the Gardens.

proposals and his conditions regarding 80 St Stephen's Green.[53] At the time, there would appear to be no clear understanding as to just what should be done with the Hatch Street frontage which formed part of the Iveagh Gardens.

At the same time, pressure for space in University College was becoming acute. Three days after the cabinet had approved and accepted Lord Iveagh's proposals, the Taoiseach met a sub-committee of UCD's Academic Council led by Dr Coffey.[54] They expressed the hope that at some stage, Iveagh House and its grounds would be made available for college purposes as there was an urgent need for new buildings. The deputation suggested that the transfer of the Engineering and Science Department from the College of Science in Merrion Street would make space available for government offices. De Valera made it clear that the house and its immediate garden would be used for the accommodation of the Department of External Affairs '...for some years to come... for which it was very suitable'. However, he would endeavour to secure that, in taking over the property, the state would not be hampered by any conditions which might, in the future, prevent any part of it being made available for the purposes of UCD if this should 'be in the public interest'.

Shortly after taking office, Dr Coffey's successor, Dr Arthur W. Conway, received a letter from his former pupil, Éamon de Valera. The Taoiseach stated that the government would agree to make a grant available to UCD for the building and equipping of a new Engineering or Science Building on a site adjoining the Hatch Street side of the grounds originally acquired from Lord Iveagh. Once the new building was completed, the existing lease of the College of Science in Merrion Street would be terminated. In addition, the government would also be prepared to lease Lord Iveagh's riding school and the covered court at Earlsfort Terrace to the college but would reserve, on behalf of the state, a right-of-way for traffic to the rear of Iveagh House.

The government would also be willing, de Valera continued, to make arrangements whereby the college would have access to and use of the Iveagh Gardens, other than the small garden sited at the rear of Iveagh House. De Valera also understood that the college authorities wished to establish a passage through the gardens from 86 St Stephen's Green to the college buildings at Earlsfort Terrace.

In an effort to uphold these proposals, de Valera wrote to Lord Iveagh asking if it would be possible to leave not only the frontage on Hatch Street but also the space occupied by the riding school and the entrance available for building purposes.[55] Lord Iveagh agreed to the Taoiseach's request and pointed out again that it was his earnest wish that the Iveagh Gardens should always provide a 'lung' for the people of Dublin and that they should never be built upon.

At an important cabinet meeting held on 15 October 1940, the government took the decision to lease the riding school and covered court section to UCD. They further agreed to formalise an arrangement whereby UCD could have the use of the grounds ...'on agreed conditions'. It was also proposed that the portion of the grounds bordering Hatch Street should be transferred to UCD for the purpose of the erection of a building to replace the present College of Science. UCD should be allowed a passage through the Iveagh grounds from the premises at Earlsfort Terrace to 86 St Stephen's Green.[56] It was also suggested that negotiations should be initiated for the transfer of the College of Science in Merrion Street to the government, in exchange for a grant to build new accommodation on a site in the Iveagh Gardens (on the Hatch Street side) at Earlsfort Terrace. It was left to the Minister for Finance to decide whether or not the state should maintain the Iveagh grounds and obtain contributions from UCD for their upkeep.

From the beginning, however, Dr Conway made it clear that UCD would not be prepared to carry the burden of financial responsibility for the gardens' maintenance:

As you are aware, we are not in a position to promise to contribute to the upkeep of the grounds. The most we could do would be to provide some man as a park keeper to control the students.[57]

Sympathetic towards the university's plight, de Valera overruled the Minister for Finance's view that UCD should be held entirely responsible for the maintenance of the grounds once the transfer had taken place. It was the Taoiseach's view that the college should be required to pay only a nominal rent for the use of the gardens and that the Office of Public Works should undertake 'full liability for the maintenance of the Grounds and for all outgoings on rent and rates'.[58]

Other details were given careful consideration, such as the occupancy of the lodge in Clonmell Street at the entrance to the gardens. This should only be occupied under the terms of a caretaker's agreement 'so that if it becomes necessary at any time to have it vacated, this can be readily achieved'.[59]

By September 1941, a formal licence agreement had been drawn up between the Minister for Finance and UCD relating to the legal position of the Iveagh Gardens. The agreement underlined many of the points mentioned above and also included provision for UCD to construct two gates; these would provide access from the college buildings in Earlsfort Terrace and from 87 St Stephen's Green to the gardens. The college also agreed to undertake the rebuilding of a boundary wall and the removal of buildings which had been erected in the gardens of 82 and 83 St Stephen's Green in order to facilitate the future plans of the Department of Finance.

On 6 October 1941, Éamon de Valera, as both Taoiseach and Chancellor of the National University of Ireland, was presented with a silver key by Professor R.M. Butler[60] with which to open the small, newly-built gateway at the eastern end of Iveagh Gardens. The ceremony continued beside the archery grounds where the second gate which led to Newman House was unlocked. Over a hundred guests attended this distinguished gathering, including professors from both UCD and Trinity College.[61]

The gardens now provided a welcome link between 85/86 St Stephen's Green for both lecturers and students. They also served as a haven of peace and relaxation amidst the noise and bustle of city life. Plays were performed on a circular platform on the site of the rosarium together with other college events, including concerts.

Down through the years, the possibility of building in the Iveagh Gardens was considered; in many people's eyes, the whole area was a potential site for development. In the spring of 1945, for example, the University College authorities felt that if the gardens, together with the riding school, were placed at the disposal of the college for building instead of being devoted entirely to 'pleasure', it might be feasible to use the extended Earlsfort Terrace site for all the building requirements demanded by the college's ever-growing pressure for space. The president of

University College, Dr Conway, was anxious to see a new School of Architecture on the site of the tennis courts behind Iveagh House and stated this in a letter to the Taoiseach, dated 6 September 1945. The response was not encouraging. The Office of Public Works requested that a fifteen-year guarantee against any further extension of UCD's interests in the direction of Iveagh House be complied with by the college.[62]

Situated in the heart of Dublin, the Iveagh Gardens remained largely undisturbed until 1990 when they were formally placed under the management of the Office of Public Works. Under the careful guidance of the Superintendent of Heritage Properties, OPW, John McCullen,[63] the restoration of the Iveagh Gardens is being co-ordinated by Margaret Gormley, Parks Superintendent. Work on the fountains, maze, rose garden and cascade has already been completed. Its 700 trees are also being carefully tended by the OPW's arboricultural management team.

This 'special, secret place' will soon be restored to its former glory, a fitting memorial to its creator, Ninian Niven. Not only do the Iveagh Gardens demonstrate the art of the Victorian landscape professional but will, in the future, provide a splendid setting for outdoor musical concerts and other events.[64]

In the days when Dublin was known as 'the Second City of the Empire', musical events abounded in places whose names still ring today – Smock Alley... Crow Street... even family names such as Pigott, so closely linked with Dublin music, go back nearly two centuries. Chapter 2 tells the story of those days.

CHAPTER 2
DUBLIN'S EARLIEST THEATRES AND MUSIC HALLS

In 1974, the government of the day decided to adapt the Great Hall of University College, Dublin, for use as a concert hall, thus concluding a chapter in a long history of debate. That the nation's capital city had been without a concert hall until then is only partly correct, however. When Dublin's musical life prior to the foundation of the state is retraced, one discovers an unusual variety of venues for music-making.

Smock Alley and Crow Street

Interestingly, the only pre-Restoration theatre erected outside London was in Dublin's Werburgh Street, adjacent to Christ Church Cathedral and Dublin Castle. Built around 1634 on the initiative of Scotsman, John Ogilby (1600-1676), it operated until the Rebellion of 1641 when it was closed down by the orders of the Lords Justice. Having lost a virtual fortune because of this, Ogilby returned to London. While his Dublin theatre was ostensibly for plays, these would have been interspersed with songs and musical interludes. From 1649 to 1659, during the period of the Commonwealth when plays were forbidden, the Werburgh Street playhouse fell into ruin.

With the restoration of the monarchy in 1660, Charles II granted the same John Ogilby a patent for the monopoly of theatrical interests in Ireland. Charles also decreed that there should be 'an Office of the Master of the Revels and Masques' and duly appointed Ogilby, who returned to Dublin and opened a new theatre in Smock Alley, also near Christ Church Cathedral. The first play to be presented there, in 1662, was *Othello*, the first recorded production of Shakespeare in Ireland.

During a performance of Ben Jonson's *Bartholomew Fair* on St Stephen's Day 1671, part of the theatre collapsed, leading to the deaths of at least three persons. Re-opening the following year, the Smock Alley Theatre flourished until 1676. It then appears to have gone through a period of spasmodic business, finally closing at some time between 1687 and 1691. A new lease of life for Smock Alley began on 23 March 1692 under a new Master of the Revels, Joseph Ashbury. The first production was also *Othello*, with Ashbury himself as Iago; a 'scratch orchestra' played during the interludes.

Tragedy struck Smock Alley again on St Stephen's Day in 1701 when, during the first night of Shadwell's *The Libertine*, the galleries gave way, without loss of life this time, although many were injured in the ensuing scramble to escape. The upholders of Dublin's morality considered

Shadwell's work to be 'a play extremely loose and improper' and declared that the accident was a judgment on the spectators. The theatre was forced to close for renovation, after which it continued for almost thirty years.

During that time, operas, ballad operas and concerts were also presented at Smock Alley. In 1711, the male contralto, Nicolo Grimaldi (1673-1732), also known as Nicolini, brought his opera company from London's Haymarket with productions of Handel's *Rinaldo* and Bononcini's *Trionfo di Camilla de Volsci*. In 1713, the Peace of Utrecht was marked with an interlude, *Peace Triumphant*. This followed the official Christ Church celebration which had included a *Te Deum* by Johann Sigismund Cousser, Master of the State Musick in Dublin, and an anthem by Daniel Roseingrave.

There was a season of Italian opera in 1725. Three years later, a production of John Gay's *The Beggar's Opera* created a sensation when it played to packed houses. It even found favour with Jonathan Swift who excused those of his clergy who ventured to see it.

Crazy Crow, one of Dublin's musical characters in the eighteenth century.

[While not pretending] to vindicate a clergyman, who would appear openly in his Habit at a Theatre, among such a vicious Crew, as would probably stand round him, and at such lewd Comedies, and prophane Tragedies as are often represented... [Swift gave his judgment] ...that nothing but servile Attachment to a Party, Affectation of Singularity, lamentable Dullness, mistaken Zeal, or studied Hypocrisy, can have the least reasonable Objection against this excellent moral Performance of the Celebrated Mr Gay.

Fears about the theatre's safety arose from time to time and it eventually closed in 1735 to allow for the building of a new auditorium. This took less than a year and the new Theatre Royal, Smock Alley, ran for over fifty years until its demise in 1787. During this time, a number of other theatres sprang up in Dublin. One in Rainsford Street, close to the Guinness Brewery, was active between 1732 and 1736. Another, in Aungier Street close to Dublin Castle, was open from 1733 to 1746. Two others stood on Capel Street which faces City Hall from the north side of the Liffey. These operated during the second half of the 1740s and from 1770 to 1784.

Dublin's most famous theatre was in Crow Street, in what is today's Temple Bar area. It ran from 1758 to 1820 and saw the first Irish performances of Mozart's *Le Nozze di Figaro* and *Don Giovanni* in the autumn of 1819. Crow Street was replaced by the Theatre Royal in Hawkins' Street which operated from January 1821 until destroyed by fire in 1880. The seeds of operatic appreciation by Dublin audiences, sown in both Smock Alley and Crow Street, would reap rewarding harvests over a number of years.

With so many theatres, there was considerable rivalry as one tried to outdo the other. This led to the Crow Street Theatre being leased to the English composer, Michael

Arne (1741-1786). On 4 January 1776, *The Freeman's Journal* carried a piece which said that Arne had

> undertaken the Conduct of English Opera both serious and comic; burlettas and all musical performances, to be represented every Monday and Thursday evening during the season. He has for this purpose engaged the Theatre in Crow Street, together with a complete Company of Vocal and Instrumental performers.

Arne opened with his dramatic romance *Cymon*, described by *The Freeman's Journal* as 'chaste and elegant from first to last with the addition of a noble band, conducted by Mr Arne and led by Mr Pinto'. Tommaso Pinto (1714-1783) had come from London in 1773 and led the orchestras of both Smock Alley and Crow Street. He conducted at the Rotunda from 1780 to 1782 and died in Dublin the following year.

However, Arne's season had not proved a financial success when it ended in May 1776. He then gave private lessons but paid little heed to his students and eventually spent time in the Debtors' Prison. The father of tenor Michael Kelly, who merited fame at home and abroad, supplied Arne with wine and a piano, enabling him to devote his time of incarceration to composition.

Fashionable Venues

The idea of giving public concerts stemmed from those given at private gatherings where some professional musicians were assisted by amateur artists. Both classes of performer enjoyed close connections with the court society of Dublin Castle. The eighteenth century saw an expansion of this activity for charitable purposes when concerts were given for some specific reason – the relief of deprivation or the benefit of one of the city's hospitals or institutions.

In 1974, Brian Boydell, Professor of Music at Trinity College Dublin, read an interesting paper to members of the Old Dublin Society in which he mentioned a number of venues which had become fashionable resorts for such activity. Among these was Mr Johnston's 'Great Room' in Crow Street, built in 1731 at the request of the Musical Academy for 'the practice of Italian Musick'. It was here, on 8 April 1736, that Handel's *Utrecht Te Deum and Jubilate* and *Coronation Anthem* were heard in Dublin for the first time. The proceeds went to Mercer's Hospital.

Following the building of the New Musick Hall in Fishamble Street in 1741, the Crow Street 'Great Room' continued to be used for over a decade. After 1743, many of its concerts were to the benefit of the Hospital for Incurables. The hall closed in the mid-1750s and was rebuilt as a playhouse and opera house.

The world-wide fame of Fishamble Street stems from the premiere of Handel's *Messiah* which took place there in April 1742. The street, which runs from Christ Church Place to the River Liffey, had in fact two halls. One was the 'Philharmonic Room' which appears to have had a connection with the Musical Academy which moved its concerts there in the early 1740s. The other was the 'Musick Hall'. Built at the insistence of the Charitable Music Society, it was known variously as 'Mr Neale's New Musick Hall', 'Mr Neale's Great Room' or the 'New Musick Hall' to distinguish it from both the Philharmonic Room and the Great Room attached to the Bull's Head tavern in Fishamble Street where, for a while, the Charitable Music Society had its headquarters. William Neale, who was the society's treasurer, ran a music publishing business from his shop in Christ Church Yard.

The Musick Hall was designed by Richard Castle, architect of the Rotunda Hospital and Russborough House in Co. Wicklow, both of which stand to his

The Music Hall in Fishamble Street, where Handel's Messiah *was first performed in April 1742.*

worked with Dubourg were Nicolo Pasquali (1718-1758) who also conducted at Smock Alley, and Gian Battista Marella who conducted the Charitable Music Society concerts, introduced the *viola d'amore* to Dublin and married the popular Dublin singer, Eleanora Oldmixon.

After this active period, the Musick Hall went into a decline until January 1777 when it became a public theatre and saw the first complete season of Italian operas without burlesques or other such inserted material. However attendance dropped, the ceiling of the adjoining supper room collapsed, and from 1792, its role was that of a purely private theatre. The hall closed in the year of rebellion, 1798, and in time was sold to Kennan and Sons who carried out an ironmongers' business there for almost two centuries.

Among the other small music venues in Dublin around this period were Taylor's Hall and Mr Geminiani's 'Great Room' in Spring Gardens off Dame Street. The most intriguing of all, however, was the 'Commodious Booth' erected by a Madame Violante in George's Lane beside Dublin Castle. This lady assembled a company of child actors through which she discovered Peg Woffington, who, in her adult years, would achieve considerable acclaim in London and elsewhere. According to Professor Boydell, Madame Violante performed various exhibitionist feats (not detailed, alas) on a tightrope which so shocked the Lord Mayor that her 'Commodious Booth' was closed down. Madame Violante departed in 1732 but her booth was used for occasional concerts until 1745 when its character totally changed. Then, Dr Bartholomew Mosse converted it into Europe's first hospital for 'Poor Lying-in Women'. This, and Dr Mosse's love of music, would have a remarkable effect on music in Dublin for the next 150 years.

memory. The hall could hold 700 persons, provided 'gentlemen were unencumbered with swords and ladies removed the hoops from their skirts'. Its orchestra was led by London-born Matthew Dubourg (1703-1767). A pupil of Francesco Geminiani, Dubourg was the eminent violinist and composer who became leader of the Viceroy's band in 1728. He composed *Birthday Odes* for various monarchs between then and 1764, returning to London the following year. Under his direction, the Musick Hall ran successful seasons until the opening of the Rotunda Concert Rooms in 1767. Others who

The Rotunda

Open-air summer concerts offered a pleasurable pastime to Dublin's nobility and gentry. These took place mainly in the Spring Gardens in St Stephen's Green, the City Basin in James' Street (where at one point in 1756 there was a floating orchestra in the 'Chinese Taste'), and the Marlborough Bowling Green. Many were for charitable purposes or for the benefit of the performing artists. Occasionally, proceedings were enlivened by fireworks during the intervals. Events such as these were extremely fashionable: one went to see as well as to be seen.

In 1768, new gardens near the village of Ranelagh were completed by the organ-builder and impresario, William Hollister, who illuminated the route from the city with lighting which was erected at his own expense. The Ranelagh concerts continued for nine years, during which time their initial popularity waned.

Before that, however, Dr Mosse had secured the lease on a plot of land on Great Britain (now Parnell) Street. In 1748, Mosse laid out new gardens which were suitable for stylish entertainment. It was a clever move, as the speculator Luke Gardiner was developing Sackville Mall (now O'Connell Street) as a residential area. Mosse's Garden Concerts, with Handel's *Music for the Royal Fireworks* invariably a crowd-puller, were exceptionally successful, and by 1751, Mosse was able to instruct the architect Richard Castle to prepare plans for the building of a hospital on a portion of the site. With his concerts' continued success, Mosse decided to extend his plans to include an indoor concert venue in Great Britain Street. The result, which had some financial assistance from the government, was the Rotunda.

Based on the circular amphitheatre built at the Ranelagh Gardens in London, the Rotunda's architect was John

Dr Bartholemew Mosse, founder of the Rotunda Hospital and one of the most influential men of his time. (The Governors of the Rotunda Hospital)

Ensor, a pupil of Castle who had also completed the hospital's design following Castle's death in 1751. The Round Room, measuring 80 feet in diameter and 40 feet in height, opened on 5 June 1767. The open auditorium caused continuing acoustic problems, however. An advertisement for concerts conducted by Johann Peter Salomon (the same who commissioned Haydn's *London* symphonies) in *The Freeman's Journal* of 20 June 1789 mentioned that 'a large canopy is erected over the orchestra in the Rotunda, to give the music its proper effect'.

Alas, Mosse did not live to see the fruits of his ambitious plans: he died in 1759. After that, the Rotunda concerts were run by a committee of 'Gentlemen of Approved Taste', including Lord Charlemont whose own house on nearby Parnell Square is now the Hugh Lane Municipal Gallery of Modern Art. Charlemont had influence at home and useful London contacts, which explains the constant stream of visiting artists to the concerts.

Mosse himself had started this trend of visiting musicians when he engaged Gian Battista Marella, of the Paris Spiritual Concerts, for all the 1751 concerts in the Rotunda Gardens. In fact, Marella remained for four years when he was replaced by Fernando Arrigoni, whose father Carlo had already played in Dublin. Arrigoni stayed for five seasons, to be followed in 1763 by Charles Claget (1740-*c*.1795), the first native musician to conduct at the Rotunda. Born in Waterford, Claget's incumbency lasted six years but initially, advantage was taken of his youth by the older band members. This drew the odium of the directors who insisted that

> *the Register be desired to acquaint the musicians, that they are to follow the directions of Mr Claget, the Conductor of the band, under pain of the displeasure of the Governors.*

Claget's younger brother, William, joined the Rotunda's cellos and one of his operas, *The Power of Sympathy*, or *The Innocent Lovers*, was staged at Smock Alley in 1767.

By the time Charles Claget's tenure ended in 1769, the number of foreign artists visiting the Rotunda had increased. The Neapolitan, Tommaso Giordani (*c*.1733-1803) returned for the next season and finally settled in Dublin in 1783. The virtuoso French violinist, François Barthelemon (1741-1808), conducted during 1771, 1782 and again in 1784. The popularity of Handel's music continued, with movements from his concertos being regular features. *Alexander's Feast* and *Acis and Galatea* also found favour, as did the music of Corelli. Works by J.C. Bach began to appear with the engagement of Johann Christian Fischer (1733-1800) in both 1771 and 1776. One of the finest oboists of the century, Fischer married the daughter of the painter, Thomas Gainsborough (1727-

The Rotunda, scene of many Georgian musical events, after an aquatint by James Malton.

1788). The German violinist, Wilhelm Cramer (1746-1799), who had played in the famous Mannheim orchestra, conducted during the 1774 season; the brilliance of his playing seems to have obscured Barthelemon somewhat. The following year brought another French artist, Pierre Vachon (1741-1803), who would eventually lead the Royal Orchestra in Berlin.

Between 1776 and 1782, the Rotunda concerts were in the hands of Thomas Pinto (1714-1783) and it was he who introduced the music of Haydn to Dublin. On 8 August 1776, it was announced that a 'New Overture by

Mr Hayden [*sic*]' would be played. This programme also included music by J.C. Bach, Arne, Fischer, Jomelli and Pinto himself. As Pinto's standards were particularly high, he employed a number of expensive artists during his term of office, to the detriment of the Rotunda's finances. An unprecedented loss in 1782 forced stringent cut-backs, leading to the employment of what Brian Boydell has called 'Army Music' – musicians from the garrison bands. From just two concerts in the summer of 1782, these increased to fourteen in 1784, the year which saw the return of Barthelemon (but at a smaller fee than he had received twelve years earlier). The soloists for these concerts were often employed for a number of weeks rather than the current 'one-night-stands'. For example, the singer Elizabeth Billington was engaged for three months from the beginning of the 1784 season. She was the daughter of Carl Weichel, an oboist in Smock Alley. Her brother Charles was conductor and violinist at the Rotunda between 1786 and 1788.

In 1790, after a six-year construction period due to the vicissitudes of funding, a 'New Room' at Rutland (now Parnell) Square opened beside the Rotunda. Later referred to as the 'Assembly Rooms', it was fully completed in 1791: its two apartments still stand as the Gate Theatre and Pillar Room underneath. Used for smaller events, the lower was the ballroom-cum-concert hall while the upper served as a supper and tea room.

With a reduction in the Rotunda's hiring charges around this time, a larger number of outside artists and promoters became involved in its concerts. Among these was Langrishe Doyle, organist at Christ Church Cathedral who conducted a benevolent performance of *Acis and Galatea* in aid of the Meath Hospital on 22 May 1790. The organist, pianist and composer Philip Cogan conducted a number of benefit concerts between 1782 and 1791. A notable event on 24 March 1792 was the

debut of ten-year-old Master John Field (1782-1837) playing 'Madam Krumpholtz's difficult pedal harp concerto on the Grand Pianoforte'. Despite a chequered career as pianist and composer, Field would have a lasting place in the history of European music.

While audiences are now familiar with female orchestral leaders (Terry O'Connor, Nancie Lord, Geraldine O'Grady, Audrey Park, Mary Gallagher, Thérèse Timoney and Fionnuala Hunt spring to mind), the first such woman in Dublin was the French virtuoso violinist, Madam Louisa Gautherot (d.1808), who broke the taboo of ladies playing only a keyboard instrument or guitar. She led the Rotunda Orchestra in 1791 and her influence meant a decline in the performance of Haydn in favour of Ignace Pleyel. Gautherot also led the orchestra in Master Field's debut.

Madam Louisa Gautherot (died 1808), an unusual example of a female virtuoso and the first such woman to perform in Dublin. (The British Museum)

Irish Musicians and Composers

The Act of Union of 1800 brought many changes to Dublin. Artistic patronage shifted from the upper to the middle classes, but the next thirty years or so found considerable activity centred on local artists and a number of native composers. Among these were Garrett Wellesley (later Wesley), Earl of Mornington (1735-1810), the first professor of music in Trinity College and father of the Duke of Wellington; Philip Cogan (1748-1833); John Stevenson (1762-1833); and Thomas Cooke (1782-1848).

Born Garrett Colley Wellesley in 1735 at Dangan Castle, Co. Meath, the Earl of Mornington was something of a musical child prodigy, playing the violin, harpsichord and organ and extemporising fugues. Before his appointment to Trinity College in 1764, he was one of the founding members of the Dublin Academy of Music.

When in London, Mornington visited the hymn-writer Charles Wesley for breakfast on one morning a week, when he invariably made music with the Wesley boys, Charles and Samuel. He is reputed to have been the first member of the British aristocracy who dared to walk openly and unashamedly through the London streets carrying a violin case.

Cork-born Philip Cogan moved to Dublin where he was organist of St Patrick's Cathedral from 1780 to 1820. A fine teacher, he numbered Michael Kelly and Thomas Moore among his pupils. He was one of the founders of the Irish Musical Fund Society and a regular performer at the Rotunda. A fairly prolific composer, his music is currently enjoying a limited revival.

The son of Bartlett Cooke, an oboist in the Dublin theatre orchestras, Thomas Cooke was a versatile musician and composer. He played all the instruments in his *Concertante* for violin, viola, cello, flute, clarinet, trumpet, piano and pedal harp. This feat was ridiculed by J.W. Croker in his *Familiar Epistles*:

> *The modest and diffident Mr Cooke... played on eight instruments for his own benefit – I am sure it was neither benefit nor pleasure to anyone else.*

But Cooke also had his supporters, none more so that the famous soprano, Angelica Catalani. Cooke led the orchestra on her first appearance in Dublin in 1807, and she maintained that he 'evinced the possession of no common talents particularly in so young an artist'. A singer himself, Cooke spent twenty years as principal tenor of London's Drury Lane Theatre, all the while continuing his violin playing and conducting.

Principal among Irish singers was Michael Kelly (1762-1826). He made his debut in Smock Alley in 1777, aged fifteen, when he took over a role in Nicola Piccinni's *La Buona Figliuola* after the castrato Gaspero Savoi was taken ill. This led to engagements in Crow Street and, on the advice of the singers Venanzio and Matteo Rauzzini who were in Dublin at the time (in fact Matteo settled here), Kelly went to study in Naples. His long career included a stay in Vienna where he sang the roles of Don Curzio and Don Basilio in the premiere of Mozart's *Le Nozze di Figaro*.

While concerts were given in the Crow Street Theatre and at the new Royal when it opened in 1821, many regular play-goers felt such events were intrusions on their patch. One critic in *The Theatrical Observer* reminded the musicians that:

Fashionable music lovers at the Rotunda in July 1790. (Walker's Hibernian Magazine)

they had the Rotunda and various other public places where they could warble and pipe until they were tired.

Visitors from Abroad

A musical highlight of 1824 was the August visit of the German pianist and composer, Friedrich Wilhelm Kalkbrenner (1785-1849). Admired by Chopin and to whom the Polish composer dedicated his E minor Concerto, Kalkbrenner was the star of a concert at the Rotunda. This was directed by the composer Jonathan Blewitt (1782-1853), the London-born organist of St Andrew's Church (now the headquarters of Dublin Tourism) and conductor of the group, the Sons of Handel. Kalkbrenner played a number of his own pieces, including the *Variations on an Irish Air* and on *God Save the King*, both for piano and orchestra. His appearance created such

a stir that he played again at the Rotunda on 6 September with his Grand Concerto. Due to popular demand, he repeated the *God Save the King* variations and gave a number of extemporaneous performances.

Another composer/pianist to visit Dublin was Ignaz Mocheles (1784-1870) who gave two concerts at the Rotunda in January 1826. (The pre-concert advertisement announced, rather strangely, that 'the band would be complete'.) Mocheles played his Grand Piano Concerto, his Piano Concerto (dedicated to the Empress of Austria) and his *Variations on the Fall of Paris*. In a *Concertante* for piano and cello by the Viennese composer, Josef Mayseder (1789-1863), Mocheles was joined by Samuel Pigott, an influential Dublin businessman and founder of a music firm which then operated from 112 Grafton Street. A fine cellist, Pigott was described as 'having exquisite tone, faultless execution and classic style'. He was also secretary of the Anacreontic Society, a mainly amateur orchestral group which was named after the sixth-century Greek lyric poet and musician. Other artists at the Mocheles concerts were Haydn Corri, later organist at Dublin's Pro-Cathedral, and his wife.

Philharmonic Society Concerts

1826 saw the formation of the Philharmonic Society under Henry Bussell (*c*.1807-1882) who was also a piano dealer, pianist and violinist. This group was the mainstay of Dublin's concert life for the next forty years, normally giving six programmes a year between January and June under Bussell's direction. In 1856, he conducted Ireland's first performance of Beethoven's Ninth Symphony with soloists Miss Ellen Williams, Mrs Cantwell, Gustavus Geary and Joseph Robinson.

A notable visitor of the 1830s, Nicolo Paganini arrived on 30 August 1831 and stayed in Willis's Hotel in Westmoreland Street. Such was his notoriety that, on leaving his hotel for an evening stroll, he 'walked through Westmoreland Street and Sackville Street and was followed by a number of persons anxious to behold this musical phenomenon'. Paganini had come to Dublin to play at the city's Music Festival which was organised by the Philharmonic and Anacreontic societies. The elaborate original plan for the festival included the building of a 2,000-seat concert hall in Lower Abbey Street, but time and expense prevented this. Instead, the six-day festival, 'For the Benefit of the Mendicity Association and the Sick and Indigent Room-keepers' Society', took place at the Rotunda and the Theatre Royal.

The festival began with a Grand Ball at the Rotunda with Ferdinand Ries (1784-1838) conducting his own oratorio *The Triumph of Faith* – 'a splendid composition', according to *The Freeman's Journal* – at the Royal. *Messiah*, with 'Mozart's accompaniments', was heard on 1 September at a morning concert, again at the Royal, during which Paganini, mounted on a special platform, played a number of solos. That evening at a Grand Miscellaneous Concert, he offered his *Carnival of Venice* Variations and his *Sonata Militaire*. This second concert also featured Mozart's *Jupiter* Symphony, Weber's *Euryanthe* Overture and various songs and arias from supporting artists. The leader of the band was Thomas Cooke.

Anxious for other engagements, Paganini arranged to meet William Calcraft, the Royal's manager. However, when he called to the stage door and asked to be escorted in, his entrance was barred by one Peter Connell, a fellow who disliked both actors and violinists. Leaving Paganini outside, Connell climbed the stairs to Calcraft's office and enquired if he was in 'to see a foreign fiddler who was below at the door'.

'Oh,' said Calcraft, 'that must be Signor Paganini. Show the gentleman up at once.'

Connell withdrew, muttering, 'A fiddler a gentleman! Oh, Lord, since when?'

Another musical luminary to visit the Rotunda was Franz Liszt who remained in Ireland over the Christmas and New Year period of 1840-41. Prior to arriving in Dublin, he had been on a tour of the English provinces, organised somewhat haphazardly by the impresario, Louis Lavenu. A number of other artists travelled with Liszt, among them the Welsh harpist/composer, John Orlando Parry. On 21 December, Liszt played his *Grand Galop Chromatique* and arrangements of Rossini's *William Tell* Overture and Donizetti's Andante and Finale from *Lucia di Lammermoor*. He was joined by Samuel Pigott for a 'Grand Duet'.

On the 23rd, Liszt was heard in his *Hexaemeron Variations*. His fellow-artist John Parry wrote in his diary:

Liszt played for the first extemporaneously, and a most wonderful performance it was. When Lewis [Louis Lavenu] asked the audience if they had any themes ready written – one was handed only – but Mr Pigott gave him the Russian Hymn in addition. This was not enough – so after talking to the audience in the most familiar way and making them laugh very much because he had not any lively air to work on – he turned round suddenly and said : 'I play de Wanted Governess!' and off he started with the Irish air and then the Russian Hymn and last my song, which he played most wonderfully. Not all the way thro' – but the waltz part in the first symphony. He played it at least 12 different ways and then wound up with the 3 together in a manner truly extraordinary! 'Twas received as it deserved with tumultuous applause.

Liszt spent Christmas in Dublin before setting out for Limerick, Cork and Clonmel. Returning in the new year, *The Freeman's Journal* announced:

In compliance with the wishes of several families of distinction [Liszt would give a] Grand Morning Recital on 7 January 1841 at two o'clock. Mons Liszt will play extemporaneously.

There was a final recital on 12 January when he repeated the *Hexaemeron Variations* and the *Grand Galop Chromatique*, again accompanying Mr Pigott. According to *The Freeman's Journal*:

Mons Liszt's concert was attended by a brilliant assemblage of rank and fashion... everything was encored.

February and March 1855 brought concerts by the Jullien Orchestra at the Rotunda with Marie Pleyel, piano, and Charlotte Helen Dolby, alto, as soloists. The programme included a number of Jullien's own arrangements of popular pieces as well as the *Allegro vivace* of Mendelssohn's Third Symphony. Pleyel, who 'had the audience under a spell of wonder and delight', played Weber's *Concertstuck* and Liszt's *Les Huguenots* Fantasy while Dolby sang Mozart arias, among other pieces.

Louis Jullien (1812-1860) was an eccentric, extravagant and profligate Frenchman. He would conduct Beethoven's symphonies with a jewelled baton, wearing a new pair of white gloves presented to him on a silver salver.

Marie Pleyel (1811-1875) was a pupil of Kalkbrenner. She had an affair with Hector Berlioz to whom she became engaged, but in 1831 she married Camille Pleyel, the pianist, music publisher and piano-maker. She insisted, however, on pursuing a flirtatious lifestyle and was professor of piano at the Brussels Conservatoire for twenty-four years.

Charlotte Helen Dolby (1821-1885) was an able singer as well as a composer. Highly regarded by Mendelssohn, he had her in mind when composing the contralto part in *Elijah*. She married the French violinist, Prosper-Philippe-Catherine Sainton. She was the teacher of Fanny Moody who, with her husband Charles Manners, would bring their own opera company to Dublin.

The Antient Concert Society

The 1840s saw Dublin acquiring a new concert hall. In 1837, a number of influential businessmen and musicians formed the Antient Concerts Society for 'the cultivation of vocal, especially choral, music of the Old Masters', i.e. the 'Antients'. The first meeting of the society took place at 85 Lower Mount Street, the home of Francis Robinson, an eminent professor of music in Dublin and the son of a Yorkshire man. In 1811, Robinson had formed the Sons of Handel which met at Morrison's Hotel in Dawson Street. Later meetings of the Antient Concerts Society were held at Northland House, now the Royal Irish Academy, in Dawson Street. In 1837, the society had sixty members, half of whom were performers. These came from the cathedrals with their choir boys, with two ladies engaged for special occasions. Unless a full oratorio was given, the concerts were usually divided between oratorio selections and unaccompanied glees.

Francis Robinson had four sons – Francis, William, John and Joseph – who formed an admirable quartet which popularised German part-songs, then rarely heard in Ireland or England. Joseph (1815-1898), the youngest baritone son, had been a chorister in St Patrick's Cathedral from the age of eight. He conducted the Antient Concerts Society from its foundation for twenty-nine years. When the premises of the Dublin Oil Gas Light Company of 52

Brunswick (now Pearse) Street became vacant in 1835, Joseph Robinson bought it. Some nine years elapsed before the Antient Concert Rooms (ACR), called after the society, opened there with a performance of *Messiah* under Joseph Robinson's direction on 20 April 1843. Francis and William Robinson were among the soloists. It was a glittering occasion, and the cognoscenti were reminded to avoid traffic chaos with this notice:

All parties attending the oratorio this evening, will proceed by Brunswick Street, in order that the carriages may set down with the horses' heads toward Westland Row.

The main auditorium of the Antient Concert Rooms was in the Ionic style and, like the current National Concert Hall, was nearly a double cube of forty-three feet, or eighty-six feet long. It could accommodate an audience of between 900 and 1,000 and had a large organ, built by Telford's, at the back of the orchestra (platform). With its opening, and because it provided more comfortable seating than the Rotunda, Dublin's music focus shifted from the Rotunda to the ACR where there were almost daily concerts in 1844. Its use as a concert hall continued for almost seventy years. The old building, which also had

The Antient Concert Rooms, once one of Dublin's most important music venues. (Shaw's Directory, 1850)

a life as the Academy Cinema, still remains in Pearse Street, but in a sadly dilapidated condition.

The young violinist Joseph Joachim, then sixteen, played at the ACR in June 1847. A friend of several composers including Brahms and the dedicatee of many works, Joachim visited Dublin on a number of occasions over the next thirty years or so.

In December 1847, the ACR played host to the first Irish performance of Mendelssohn's *Elijah*, a work still popular with Dublin audiences. At a Philharmonic Society concert in the ACR in March 1852, conducted by Henry Bussell and 'applauded to the echo', the artists included violinist, Ernesto Sivori (1815-1894), and contrabassist Giovanni Bottesini (1821-1889). Sivori was the only direct pupil of Paganini and had been something of a child prodigy. Bottesini was the champion double bass player of the day. At the age of eleven, apparently, he applied for a place in the Milan Conservatory where the only position left was for the double bass. Naturally, the instrument was taller than the fledgling player but realising he would grow, Bottesini made necessity the mother of invention.

The violinist Eduard Remenyi (1830-1898), with whom Brahms toured extensively as a young pianist, was at the Philharmonic Society in the ACR in January 1855 where he played Spohr's First Violin Concerto and music by Paganini. *The Freeman's Journal* review thought the performance of the Spohr 'the most perfect execution' but that elsewhere, there was a 'little coarseness, too much rapidity and a sentimentalism bordering on sickliness'.

On 30 May 1856, Henry Bussell conducted the Philharmonic Society at the ACR when the celebrated pianist Clara Schumann (1819-1896) was one of the soloists. She played Mendelssohn's Concerto in D minor and two pieces by Robert Schumann (this was just two months before Schumann's death on 29 July 1856).

The other artists in this concert included Emilie Krall of the Dresden Opera and Signor Picco who played Bellini's *Casta diva* 'upon a little whistle only the length of one second finger'. Picco was the 'blind Sardinian minstrel' who appeared at Covent Garden and after whom the picco flute is named. The lengthy programme also offered Stephen Heller's arrangement of the finale of Mendelssohn's Fourth Symphony, one of Beethoven's *Leonora* Overtures, a symphony by Spohr, and numerous arias and songs from Frau Krall and the well-known local singers, Gustavus Geary and Richard Smith.

Another popular ACR visitor was the Russian composer/pianist Anton Rubinstein whose first appearance in May 1858 came under the banner of the Philharmonic Society.

The Irish Academy of Music

But to retrace our steps – 1848 was of particular importance to musical Dublin with the foundation of the Irish Academy of Music (IAM). One of its aims was 'the cultivation of instrumental music' through the training of orchestral musicians. It was also hoped that such an academy might help the choristers of Dublin's three cathedrals in perfecting and completing their musical education.

Among the initiators of the IAM were Henry Bussell and Samuel Pigott, William Hudson (a barrister who had close links with the patriot, Daniel O'Connell), and Hudson's brother Henry – both were collectors and arrangers of folk songs. Also involved were the violinist Richard Michael (R.M.) Levey, brothers Francis and Joseph Robinson, and John Smith who had been recently appointed to the chair of music in Trinity College. The IAM, which became

'Royal' (RIAM) during the Duke of Edinburgh's visit to the 1872 Exhibition, would soon become an integral part of Dublin's musical life. Later, it would have a number of European musicians on its teaching staff, the first of whom was the German-born cellist, Wilhelm Elsner, who arrived in 1851. These Europeans would bring considerable influence to bear on Dublin's musical life, although before them, it was Levey, Joseph Robinson and Smith who were the linchpins in the city's music-making.

R.M. Levey (1881-1899) was the backbone of many a Dublin orchestra; in 1834 he was appointed leader of the Theatre Royal's band, a position he held until the theatre burned down in 1880. According to Dublin-born composer, Charles Villiers Stanford, Levey 'was a rough player, but an admirable leader of an orchestra, and often as a conductor managed to make sows' ears like silk purses'. Born O'Shaughnessy, he styled himself as 'Levey', believing it to be more musical-sounding. He was a fellow student of composer Michael Balfe and the two remained life-long friends. In 1840, Levey conducted the Irish premiere of Balfe's *The Maid of Artois* and produced several volumes of his own *Dance Music of Ireland*. He married three times and had a large family thereby, a number of whom became musicians. William Charles Levey (1837-1894) conducted at Drury Lane and Covent Garden, while his twin John (1837-1891) was an author and comedian. Richard Levey played the violin and harp and appeared with Clara Schumann on her visit to Dublin in 1856. He later adopted the stage name 'Paganini Redivivus' and appeared in the Exhibition Palace in 1866.

A Craving for Opera

Nineteenth-century Dublin continued its love of opera, and the Theatre Royal in Hawkins Street, which opened in 1821, was to the forefront in satisfying that desire. In

GEORGE BROWN Musical Instrument Maker, dwelling at Mr, Hyena's, Cutler in Crane-lane, Dublin. has by his Skill and Industry, brought that Instrument call'd the German Flute to that Degree of Perfection, that the most Knowing in that Art can find no Defect in them, and by a new Machine of his own Invention, Gentlemen may with the greatest Facility found all the Notes of the said Instrument, from the highest to the lowest. He also makes excellent German Cane Flutes, for the Accommodation of those Gentlemen that wou'd recreate themselves abroad, and as he has been for this considerable Time past a successful Practitioner in his Art, and has wrought for the most eminent Masters in his Travels through Germany, Holland, Flanders and England, humbly hopes, Gentlemen, such as have occasion for said Instrument will favour him with their Custom, and they may be assured of getting as good Instruments from him as is possible to be made.

An advertisement for George Brown, one of Dublin's instrument makers in the nineteenth century.

August 1848, for example, *The Freeman's Journal* advised:

Mr Calcraft begs respectfully to announce that he has, at ENORMOUS EXPENSE, effected the engagement of unrivalled artists for the production of Italian opera for eight performances commencing on Tuesday 29th August and terminating on 9th September. The chorus and orchestra will be full and efficient under the immediate superintendence of Mr Levey.

The artists responsible for such 'enormous expense' included one of the nineteenth century's most celebrated prima donnas – Giulia Grisi (1811-1869). She created the roles of Adalgisa (*Norma*) and Elvira (*I Puritani*) and made her London debut in 1834 in *La Gazza Ladra*. She married the equally renowned tenor, Giovanni Mario, in 1844; he was also on the singers' Theatre Royal roster. Like Angela Gheorghiu and Roberto Alagna today, it was quite common to find husband and wife on stage together. The season's conductor was Julius Benedict (1804-1885), a pupil of Weber's and a particularly fine opera conductor. His *The Lily of Killarney*, after Dion Boucicault's *Colleen Bawn*, remained a firm favourite with Irish opera-goers for almost a century.

The operas presented at the Theatre Royal for this 1848 season were *Norma, I Puritani, La Gazza Ladra, La Sonnambula* and *Don Pasquale*. On 6 September 1848, *I Puritani* was compressed into two acts and the evening concluded with Act III of *Don Pasquale*. Grisi and Mario appeared each evening, with Mario's singing of 'Com'e gentil' in *Don Pasquale* repeated three times to satisfy audience demand. The couple returned 'at unprecedented expense' for a number of further Royal seasons.

Another period of Italian opera in October 1848 introduced Jenny Lind (1820-1887) to the Theatre Royal where she sang Amina in *La Sonnambula*, Elvira in *I Puritani*, Marie in *The Daughter of the Regiment* and the title role in *Lucia di Lammermoor*. The 'Swedish Nightingale' had demanded and received an enormous fee – £500 per performance. And this, it should be remembered, was one of the years of the Great Famine. Box office receipts on the opening night were in the region of £1,600.

Lind and her company, which included her conductor, the Dublin-born composer Michael Balfe, stayed in Morrison's Hotel where it was reported she gave an impromptu ballet performance for a very select company. One of the hotel waiters, entering the room in a professional capacity, was apparently pressed into service at a crucial moment, although the exact nature of his new role has not been revealed. In the Rataplan of Act I of *The Daughter of the Regiment*, Lind accompanied herself on her own small side-drum, playing, it is said, like an experienced *tambouriere*. So great was the rush for tickets that extra performances of both *Lucia* and *The Daughter* had to be given on 19 and 24 October respectively.

The legendary Jenny Lind (1820-1887), the 'Swedish Nightingale'. Her performances in Dublin always caused a sensation.

Lind's concert in the Rotunda on 21 October 1848 also brought an overwhelming demand for tickets from throughout the country. She returned to Dublin for a *Messiah* at the ACR in aid of the Irish Musical Fund Society (set up in 1787 to help musicians who, through old age or misfortune, were reduced to poverty) and Mercer's Hospital, one of the beneficiaries of its premiere in 1742. The net result was £940 between the two charities.

This operatic craving continued, spilling over into concerts and recitals where instrumental fantasies on themes and arias invariably formed part of the repertoire. Such was the case when the brilliant pianist, Sigismond Thalberg (1812-1871), came to the Rotunda in February 1849. He had a brief but dazzling career as a touring pianist throughout Europe and the Americas; he married Nicola Lablache, the daughter of the great bass of French and Irish extraction, Luigi Lablache, who sang with Guilia Grisi and Giovanni Mario in *Anna Bolena, Norma, I Puritani* and *La Sonnambula* in the Royal seasons of 1840 and 1841. Later, Zara Thalberg, the pianist's daughter, would become a popular soprano with the Italian operas visiting Dublin. Thalberg's brother-in-law, Frederick Lablache, and his wife, Madame Emilie de Meric Lablache, would also enthral Dublin audiences.

Concert-goers of Dublin, Ireland and the Continent would be further enthralled with the arrival of the International Exhibition Movement. The Great Dublin Exhibition of 1865 would also have a lasting effect on the Iveagh Gardens and the location of the National Concert Hall over a century later.

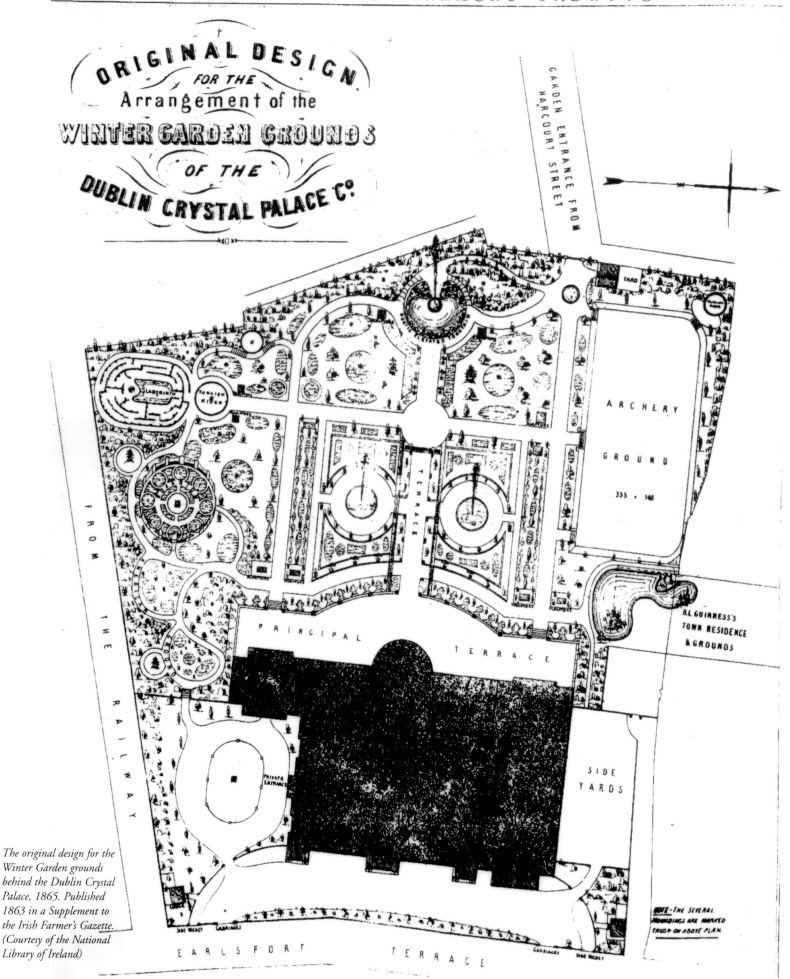

ORIGINAL DESIGN
FOR THE
Arrangement of the
WINTER GARDEN GROUNDS
OF THE
DUBLIN CRYSTAL PALACE Cº

GARDEN ENTRANCE FROM HARCOURT STREET

ARCHERY GROUND

335 × 140

LABYRINTH

TURKISH KIOSK

TERRACE

PRINCIPAL TERRACE

B.L. GUINNESS'S TOWN RESIDENCE & GROUNDS

FROM THE RAILWAY

PRIVATE ENTRANCE

SIDE YARDS

SIDE WICKET   CARRIAGE

EARLSFORT TERRACE

CARRIAGES   SIDE WICKET

NOTE - THE SEVERAL BUILDINGS ARE MARKED THUS ▪ ON ABOVE PLAN.

The original design for the Winter Garden grounds behind the Dublin Crystal Palace, 1865. Published 1863 in a Supplement to the Irish Farmer's Gazette. (Courtesy of the National Library of Ireland)

CHAPTER 3
THE EXHIBITION ERA IN VICTORIAN IRELAND

The Origins of an Idea

The International Exhibition Movement which swept through nineteenth-century Europe became the vehicle for international exchange in both art and technology. One of its principal, more lofty, aims was to 'forward the upward progress of industrial civilisation'. The Victorians were keen to build on the scope and reserves of the British Empire and to contain it within the framework of the intellectual and social outlook of the times.

International exhibitions guaranteed that manufactured goods from countries around the world would be viewed in one place and in sorted categories, ensuring that easy comparisons could be made. As part of its main agenda, it would appear that each exhibition had to be bigger and better than the previous one.

International exhibitions had their origins not in Britain but in France. Shortly after the French Revolution, a severe depression occurred which necessitated finding new markets for French goods. The Marquis d'Avèze, commissioner of three former Royal Manufactories,[1] found himself with a surplus of items from these prestigious establishments – and no buyers. In an attempt to find a market, he organised[2] the first successful 'Exposition of Industry' which was held in 1798 in the Hotel d'Orsay in Paris. A series of similar exhibitions followed at irregular intervals, each of which was devoted to the glory of the art and industry of France. Financed by

The key used by the Prince of Wales to open the Dublin International Exhibition of Arts and Manufactures at Earlsfort Terrace on 9 May 1865 and illustrated in the official catalogue. (Courtesy of the National Library of Ireland)

the French government, they culminated in the Paris *Exposition Universelle* held in 1855.[3]

The French had taken the lead in the exhibition arena, and although several attempts had been made to organise similar exhibitions in England,[4] it was the Royal Dublin Society – the RDS – and not members of the British government who took the initiative in exhibiting arts and industries, earning for Ireland an honourable place in Victorian exhibition history. It was the RDS who were to influence the Prince Consort when he, together with Victorian educationist, Sir Henry Cole, introduced the idea for the famous 1851 Crystal Palace Exhibition in London. This would set the standard for all subsequent exhibitions around the world and celebrate British achievement in the field of industry.

As far back as 1829,[5] the idea of a general exhibition, organised on the Parisian plan, had been contemplated by the RDS. In 1833, a committee was appointed to study the possibility of a yearly exhibition of manufacturers and products which would demonstrate 'what Ireland is capable of affording from native production and native talent'. In May 1834, the concept was realised when the first exhibition of arts and industries was held in the RDS premises at Leinster House, Kildare Street. From then on, such exhibitions were triennial and became a regular feature of the Society.[6] These exhibitions exercised a considerable influence on manufacturing progress, ensuring that only high-standard goods made in Ireland should be placed on display.[7] The RDS series culminated in 1850 with an exhibition held on a site between Kildare Street and Merrion Square which was more prestigious and comprehensive than any of its predecessors. Attracting some 300,000 visitors with receipts in the region of £10,000, a more liberal approach was adopted, with foreign entries being admitted for the first time. Awards were made to all, despite the 'rivalry of other nations'. 1853 was the year selected by the RDS for the eighth in its triennial series of Irish National Exhibitions of Manufactures.

'The Man Who Built the Railways'

After the Great Famine of the 1840s, poverty was beginning to make way for prosperity, with the railway boom having a startling impact on the nation. As a result, the 'Father of the Irish Railways', industrialist and surveyor, William Dargan (1799-1867),[8] had made a considerable fortune. Dargan had been impressed by the Crystal Palace Exhibition of 1851 and by the small-scale Cork Industrial Exhibition of 1852.[9] He saw them as a means with which 'to elevate the country to a position it had never before attained'[10] and as arenas in which to demonstrate peaceful international co-operation. The effects of the Famine on agriculture had been severe: perhaps Irish industry could be encouraged and boosted by having a platform on which to display its products.

On 11 June 1852, Dargan wrote to the RDS offering to contribute £20,000 towards the cost of a major exhibition the following year, subject to certain conditions. He required no return unless there was a profit. His offer to sponsor, single-handedly, the Dublin International Exhibition of 1853 was immediately accepted, with Dargan generously agreeing to donate a further £20,000, thus doubling his original offer. (It is worth noting that with subsequent exhibitions on this scale, it was private individuals and private initiative, rather than state encouragement, which supported and made these ventures possible.)

The 1853 Exhibition

A competition organised for the design of the pavilions was won by John Benson (1812-1874) of Cork. Benson's design appears to have been based on Joseph Paxton's 'Cristal Exhibition' structure of 1851[11] and made maximum use of the 6½ acres on both sides of Leinster House. It covered both the forecourt of Leinster Lawn looking out on to Merrion Street and stretched back as far as Kildare Street.

Less than twelve months after the project had been initiated, the exhibition was opened on 12 May 1853. The music was provided by Joseph Robinson who conducted one thousand performers in the largest band and chorus ever assembled in Dublin up to that time. The ceremony was performed by the Lord Lieutenant, the Earl of St Germans, with Queen Victoria and Prince Albert visiting the exhibition on 30 August.[12] Displays were divided into four distinct categories – Raw Materials, Machinery, Manufacturers, and Fine Arts and Antiquities. A major difference from previous exhibitions was the absence of awards or medals. Exhibits included a grand medieval court, naval, railway and agricultural machinery, minerals, silk and wool. The Fine Art and Antiquities section displayed a set of geological specimens which had been sent by Richard Griffiths, Chairman of the Board of Works. Several European monarchs also contributed – Royal Berlin iron and porcelain vases came from the King of Prussia, and Sevres and Gobelins from Napoleon III.

The Great Exhibition continued until 31 October and succeeded in going far beyond Dargan's intention of opening it to 'the three Kingdoms' of Britain. Attracting entries from as far afield as Japan and India, it gave many members of the public an opportunity to view arts and crafts from these countries for the first time. When it closed, attendance had almost reached the million mark. Losses had amounted to nearly £19,000, with all costs being carried by Dargan himself. Today, this clearing of debts and complete financing of an international exhibition by one single individual seems extraordinary. Dargan had made a magnanimous contribution to the promotion of his country and, as a result, incurred a substantial loss. A knighthood had been offered and refused. However, it was widely felt that Dargan's efforts should be commemorated in some way and in his honour, a public testimonial fund was started. A sum of £5,000 was allocated in 1854 towards the building of a Public Gallery of Art, and in 1864, the National Gallery of Ireland opened. A single memorial to William Dargan

remains today – a bronze statue by John Edward Jones (1806-1862) which stands on the front lawn of the National Gallery of Ireland.

The year 1858 saw a small art exhibition taking place in Dublin which did, in fact, succeed in making a profit. This led to a more ambitious one, organised by the RDS three years later which carried the rather lengthy title – the Exhibition of Fine Art and Ornamental Art. It was held on the site now occupied by the National Museum of Ireland and also proved to be a success, attracting over 200,000 and enlivening Dublin society with its concerts, illuminations and promenades.[13]

The final triennial exhibition organised by the RDS took place in 1864 and was devoted entirely to 'every branch' of Irish manufactures, together with an art collection on-loan. The latter appeared to disappoint the *Art Journal*, as the Irish representation was, in their opinion, below standard.[14]

'A want long felt'

The International Exhibition Movement came to a climax with the Great Dublin International Exhibition of Arts and Manufactures held at Earlsfort Terrace in 1865 on the site of the present National Concert Hall. In order to bring this about, the Dublin Exhibition Palace and Winter Garden Company (Limited) was formed in 1862. A joint stock undertaking was floated, and, armed with capital of £50,000, the company was anxious to provide

an institution to afford, to the people of Dublin and its neighbourhood, rational amusement blended with instruction and thus supply a want long felt in the city.

A list of the company's committee and trustees provides an indication of the prestigious members of society who agreed to lend their names to this new venture. They included the chairman, the Duke of Leinster, and Benjamin Lee Guinness, who acted both as vice-chairman and trustee. Among the forty-strong board were the names of William Dargan, John Switzer, the Lord Talbot de Malahide, James West, Catterson Smith, Thomas Pim, the Rt. Hon. Denis Moylan, Lord Mayor of Dublin, the Hon. St John Butler, Thomas M. Gresham, Thomas Vance, and Sir J. Jocelyn Coghill. The company's secretary, Henry Madden Parkinson,[15] elaborated on its *raison d'être*:

Not withstanding the largely increased population and wealth of Dublin within the last few years, and its rank as the second city in the empire, it has long been a matter of observation and surprise that it contained no institution where the citizens might meet for the purposes of rational amusement blended with instruction – no garden or place of public assembly of a character similar to those existing in many of the Continental cities... [The intended buildings] will comprise a winter garden, where horticultural exhibitions and promenades may be held; a concert hall suitable for the production of the works of the great masters with an effect not hitherto attainable in this city; a smaller concert hall adapted for the musical societies of Dublin; a gallery for the exhibition and sale of pictures; a department for the display of manufactures and useful arts; a polytechnic museum and theatre for lectures on popular subjects, the whole to be placed in ornamental pleasure grounds, in which the skill of the landscape gardener will be displayed.[16]

Over 10,000 shares were sold at £5 each to approximately 600 shareholders. It was understood that a substantial dividend would be paid on the capital invested. The income would come from a variety of sources, as explained by Henry Parkinson:

The income of the Dublin Exhibition Palace and Winter Garden Company was to be derived from receipts from ordinary public concerts, promenades, musicales, subscriptions to the Institution, and the sale of season tickets; Hire of public rooms for Exhibitions, lectures, private concerts, meetings, etc.; Public lectures on Scientific and other subjects, commission on sale of paintings and other articles, rents on bazaar stalls, refreshment rooms, and of space for goods exhibited for sale. In addition to these and many other sources the Directors expect a large income will be realised from oratorios, musical festivals, and the production of the most attractive and legitimate Exhibitions and novelties which may from time to time appear in the chief capitals of Europe, and which, in the Exhibition Palace, and with the resources of the company, can be produced with much effect, and with advantage to the shareholders. The Directors, after a careful estimate of even the ordinary income of the Company, believe that it will pay to the shareholders a large dividend on the capital invested.[17]

Acquiring a Site

The vice-chairman and trustee of this new committee, Benjamin Lee Guinness, realised that the RDS site at Leinster House, Kildare Street, was severely limited as an exhibition and display area. On 5 April 1862, Guinness had purchased part of the land of the Coburg Gardens[18] from Henry, Earl of Clonmell, in order to provide a garden for Iveagh House. Part of this portion of land, comprising eleven acres and thirteen perches, was now to be leased to the Dublin Exhibition and Winter Palace Company by Guinness[19]. This included land bordered by Harcourt Street, St Stephen's Green South, Earlsfort Terrace and Hatch Street. Certain conditions were laid down, one of which stated that no buildings could be erected in the 'garden' area other than ornamental fountains, conservatories and greenhouses.[20] The agreement, which was for 999 years with an annual rent of £302 being paid by the Company to Guinness, commenced on 1 May 1862.

After completion of negotiations with Guinness, the directors of the Exhibition Palace and Winter Garden Company were anxious to extend the site and therefore set about negotiating the purchase of a portion of land which lay opposite Wellington Square (a name assigned to a planned development between Hatch Street and Adelaide Road) and which ran parallel to Hatch Street. This area bordered the land which had already been leased to them by Benjamin Lee Guinness and belonged to the Hely-Hutchinsons. After much negotiation, the family finally agreed to let it to the company at an annual rent of £243.[21] By the end of February 1863, the company had acquired the site for the second Great Dublin Exhibition, an area that would also serve as the location for the company's planned recreational and cultural centre for Dublin's citizens.

The Search for an Architect

The directors of the Exhibition Palace and Winter Garden Company ran into difficulties when selecting a suitable design. An architectural competition was held, with two premiums (prizes) only being offered.[22] Entries were to be submitted in monochrome, inclusive of proof that the proposed design could be executed for the sum of £35,000. Twenty-four entries were accepted, six of them from Dublin architects, and these were placed on view in September 1862. The *Dublin Builder* of 1 October 1862 discussed the range of drawings on public display:

...a couple of them [are] somewhat of the Crystal Palace fashion; another... on a reduced scale, of the International building at South Kensington [i.e. the buildings of the 1862

Exhibition]; another partaking more or less of its character; while others exhibit façades which might not inappropriately denote an imperial palace or great public offices; and, lastly, there are two or three extraordinary conceptions showing a regular cathedral arrangement of nave, aisles, transept, chancel, tower, etc., in debased Gothic, and a huge Oriental structure (of Turkish bath type), respectively. The authors of these can hardly have been serious; if so, there is no accounting for taste...[23]

After much discussion, it was agreed that none of the entries could be executed within the sum allowed. Rather than cancel the competition, the judges invited the architect, Alfred Gresham Jones of 3 Molesworth Street, to reconsider his design in consultation with the company architect, Frederick Darley, in an endeavour to make it more economical.[24] A folio of original watercolour drawings on paper now in the National Library of Ireland's Prints and Drawings' collection probably represent some of Alfred Gresham Jones' original external and internal plans for the proposed Exhibition Palace and Winter Garden to be sited at Earlsfort Terrace.[25] Alfred Gresham Jones' original plan for the Exhibition Palace and Winter Garden appeared in the *Dublin Builder* for 31 January 1863. Later it would be considerably modified.

The origins of Alfred Gresham Jones (1822-1915) are somewhat obscure. The first reference to him in Ireland is found in the records of the RHA which notes that he contributed to the 1850 exhibition from a London address.[26] Indeed he may have been one of the many architects who moved to Ireland during the church-building boom of the mid-Victorian period. By 1858, Jones was living and working in Dublin, a partner in the firm, Hugh Carmichael, Architects and Surveyors, of Molesworth Street.[27] In the same year, he designed

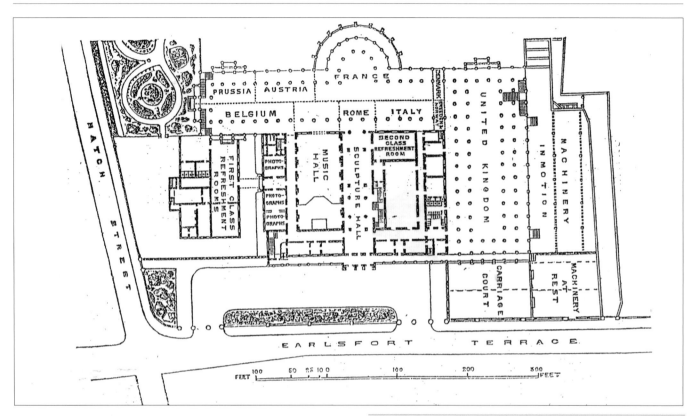

Merrion Hall (now the Davenport Hotel), Dublin, which was modelled to a large extent on the Metropolitan Tabernacle in Stoke Newington.[28] However, Jones' largest commission was the Dublin Exhibition Palace and Winter Garden which was to become notable for its use of cast-iron, employing as it did much the same technology as the Crystal Palace exhibition structure erected in 1851 in Hyde Park, London.[29]

Although he retained the affix FRIBA (Fellow of the Royal Institute of British Architects) for the greater part of his architectural career, no evidence can be found to date of Jones' membership.[30] From 1889 onwards, there appears to be no further reference to building projects designed by him in Ireland. It is possible that, around this period, he emigrated to Australia where he continued his career as an architect. He died in Melbourne, aged ninety-three.[31]

The Ground Floor Plan of the Exhibition Palace and Winter Garden in which the Music Hall had a central place. (from Parkinson and Simmonds, 'The Illustrated Record and Descriptive Catalogue of the Dublin International Exhibition of 1865', London 1866)

Construction begins

The engineers selected to build the Exhibition Palace and Winter Garden at Earlsfort Terrace were Ordish and Le Feuvre of Westminster, London.[32] Rowland Mason Ordish had been partly responsible for working out the details relating to the ironwork for London's Great Exhibition of 1851. He had supervised the erection of the exhibition building in Hyde Park and its subsequent re-erection at Sydenham. The principal contractors were a Dublin firm, James Patrick Beardwood & Company. An agreement between the Exhibition Palace and Winter Garden Company and James Patrick Beardwood & Company was drawn up in July 1863.[33] The Exhibition Palace out-offices and other outdoor constructions were to be built at a cost of £70,481, with materials supplied by James Martin of John Martin & Son.

Meanwhile, considerable labour was being injected into developing and laying out the 'pleasure grounds' – the Coburg Gardens.[34] As the gardens were taking shape, the foundation stones of the iron and glass building (the Winter Palace), together with the brick and stone building (the Exhibition Palace), were laid with great ceremony by the Lord Lieutenant, the Earl of Carlisle, on 12 June 1863. The site chosen was the south angle of the semi-circular apse of the Winter Garden.

At the proper time the first stone was gradually let down to its destined position, and his Excellency having been handed a square and plumb line of elegant workmanship, ascertained that the stone had been properly adjusted. He was then handed a mallet, made of beautifully polished wood, with which he struck the stone three times, and said 'I declare the first stone of the Exhibition Palace and Winter Garden is well and truly laid'. This announcement was received with loud and continuous cheering.[35]

A glass casket containing six Irish newspapers (only *The Irish Times* is still in circulation today) and all dated 11 June 1863, together with several coins of the realm, were placed next to the foundation stone.

Construction had already begun the previous month and would continue for the next two years. The Exhibition Palace Building, the main building, was designed in the Classical style and comprised a structure which faced Earlsfort Terrace (the east front). It was built in both brick and stone with cement lining and divided into three storeys. The basement held extensive kitchens, cellars, larders, still-room, scullery and storage rooms. On the ground floor were an elaborate entrance hall, a sculpture gallery, two concert halls, rehearsal rooms, cloakrooms, refreshment rooms and offices, together with extensive corridors which provided easy access throughout the building. On the first floor were the company's administrative offices, a dining room which could be subdivided with screens, and the company's boardroom which overlooked Earlsfort Terrace.

The second section, a building called the Winter Garden, was comprised of both iron and glass. Built by Rankin & Sons of Liverpool, the design was L-shaped and ran along two sides of the main Exhibition Palace building. An additional annexe of similar structure and covering an area of approximately 7,000 square feet provided space for displaying machinery and cars, not only in motion but also at rest. It included an air-conditioning plant for the entire collection of buildings at Earlsfort Terrace which was capable of supplying both warm or cold air, if required. A permanent steam-pumping engine, together with air conditioning, had been installed in the 'machinery in motion' section and succeeded in heating the building and operating the garden cascade and lawn sprinklers.

The Winter Garden building was ideal for displaying exotic plants and trees and provided a pleasant indoor promenade area. It also supplied the vast majority of the space for the forthcoming exhibition.[36] This iron and glass structure extended to 640 feet in length and possessed a circular transept at the centre. The materials chosen for the construction of the Winter Garden were wrought and cast iron, wooden frames, corrugated iron, glass and zinc.[37] Wrought iron lattice girders were used in both the Winter Garden and the Exhibition Palace buildings, the first recorded use of this type of girder in Ireland. The Winter Garden's unusual feature was the absence of any diagonal bracing for the arched roof as the thrust was carried by iron buttresses to the second tier of columns.

A print from a glass-plate negative in the Stereo Pairs collection, National Library of Ireland. The photograph was taken in 1865 and shows the elm tree mentioned on page 22. (Courtesy of the National Library of Ireland)

Put to the Test

In March 1865, the strength of this structure was tested to the utmost when weights to the total of thirteen tons were suspended from the joists. Then, the workmen were made to gallop along the first-floor galleries. And for one day, 7,000 canon balls were rolled around the galleries. To complete the process, 600 men of the 78th Highlanders, in full kilt and with their band, marched repeatedly all around the galleries and stairs. The structure proved to be a resounding success.

The quantities of materials used in both buildings were impressive – for example 100,000 square feet of glass; 1,333,000 bricks; 17,265 tons of granite rubble; and over 4½ miles of gas piping. A tramway was constructed to assist with the transportation of materials.

The exterior of the stone and brick building, the Exhibition Palace, consisted of a central pediment supported by both Corinthian and Doric columns. Above the pediment were three allegorical statues representing Hibernia, Industry and Commerce. The first-floor windows were in the Byzantine style, and a long glass-roofed veranda enabled carriages to deliver passengers under cover from the elements. Alfred Gresham Jones' designs also included impressive entrance gates which have survived to this day. These were hung on powerful cast-iron hinges, designed in the shape of a hand, and provided access for carriages – with, it should be noted, only one entrance for the poor, plodding pedestrian! These, together with the railings, pillars (now without their tall, elegant lamps) and the wall surrounding part of the exhibition site at Earlsfort Terrace, are still *in situ* today.

On entering the Sculpture Hall in the Exhibition Palace building of 1865, the visitor could view the majestic cascade sited at the far end of the gardens. An enthusiastic reporter in The *Dublin Builder* wrote:

Of the entrance-hall itself... it is possible to speak in terms of high praise. This hall extends through the height of both the floors of the building, and is lighted from the top only... the lighting both of the pictures and of the most conspicuous statuary, is admirable. The walls of the lower part of the hall have been decorated in dark colours, Pompeian red being the most prevalent tone, and this, deepening the gloom of the shadow thrown by the galleries, serves to throw up the sculpture, which stands well forward from the walls, in a remarkable manner.[38]

A double stairway, still there today, led to the upper, four-sided gallery which had been designed as a display area for paintings. To the right (north) of the Sculpture Hall was the smaller of the two concert halls with a three-sided gallery, able to accommodate 1,200-1,500 people. This measured 90 feet long and 50 feet wide. For the 1865 exhibition, a floor was built at gallery level to provide two rooms. In the long-term, it was intended that both rooms should become a lecture theatre and small concert hall.

South of the Sculpture Hall was the Great Concert Hall with a capacity for seating approximately 3,000, including a vast choir and orchestra space. The organ and stage were sited at the east end of the room, i.e. nearest Earlsfort Terrace. The hall itself measured 130 feet in length, was 65 feet wide and measured 59 feet in height. The design of this room, remarked The *Dublin Builder* of 20 May 1865, is similar to the interior of the Free Trade Hall erected in Manchester in 1840. The same reporter wrote:

... of the merits of [the Great Concert Hall] it is hardly possible to speak, as it is seen at present incomplete, and with its chief architectural features encumbered and concealed by a series of large cartoons, for the display of which no other place seems to have been found.

Plans Gather Momentum

The opening date, 9 May 1865, had been agreed and an independent executive committee was set up to manage and run the exhibition which included William Dargan, Sir Richard Griffiths (Board of Works) and Sir Robert Kane (President of Queen's College, Cork).[39] For the duration of the exhibition, this committee leased the grounds and building from the Dublin Exhibition Palace and Winter Garden Company for £15,000. This time, unlike the Great Dublin Exhibition of 1853, awards were to be presented. Six substantial advisory committees were established, each one in charge of one of the six main categories:

Raw Materials – Mining, quarrying processes, mineral products, chemical substances and articles of food.

Machinery – Not only machinery in motion and at rest but philosophical and musical instruments and implements of modern warfare.

Textile Fabrics – Fabrics of cotton, wool, silk, lace and leather.

Metallic, Vitreous and Ceramic Manufacture – All the multifarious production of the smith and potter.

Miscellaneous Manufacture – Included under this heading came articles required for decoration.

Fine Arts – Not only painting, sculpture, marble etc., but also jewellery and photography.

There was also a complex network of local and foreign advisory and organising committees which managed to co-ordinate thousands of exhibits from twenty-seven countries. Advice was sought from the committee

responsible for organising the London International Exhibition of 1862 as well as from the Foreign Office in London which sent circulars to the representatives of the British government abroad, inviting participation in the forthcoming exhibition. Delegates were sent abroad to enlist the support of foreign governments, among them: barrister Hercules McDonald who was closely connected with the Irish Academy of Music; and George Mulvany, director of the newly established National Gallery of Ireland. Their task was to travel to Europe soliciting support and procuring suitable items for exhibition. On his travels, Hercules McDonald had been shocked by foreigners' ignorance of Ireland, many of whom still believed the country to be in a state of rebellion and terrorism. However, his visit to the pope proved fruitful. Both the pontiff and the French emperor became liberal contributors to the exhibition, sending both sculptures and mosaics. The commercial field was also well represented and included entries from both the continent and beyond. Special railway and other concessions were

Unpacking the statues for the 1865 Exhibition. (Illustrated London News, 1865)

arranged. Concessions were also extended to the transportation of goods from abroad to Dublin; for example, Sweden despatched goods and works of art in a frigate specially commissioned by her government.

To simplify administration, the exhibition had been divided into a number of categories. The Agricultural Machinery section was to be housed in the Agriculture Hall of the RDS in Leinster House, Kildare Street[40] and not at Earlsfort Terrace. A note of discontent sounded, however, when it was agreed to exhibit Irish industry as part of British industry as a whole, rather than placing it in a separate section. This led to criticism from Irish manufacturers who felt that they were not being allocated sufficient prominence or space in an Irish exhibition.

The Exhibition Palace itself was well equipped, with a telegraph centre, post office branch and railway office (the

Harcourt Street railway line lay nearby, at the end of Hatch Street). Facilities for a substantial number of international newspaper reporters, official photographers, and the London Stereoscopic and Photographic Company were also made available. Every need was catered for, including the hiring of opera glasses through Chancellor & Son. Specialist staff were employed, along with general employees who numbered sixty-nine.[41]

The 1865 Exhibition

The opening ceremony was a glittering affair. On 9 May 1865, the heir to the throne, HRH the Prince of Wales (Queen Victoria was still in retirement following the death of Prince Albert in 1861) drove in procession together with the Duke of Cambridge, the Lord Lieutenant and Lady Wodehouse. They were escorted by a squadron of the 10th Hussars from the Vice-Regal Lodge to Earlsfort Terrace, arriving at 2pm. After the National Anthem (in a special arrangement by Joseph Robinson), the prince was greeted by the Duke of Leinster who read an address of welcome on behalf of the Dublin Exhibition Palace and Winter Garden Company from a platform resplendent with uniforms of all kinds, including the Knights of St Patrick. As the prince resumed his seat to loud applause, 'the Orchestra, Grand Organ and Chorus burst forth with the sublime and impressive music and words of the 100th Psalm'.

Mr Gilbert Sanders, Chairman of the Executive Committee, then read a lengthy report on the evolution of the building and the exhibition and presented the prince with a catalogue of the articles on display. As a souvenir of the occasion, the prince received a key, in a purple velvet case, to the exhibition building. The key, designed with a crown, harp and shamrocks, together with the Prince of Wales' feathers, had been made by Chubb of London. The orchestra played Handel's *Coronation Anthem* after which

the Lord Mayor presented an illuminated address to the prince. This was followed by Haydn's *The Heavens are Telling* after which the prince and his party made a brief tour of the exhibition to the accompaniment of Meyerbeer's Grand March from *Le Prophete*. On his return to the dais, the prince directed Sir Bernard Burke to declare the exhibition open. Then

> *Signal rockets were discharged and immediately salutes were fired from the Pigeon House in Ringsend, the Magazine in the Phoenix Park and the Royal George Yacht Club in Kingstown [Dun Laoghaire] Harbour. Three military bands, under the direction of Mr Smalley played the Danish National Song as the Prince left the building.*

The Prince of Wales and his party passing through the Sculpture Hall at the opening of the Dublin International Exhibition of Arts and Manufactures on 9 May 1865. (Illustrated London News, 13 May 1865)

The choral performances were considered to be the most outstanding aspect of the ceremony. The choir, trained by Joseph Robinson, numbered 500 and the orchestra almost as many. Amongst their instruments was a drum, the largest in the world, eight feet across, and made from buffalo skin. The excellence of the music threw *The Irish Times'* correspondent into spasms of praise:

> *... It was really a wise step to procure the services of such a musician as Mr Joseph Robinson, and it may well be questioned whether a finer chorus of 500 voices has ever been assembled or trained. This was especially manifested in the magnificent rendering of the Hundredth Psalm, the two first verses in harmony and the third in unison accompanied. The orchestra made up the number of performers to nearly a thousand, and performed its duty with remarkable purity and completeness. This was admirably displayed in Handel's magnificent 'Coronation Anthem', and in Mendelssohn's glorious 'Hymn of Praise'. Haydn's chorus, 'The Heavens are Telling', was never rendered in Dublin with such force, unity and sympathetic grace. Nor did it ever ring out with such vigour and telling effect. It was a triumph of musical skill to conduct so vast a number of performers with such ability, that not the slightest error or hesitation occurred throughout the whole of the musical programme.*[42]

The Dublin Winter Garden Palace of 1865. (Illustrated London News, 13 May 1865)

However, one London newspaper noted that, to their disappointment, no Irish music had been included in the concert programme.

The splendid day closed with a ball held in the Mansion House in honour of the Prince of Wales and presided over by the Lord Mayor to which 3,000 guests had been invited. On the same evening, queues were still assembling outside the Mansion House up to 2am.

'A Frolic on the World Stage'

A visitor to the Exhibition Palace building would have found that this housed the sculpture and painting galleries and the large Concert Hall, while the Winter Garden building and annexe was used to exhibit goods from Switzerland, Belgium, Holland, Italy, Zollverein (Prussia), Russia, Austria, France, Turkey, China and Japan, India and the British Colonies. Among the Colonial displays were goods from Africa, Australia, Canada, Ceylon, India, Jamaica and New Zealand. With the exception of the Fine Arts, exhibits were grouped by country of origin.

Around half of the exhibits came from the United Kingdom, with Irish exhibits being placed under the same heading. However, it is interesting to note that British exhibits were less than half the number of those exhibited in the Great Dublin Exhibition held in 1853. In its editorial, *The Freeman's Journal* described the exhibition as 'one of the most useful, instructive and educating collections ever brought together in any country'.[43] Many 'British' exhibitors involved names still familiar today, including Gouldings & Co. of Cork and Johnston & Matthey of London. From Dublin, whiskey was supplied by Kinahin's of Carlisle Buildings and biscuits by Jacob's. Mr Graham Lemon's confections were in great demand, while Mr Rathborne of Essex Street displayed beeswax, sealing wax, and bleached and unbleached spermaceti, both crude and refined.

The *Illustrated London News*, which provided a visual recording of the event,[44] noted that

despite Ireland's economic difficulties she has not resigned her claim to vie with other countries in great undertakings. She can take her turn with the proudest of them in providing instruction and entertainment.

The *Dublin Builder* was sharper and hard-hitting, criticising the exhibition for accommodating foreign exhibitions at the expense of Irish manufacturers.[45] The Sculpture Court was praised but the absence of a specifically Irish section was noted and again came under fire. Praise was awarded for the classic tradition of design displayed in the exhibits, whereas 'the great mass of the Gothic furniture exhibited is bad beyond belief in design'. Architecture was meagrely represented.[46]

The *Practical Mechanics Journal* stepped up the attack.

There is a distinct room for the medieval court, where those learned in 'church millinery' or who can recognise anything more than absurdity in the priestly trumpery of the 12th and 13th centuries, revived for 'church decoration' in the 19th, may enjoy their ecclesiological predilections.[47]

Among the many companies displaying furniture was R. Strahan & Co. of Dublin. J. Maguire of Dawson Street displayed ornamental metal work. Several firms showed fabrics and textiles, including a number from Ulster displaying flax, linen and damask. Walpole & Geoghegan of Suffolk Street, Dublin, had a fine display of linen yarns and damask table linen. J.J. Barnardo of Dame Street featured among the exhibitors of furs and skins. Rowney & Co. exhibited their materials for artists.

Italy had over 200 exhibitors, with foodstuffs such as biscuits, Bolognese and Florentine sausages, Cremona pickles, chocolate, coffee, creams and condiments as well as liqueurs, wines, olive oils and cheeses. There were fine silks, beautiful brocades and embroidery, while 'The Italian Fine Arts' section had some unique coral work and watercolour miniatures executed on marble and inlay furniture. Their ceramic section included porcelain, terracotta and mosaic work.

Around a hundred exhibitors participated from France. Notable were the exquisite specimens of Gobelin tapestry

The Picture Gallery at the 1865 Exhibition where works such as Sir Frederick William Burton's 'Meeting on the Turret Stairs' were exhibited for the first time. (Illustrated London News, 13 May 1865)

and a fine collection of musical instruments, particularly from Paris. There were bronzes, lamps and candelabra, as well as wines, liqueurs and alimentary produce. The Roman display included fine engravings based on work by old masters, medals, fine lace and embroidery (executed by the female prisoners in the Termini penitentiary), imitation marble tiles, mosaics, tapestries and a colossal statue of the reigning pope, Pius IX. Various sweetmeats and olive oil were also mentioned.

From Austria and the Zollverein came the china and porcelain for which Dresden is famous. That city also sent a curious collection of baked photographs and an admirably executed map showing the Prussian coal and mining districts. There were examples of exquisite glass from Dusseldorf.

The Colonies' section included displays from Ceylon – fibres and matting, spices and fruit, basket work and pearls. Australia sent wines, silk and fibres, twenty-five kinds of wool, fifteen watercolours of Adelaide and a handsome model of the Royal Exchange in London incorporating 500 examples of, principally Australian, wood. Africa was represented by cotton, hemp and warlike weapons used by the natives, as well as rope, twine, net and fibres. Canada was represented by leather, seal skins, oil and fur, and India by collections of cloths of gold and silver, weapons of warfare, suits of armour and carpets, together with a large selection of different fibres. The exhibition's

greatest attraction is, without doubt... the fine art galleries. These contain collections that for variety, beauty and excellence have never been equalled by similar exhibitions.[48]

A number of different rooms were assigned to the Fine Arts section. A room ninety-four feet in length which stretched along the gallery of the eastern court was occupied solely by old masters. Exhibits included works by Masaccio, Botticelli, Giorgione, Titian, Van Dyck, Rembrandt, Romney and many other examples from the Spanish, Italian, French and English schools. Pictures from the modern English School were hung in the lofty chamber which formed the upper part of the small Concert Hall. Scandinavian art had a room allotted to itself in the eastern corridor, while the northern corridor of the gallery led to the room set apart for work in watercolour. The art of photography was also illustrated and a small chamber was set aside for pictures describing heroic achievements which in turn had merited the Victoria Cross.

This exhibition saw an increase of around one-third in the number of works of fine art being submitted, particularly in the Sculpture Court, compared with the Exhibition of 1853.[49] An exhibition of 'Paintings in Water Colours' revealed to Dubliners for the first time work by such artists as J.M.W. Turner (*On the Rhine*, No. 24) and Co. Clare-born Sir Frederick William Burton (*Meeting on the Turret Stairs*, No. 56). These, together with J. Hungerford Pollen's design for the ceiling of the Great Gallery at Kilkenny Castle (No. 17, *The Golden Age* – Design of Painting on roof of Great Gallery, Kilkenny Castle), ensured that a high standard was maintained throughout. Other sections were devoted to bronzes, engravings and enamels.

Substantial pieces were loaned by Queen Victoria, including a selection from the British School, together with portraits of the royal family. Entries were also received, among others, from Lords Charlemont, Portarlington and Powerscourt, the Duke of Leinster, Sir Charles Coote, the Knight of Kerry, the National Gallery, London, the Royal Academy, and the South Kensington Museum.

Almost immediately after the opening, 'the Palace' settled into a routine of concerts but not, however, before a Grand Ball which took place on 12 May 1865

The height of Victorian fashion at the Grand Ball on 12 May 1865, in aid of the Irish Academy of Music.

in aid of the Irish Academy of Music (IAM). The list of supporters was impressive and included the Lord Lieutenant's wife, Lady Wodehouse, and a clutch of countesses, along with a bevy of marchionesses who endeavoured to mingle with the crowds.

In the opinion of *The Freeman's Journal* (13 May 1865), at least 3,000 people had attended the glittering evening which was 'a scene of splendour and festivity that dazzled and delighted...'.

On 31 May, the Philharmonic Society presented Joseph Joachim, violin, and Louis Brassin, piano. Joachim ('he expressed the most tender and passionate emotions') played the Mendelssohn Concerto with Joseph Robinson 'a little too loud' on the piano. Brassin also played Beethoven's E flat Concerto with 'the orchestra' and he and Joachim were heard in the Andante Variations of the Kreutzer Sonata and some solo piano pieces. Mrs R.M. Levey (Julia Cruise), also part of the programme, regaled her audience with Wilhelm Ganz's *Nightingale's Trill*.

Music at the Great Exhibition

Throughout the Exhibition months, the grounds resounded to the sounds of the military bands performing each evening at 7pm. Indoor concerts and recitals demonstrated the various musical instruments which were on display, beginning with Miss Rose O'Toole playing a selection of Edward Bunting's *Ancient Music of Ireland* on 'Caldey's Boudoir Grand Piano'.

A performance by the brother and sister duo – William Charles Levey, by then a member of the Society of Composers in Paris, and Mrs H.A. Cruise (Emma Levey) – took place on 21 July and included a performance of a 'Grand Duet for Two Pianofortes on motifas from *Il Trovatore* at the conversazione at the Exhibition Palace'. Members of the famous Levey family, they presented a number of programmes over the coming months. At times, they were joined by regimental bands and, on 5 September, by the precocious Master Stradiot, son of the bandmaster of the 8th Regiment.

On 23 July, Pauline Elsner, the fourteen-year-old daughter of Wilhelm Elsner, professor of cello at the IAM, gave a recital on 'Hopkinson's Patent Grand Piano'. Miss O'Toole returned to Earlsfort Terrace on 12 September to play the only 'duet piano' on display, built by Edward Charles Locke of Manchester. Later in the month, Rust & Co. of London announced that Mr Fletcher Baker would give a recital on their 'Royal Patent Tubular' and 'Telescopic Desk-Front' pianoforte – said to be an entirely new, modern and elegant drawing room instrument. This was allegedly 'the most perfect piano produced'. The Grand Organ of 'the Palace' was the centre of attraction on a number of afternoons, as on 17 August when Mr R. Sutton Swaby of Wexford gave a recital.

The exhibition continued until 9 November with the final concert held that evening. The New Philharmonic Society was under the direction of Robert Stewart, the Dublin-born conductor, composer and teacher who had been organist of Christ Church Cathedral and Trinity College. The closing programme included Handel's *Coronation Anthem*, oratorio selections and a new cantata by Stewart which was described as 'peculiarly rich in choral and orchestral effects and its general merit bears excellent testimony to the eminent abilities of its composer'. So crowded was the audience that it was 'found necessary to throw open the huge folding-doors dividing the hall from the nave and western gallery'. Following the formal concert, the bands of the 14th Hussars and 17th Lancers performed in the nave 'to an immense audience'.

Nearly a Million Visitors

A total of 932,662 visitors attended the Great Exhibition[50] between 9 May and 9 November 1865. In terms of national impact, the 1865 Dublin International Exhibition of Arts and Manufactures had been considerably less successful than the Dublin International

Photograph showing crowds strolling in the exhibition grounds, with the Winter Garden in the background. Earlsfort Terrace, 1865. (William English, Getty Images)

Exhibition of 1853. Total receipts were down – £45,000, substantially less than £53,000 in 1853. The number of British exhibitors had been reduced by half, although the display of luxury goods had increased. However, many of these prestige exhibits had little relevance for the average visitor. In the view of many, the Dublin International Exhibition of 1865 had not lived up to expectations.

At the official closing ceremony, F.W. Brady, QC, spoke on behalf of the Executive Committee of the Company:

> *[the members of the Committee] now resign the trust committed to them with the less regret, that these extensive halls are not to be taken away but will soon be re-opened, and form a permanent centre of recreation and instruction where for years to come the people of Ireland may find many agreeable associations to recall the International Exhibition of 1865.*[51]

Such sentiments were universally held.

CHAPTER 4
AN ERA COMES TO AN END

Events at 'the Palace'

Shortly after the close of the 1865 exhibition, 'the Palace' reverted to its original, intended role as a venue for popular entertainment which included lectures, concerts, shows, recreations and 'rational enjoyment'. The *Dublin Builder* of 15 February 1866 reported on a recent 'Conversazione at the Exhibition Palace' which attracted 6,000 people for an evening of music, poetry, singing and the fine arts. However, *The Freeman's Journal* looked on these amusements as being 'tenth-rate in character, English in kind, suitable perhaps to the great manufacturing towns',[1] but had to concede that

> the large concert hall also looked to great advantage. Mr Jones, the architect, deserves high praise for the tasteful and elegant design of the galleries now completed and contributing much to make the large concert hall by far the most elegant and spacious apartment in the Kingdom.

From May 1866 onwards, it was announced that a series of 'Grand Musical performances' would begin at Earlsfort Terrace, to be followed by summer promenade concerts which would include choir and orchestra of 150 persons and soloists. A Grand Ball, the first of many, took place in the Palace on 2 July, while *The Freeman's Journal* of 9 July carried an advertisement announcing that the Management Committee intended forming a chorus under the direction of John O'Rorke and were seeking applicants.

Other events held during the season included Richard C. Levey's first appearance in Dublin. Entitled 'Paganini Redivivus', it introduced

effects never heard before and variations of unprecedented beauty and difficulty... offering the most wonderful musical feat on record, one string only and a bow without any hairs.

Allan James Foli — 'Signor Foli' (1835-1899). Born 'Foley' in Cahir, Co. Tipperary, he was a carpenter before moving to Naples to study singing. He had a voice of enormous power and richness in over sixty roles.

The popular Christy's Minstrels also held a series of concerts which 'in consequence of enormous receptions moved to the large Hall'. The Minstrels performed a number of operatic burlesques, including *Lucia di Lammermoor*, on 19 October when the 'Grand Fireworks Night of the Season' took place along with six military bands. Prior to Christmas, fashionable afternoon promenades were held when 'the building [was] comfortably warmed with new heating apparatus'. After Christmas, Blondin, the hero of Niagara, performed marvellous feats of high-rope expertise.

The new year, 1867, brought the first appearance of the Exhibition Palace Choral Union with two performances of Handel's *Messiah* on 15 and 19 January conducted by John O'Rorke with local artists Elizabeth Fennell (later Scott-Fennell), Richard Topham and Grattan Kelly. A review at the time mentioned

> the numerous and fashionable audience, attracted from their warm and cheerful firesides on a night worthy of Siberia. The oratorio was performed most respectfully. The absence of a band was a great drawback but the great organ was worthily presided over by Mr Houghton. The choruses, though not sufficiently full, were admirable, all things considered, and indeed one must confess to being agreeably surprised at the excellent manner [in which] the portions of the Oratorio produced were performed... Mr O'Rorke acquitted himself with much ability, taste and judgment.

Finance was now becoming a major problem, as the Palace was proving unremunerative and difficult to maintain. Management was poor and uncoordinated, and as a result, the debts had grown alarmingly. James Beardwood, who had been responsible for the construction of the main building, had not been paid in full; he died in October 1865 without having been reimbursed for his substantial contribution.[2]

In December 1867, debts had reached a total of £44,367. It was therefore felt that the company could no longer continue in business, and voluntary liquidation was advised. Charles Cummins of Westmoreland Street was appointed official liquidator for a fee of £100. A summary valuation of chattels was carried out which amounted to £56,789/6/0d, with the organ being valued at £1,000. On 19 December 1867, shareholders voted for the winding up of the Exhibition Palace and Winter Garden Company (Limited).

'What will become of the Palace?'

The papers of Richard Southwell Bourke, 6th Earl of Mayo (National Library of Ireland Manuscripts' Collection), provide a detailed and comprehensive chronology of events relating to the debate concerning the future of the buildings and garden at Earlsfort Terrace in the years immediately following the close of the Great Exhibition of 1865. Mayo had been appointed Chief Secretary to the Lord Lieutenant on three separate occasions between 1825-1868. Among Mayo's proposals for the future use of the Earlsfort Terrace site was the transformation of the exhibition building into a centre for scientific education.[3] On 4 October 1867, a W.H. Kerr of 3 Walpole Terrace, Clontarf, wrote to Mayo, offering to buy the exhibition building in order to secure a permanent venue for the exhibition of products manufactured in Ireland. This was to be modelled along lines similar to the Department of Science and Art in South Kensington, London.[4] *The Irish Times* of 5 October 1867 took up the cudgels and urged that

> The Committee of Directors [of the Company] ask the Government to purchase the Exhibition Palace Gardens and premises for the permanent exhibition of manufacturers, raw materials... for the delivery of lectures on arts, music etc., [and] for the erection of the Queen's University in the beautiful gardens.

The Mayo correspondence makes it clear that official government thinking did not mirror the growing popular view. In a letter to Mayo dated 12 October 1867, Under-Secretary, Major General Sir Thomas Larcom (1801-1879), stated that Ireland did not require an exhibition palace as it already possessed the Royal Dublin Society, the

Royal Irish Academy, the National Gallery of Ireland and a Museum of Irish Industry (the Royal College of Science, St Stephen's Green). Larcom argued that all of these institutions contained exhibitions and libraries which were sufficient to meet the requirements of the day. A further proposal from Sir Richard Griffith, Commissioner of Valuation, suggested that the exhibition building might serve as a site for a Queen's University, as originally proposed by *The Irish Times*.[5] On 22 October, Mr Kerr again renewed his campaign[6] and wrote to Mayo suggesting that the exhibition building be transformed into a permanent exhibition for the manufactures of Ireland. The proposal was rejected.[7]

Dublin Corporation now added their views to the debate, stating that the Earlsfort Terrace site should be transformed into a Museum of Art and Industry which might serve as a centre for the diffusion of scientific and industrial knowledge throughout Ireland.[8]

The Victorian design educationist, Sir Henry Cole (1808-1882), described by Professor John Turpin as 'a major architect of the system of art and design education in Victorian Britain',[9] also joined in the debate. In a confidential memo to the Lord President of the Council on Education, Cole referred to a report dated 2 January 1868 which proposed transferring the Royal College of Science from St Stephen's Green to Earlsfort Terrace. The Queen's University, the report had stated, should occupy the vacant building in St Stephen's Green. It should not be housed at Earlsfort Terrace.[10] The report further recommended that the Royal College of Science, the Royal Irish Academy and the Royal Hibernian Academy should all occupy the same exhibition building at Earlsfort Terrace and that, in each case, their existing current premises should be sold. The great Central Hall, together with the glass-covered portions of the Earlsfort building (the Winter Garden) were to be made available for

The destruction of the Theatre Royal in 1880 meant yet another Dublin venue was no longer available for musical events.

exhibitions of the Royal College of Science. The left wing would house the College of Science, the Royal Irish Academy and the Royal Hibernian Academy.[11]

Cole disagreed with the report's suggestions. He wished to see the Royal College of Science continue as an institution and believed that it should retain its St Stephen's Green site. He envisaged the Earlsfort Terrace building being transformed into an industrial museum and becoming a home for exhibits from the Royal College of Science.[12] On 7 March 1868, *The Freeman's Journal* confirmed that the Royal Dublin Society would not be moving to Earlsfort Terrace. The paper remarked that

even the phantom of Fenianism vanishes before the substantial realities of employment, comfort and content.

Other bodies such as the Irish Art Institute Committee envisaged that a technological museum, together with a Museum of Natural History, should occupy the site.[13]

For two years, a furious debate centred on the future of the Earlsfort Terrace Palace site and buildings. The government contemplated buying the Exhibition Palace and Winter Garden Company as a Royal Irish Institute 'for the diffusion of science and art as applied to industry throughout Ireland',[14] and the buildings, together with the site, were offered to them for £50,000. However, negotiations were interrupted by a change of government. In an article dated April 1868 and entitled 'What is to become of the Dublin Exhibition Palace?', the *Dublin Builder* describes a meeting of company shareholders, chaired by Benjamin Lee Guinness, to consider the government's offer. By now, the company's debts were in the region of £50,000, and the mood of the meeting was one of indignation at the inadequacy of the sum proposed by Westminster which it deemed to be 'shamefully insufficient'.[15] One speaker at the meeting made this point:

Alderman Manning said it was of public importance that they should keep the Exhibition open as a place for public amusement and recreation. He was never anxious that the Government should get hold of it. He would much rather they should keep the buildings [the Exhibition Palace and Winter Garden] themselves for what [they were] originally intended, and therefore, he would suggest that those who were responsible to the bank should come forward and liberally assist the concern, while the other shareholders should do likewise by purchasing the preference stock. For his own part, he was prepared to invest £100 in the purchase of shares, and he promised to get hundreds of others to do the same.[16]

In May 1869, it was suggested that the Exhibition Palace and Winter Garden be sold. The buildings were in urgent need of repair and the list of debts and claims against the company was rising steadily. An official liquidator, Edward Hudson of Gardiner Place, Dublin, was appointed[17] and the date for a public auction was set – 30

December 1869 – with George Tickell of Dublin appointed as auctioneer. The reserve price of £46,000 was to be kept in a sealed envelope until the time of the sale. The property was to be offered in one lot.

Any offers for 'the Palace'?

On the day of the auction, the highest offer amounted to £30,000 and resulted in no sale.[18] In May 1870, Sir Arthur Guinness and his brother, Edward Cecil, offered to buy the leasehold of the Exhibition Palace and Winter Garden Company and all its property for the sum of £10. They also agreed to pay all debts, including legal costs and all other legal proceedings.[19]

On 25 September 1871, *The Irish Times* announced that Sir Arthur Guinness and Edward Cecil had purchased the site. By an order dated 29 May 1871, both brothers were deemed to be the purchasers of the entire leasehold and other property.[20] They paid off the company's debts and ensured that all creditors and other parties had been reimbursed.

Sir Arthur Guinness and Edward Cecil Guinness appear to have been anxious that the original idea of the Exhibition and Winter Garden Company – to provide popular entertainment – should be carried on, and for the next ten years, public events including banquets, concerts, exhibitions, flower shows, meetings and circuses continued as before.[21]

Balloons and Circuses

One of the most exciting events to take place at the Palace during this period was a grand ascent by the famous French balloon, 'Gambetta', which had been brought to Dublin at enormous expense. This was due to take place on 29 May 1871.

Two engravings, views of Alfred Gresham Jones' Dublin Exhibition Palace and Winter Garden. His work was selected in the 1862 competition, although the plans were considerably modified. (Courtesy of the National Library of Ireland)

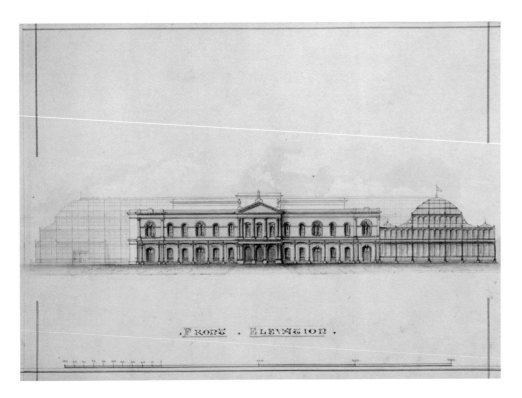

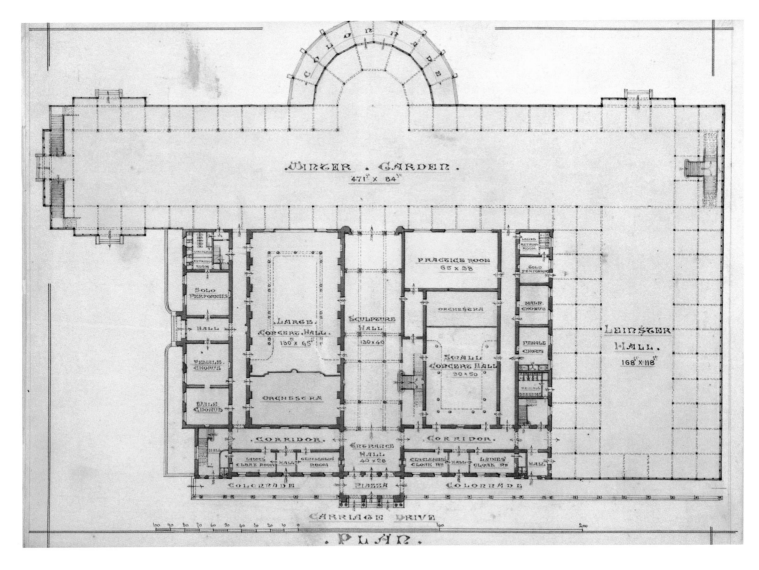

Alfred Gresham Jones' drawings for the Exhibition Palace, 1865.

Top: The Front Elevation.

Bottom: Ground Floor plan, showing the size and importance of areas devoted to music. The 'Large Concert Hall' and 'Orchestra' (left of centre) and the 'Small Concert Hall', 'Orchestra' and 'Practice Room' (right of centre).
(Courtesy of the National Library of Ireland)

Three views of Alfred Gresham Jones' Dublin Exhibition Palace and Winter Garden, Earlsfort Terrace. Top: Elevation of the Winter Garden; Bottom left: Side Elevation of the Main Building; Bottom right: Front Elevation of Interior. Watercolour on paper. (Courtesy of the National Library of Ireland)

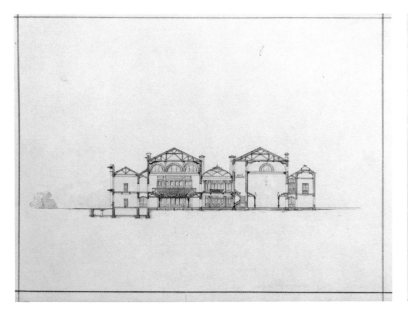

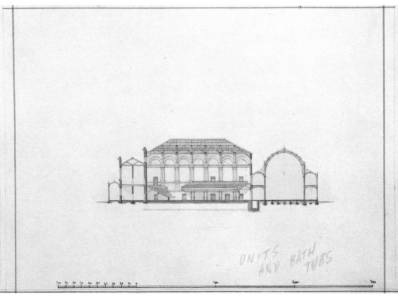

An interior view of the stands at the 1865 Dublin Exhibition. (from The Supplement to The Illustrated London News, August 1865)

The Coldstream Guards' fancy dress ball at the Exhibition Palace in 1873.

The Iveagh Gardens which lie behind the National Concert Hall are now used for NCH concerts and Outreach programmes. (Photo: Eugene Langan)

The fountain overflows: A water display in the Iveagh Gardens, recalling W.B. Yeats' symbol of 'the richness of artistic endeavour'. (Photo: Eugene Langan)

R.M. Butler's own impression of the new National University of Ireland at Earlsfort Terrace, 1914. Butler's original designs paid tribute to elements of eighteenth-century Dublin architecture, particularly that of James Gandon and his Custom House. (Courtesy of the Irish Architectural Archive)

Alfred Gresham Jones' designs for the 1865 Exhibition Palace included impressive entrance gates. Surviving to this day, they were hung on powerful cast-iron hinges and formed in the shape of a hand, as shown here. (Photo: Eugene Langan)

Details of Columns at the NCH.

Richard J. King's stained glass memorial window to Kevin Barry.

Mr J. Hodsman will ascend [from the grounds of the Exhibition Palace] with a young lady, a native of Dublin. During ascent the aeronauts will dislodge ornamental parachutes. Letters will be received and delivered by 'Balloon Post', according to the latest Parisian system.

Due to some undisclosed accident, the project had to be abandoned. However, Hodsman and his daughter eventually became the first persons to cross the Irish Channel by balloon.

October 1871 saw the appearance of Maskelyne and Cooke and their talented London Company, in what *The Freeman's Journal* described as 'original, popular and refined entertainment of science, mystery, mirth and amusement'. This included 'the most marvellous phenomena, Japanese Juggler, Exposé of Spiritualism, Decapitation Extraordinary and Startling Metamorphosis'. Whether this led, a year later, to a series of twelve lectures on Sanitary Science by Dr Charles A. Cameron, Professor of Science at the College of Surgeons, is a matter for conjecture.

In December 1871, Sir Arthur Guinness and Edward Cecil decided to place both the glass and masonry buildings (the Exhibition Palace and Winter Garden), together with the site, at the disposal of a committee which would be responsible for organising a National Exhibition of Arts and Industries. This was officially opened by the Duke of Edinburgh on 5 June 1872, with music supplied by the New Philharmonic Society and Orchestra. One of the principal aims of the exhibition was the advancement of Ireland and its industries. An area entitled 'The Leinster Hall' was set aside for the promotion of Irish manufactured products. A second section dealt with Industries and Manufacturers. The third, relating to Fine Art, included the loan collection of national portraits, 'The Irish National Portrait Gallery', similar to the English National Portrait Gallery in London. Nationalist figures were included – O'Connell, Emmet, Davis, Sarsfield. Artists, actors and writers were not overlooked and included the artist William Ashford, actor Charles Macklin, and writer Edmund Burke.[22] (This collection was to serve as the nucleus of the Irish National Portrait Gallery belonging to the National Gallery of Ireland.)

Also included was a collection of ornamental art of which the *Art Journal* remarked: 'There is good reason to believe that there are ample materials for a Dublin South Kensington'. A number of works in watercolour were also placed on view[23] with leading members of the Old Water-Colour Society contributing. The strong emphasis on Irish painting and sculpture led to an increased awareness of the heritage of Irish art and what Irish artists were capable of producing.

The Musical Tradition Continues

Music continued throughout the exhibition period with band concerts, a choral recital of secular music, an organ recital and concerts by students from the Royal Irish Academy of Music. The proceedings were considerably enlivened by the appearance of Miss Sophie Flora Heilbron, who described herself as 'pianist to the Empress of Russia and Austria, the King and Queen of Prussia and the Queen of Portugal, having just completed an engagement of the International Exhibition, South Kensington'. The exhibition was brought to a close on 30 November with an evening concert. An 'Ode' written especially for the occasion by John Francis Waller, set to music by Robert Stewart, was performed by the New Philharmonic Band and Chorus

Barton McGuckin (1852-1917), a singer much admired by Dublin audiences at the end of the nineteenth century. He was the model for Bartell D'Arcy in James Joyce's story, 'The Dead'.

numbering five hundred on the enlarged orchestra (stage) at the north end of the Winter Garden.

However, the event had not been without controversy. Many felt that the section relating to Irish manufactured goods should have been substantially larger; Belfast firms had not been adequately represented and the response from manufacturers, particularly those engaged in large-scale factory production, was deemed petty.

Renovation of 'the Palace'

In order to bring the Exhibition Palace and Winter Garden up to an improved standard, the Guinness brothers had employed a London architect, William Emden, who was to be responsible for the interior

decoration and general refurbishment of both the Winter Garden and the Exhibition Palace. Emden's work included designs for two large fountains to be erected in the central hall and made in 'marezzo marble'.[24] Emden employed mainly English and French craftsmen and workers[25] which led to ill feeling. A 'Pupil of the Dublin School of Art', writing in the *Irish Builder* in May 1872, expressed the widespread confusion and resentment.

> *Sir, Does it not seem somewhat paradoxical that while the newspapers, on the one hand, tell us that native genius and talent is capable of achieving almost everything in the circle of the arts, that the promoters of our exhibition, on the other hand, are doing their very best to make us ridiculous as a people, why, in the name of common sense, did they send over across channel to procure third-rate artists, and some second-rate manufacturers?* [26]

This air of discontent had been evident even before the National Exhibition of Arts and Industries had opened on 5 June 1872, with acrimonious exchanges flying back and forth between Emden and his employers in relation to Emden's accounts. These ranged from 'the absurd price of £9 for tree ferns' to disputes relating to designs for the fountains; Sir Arthur Guinness and Edward Cecil considered these to be outrageously expensive and were reluctant to pay.[27]

In 1873 a small-scale exhibition was organised at Earlsfort Terrace and opened with a performance of Mendelssohn's *Athalie* conducted by G.V. Lee. The soloists included Emilie de Meric Lablache and Signor Foli. In the evening, the musicians appear to have stunned their audience – 'a band of fifty, which agreeably surprised us' by playing Haydn's *Surprise* Symphony in a programme under R.M. Levey. Earlier that afternoon, a new organ had been inaugurated by W.H. Gater. *The Freeman's Journal* of 15 May reported:

The organ stands at the rere of the Orchestra, at the junction of the nave and Leinster Hall, all is contained in a case which bears on the front pipes some of the specimens of art illumination after the medieval patterns. Gater displayed the resources of the new organ to the best advantage. It possesses high merit in softness and tone, and its power is remarkable for an instrument of its compass.

[In the evening] At seven 'clock the doors were thrown open again and there was a genuine rush to the Concert Hall as all believed a rich treat was in store for them. The pressure from behind became so great that very many persons found their way over the barriers dividing the reserved seats from the body, and the Hall was filled to the doors on floor and balconies with surprising quickness.

Critical Voices

Structural improvements at the Palace buildings had not succeeded in dampening criticism of events being held there. On 18 November, the second of two Grand Concerts was presented by Cramer & Co., the music store in Westmoreland Street. The soloists were Carlotta Patti (1835-1889), an elder sister of Adelina Patti, the great Parisian pianist Theodore Ritter (1841-1886), a pupil of Liszt, and the violinist Carl Berzon, who would join the teaching staff of the RIAM. *The Freeman's Journal* reported:

Several hundred were in the Palace shortly after one o'clock and not to have got away before a quarter to five was something like imprisonment.

The RIAM gave a series of choral concerts between January and June 1875 with Joseph Robinson conducting. The programmes covered Beethoven's Mass in C and

Choral Fantasia, selections from Irish composers, and the ubiquitous Mendelssohn, *Lauda Sion* in the first concert and the lyric Odes from his *Athalie* in the second.

Through the determination of Joseph Robinson, 1876 saw the birth of the Dublin Musical Society (DMS). Robinson would remain in charge for almost fourteen years and most of the choral body's public appearances would be in Earlsfort Terrace. Their first concert in May 1876 included Gounod's *St Cecilia Mass*, and saw every seat occupied. *The Freeman's Journal* stated that 'the Hall looks as cheerful and gay as ever we remember seeing it'.

A programme for a concert at the Exhibition Palace on 28 February 1881 in which Madame Zelia Trebelli, pictured here, was the soloist. Part One of the concert was devoted to Rossini's 'Stabat Mater', with a 'Miscellaneous Selection' for Part Two.

The highlight of 1877 may well have been Anton Rubinstein's piano recitals on 2 and 3 April. Including Schumann's *Carnaval* and music by Chopin and himself, he played on an Erard piano, and 'When all was over the audience were in an ecstasy of delight'. May Day was celebrated with a Festival of Flowers and Song in the Winter Garden, including 'May-Pole on the Village Green', 'The Chimney Sweepers May-Day Glee' and a juvenile choir of some seven hundred voices.

In January 1878, an odd variety of events at the Exhibition Palace began with the Hague Minstrels, the 'original slave troupe of sixty performers'. The Irish Billiard Championship took place in February and the Murrill Collection of Modern Paintings and Raphael Cartoons was exhibited throughout the summer. The Irish Kennel Club had its first show in early August and there was a civil and military gymnastic contest by electric light in December. Over the Christmas and New Year period, there were 'attractions never before rivalled in the City of Dublin when Zazel will be fired from the cannon'.

The Hallé at the Hall

A major musical attraction during 1878 was the first ever visit to Ireland of the Hallé Orchestra in October. They gave two concerts at the Exhibition Palace on the afternoon and evening of the 26th. Conducted by Charles Hallé and with Hallé himself and his second wife, Madame Norman-Neruda as soloists, the concerts had a profound effect on the musical life of Dublin despite the fact that they were poorly attended.

The advertisements for the concerts included the complete list of orchestra members as well as the programme details. Hallé played Mendelssohn's *Serenade* and *Allegro giocoso* in the afternoon and Beethoven's *Emperor* Concerto in the evening. Mrs Hallé was heard in Spohr's *Concerto Dramatico* and the *Adagio* and *Rondo* from Vieuxtemp's E major Concerto. On the symphonic front, it was Beethoven's Sixth before tea, followed by Mozart's *Jupiter*, While the performances received unstinted praise, it was felt the small assembly was due to lack of vocal items on the programmes.

An Era Ends

Exhibitions and recitals continued at Earlsfort Terrace for the next two years. Then, in May 1882, Edward Cecil Guinness sold the glass and iron building – the Winter Garden – to John Orrel Lever (1824-1897), MP for Galway,[28] for £8,200. The conditions specified that the building had to be dismantled within three months and that no part of the materials were to be used in Ireland; all had to be 'removed with dispatch to England'.[29] The agreement covered all glass and iron works, although grottoes and fountains, together with the gas and heating pipes, were excluded. Estimates were received for the dismantling of the building and the shipping of the materials to London.[30] The Winter Garden was subsequently erected in Battersea Park, London, on a site extending to just over ten acres and known as the Albert Palace of Science and Art. It was demolished 1894.[31]

As part of their joint agreement,[32] Guinness and John Orrel Lever agreed that Guinness would erect a nine-foot-high wooden fence at the rear of the iron and glass building in order to prevent workmen from trespassing in his garden while removing the structure.

By now, Guinness had decided not to hold further exhibitions and other events at Earlsfort Terrace and was anxious to sell the Exhibition Palace building (the remaining stone and brick portion). The Commissioners of Public Works had already made arrangements with him for renting rooms in the Palace building for University and Civil Service examinations.[33] Guinness was aware that the newly established Royal University of Ireland was anxious to build lecture halls on any vacant ground that might become available. Various approaches were made to the Commissioners of Public Works in an effort to overcome several difficulties,[34] including the removal of certain covenants which would restrict future building on the site.

On 1 March 1883, Edward Cecil Guinness instructed counsel to settle the deed for the sale of the building to the Commissioners of Public Works. The agreed sum was £27,000.[35]

With the establishment of the Royal University of Ireland, Earlsfort Terrace would take on a new life as a centre for learning.

Charles Hallé and his second wife, Wilhelmine Norman-Neruda, appeared at the Exhibition Palace on 26 October 1878. The Hallé Orchestra has continued to make frequent visits to Dublin for more than a century.

The ESB/National Concert Hall Music Residencies Project, 'In Tune', is one of the many successful Education and Outreach programmes at the NCH. (Photo: Eugene Langan)

CHAPTER 5
THE UNIVERSITY ERA AT EARLSFORT TERRACE

The Royal University of Ireland

The 1879 Act of Parliament which established the Royal University of Ireland (RUI) was a significant event in the history of the Earlsfort Terrace site as the RUI was to occupy the buildings from 1883 to 1908. A number of events led to the passing of this Act.

A proposal to establish the Catholic University of Ireland was first initiated at the Synod of Thurles in 1850. In November 1851, John Henry (later Cardinal) Newman (1801-1890), one of the leaders of the Oxford Movement which had fought for reform of the Church of England, was formally invited by Archbishop Paul Cullen to advise on the establishment of a Catholic University of Ireland and to become its rector, an office which Newman held until his resignation in November 1858. Lectures commenced at the Catholic University on the feast of St Malachy, 3 November 1854, with the main activities centred at 86 St Stephen's Green (afterwards known as St Patrick's or University House and today called Newman House) and at the Catholic University's Medical School, Cecilia Street (now part of Dublin's Temple Bar area). The latter opened on 2 November 1855 and maintained an active and flourishing existence there until 1908 when it became the Medical Faculty of University College, Dublin (UCD).[1]

The design for the Catholic University of Ireland by James Joseph McCarthy (1817-1882). The design was published, and the foundation stone was laid in July 1862. However, it was never built. The site, in Clonliffe West, Drumcondra, Dublin, was later sold to the Irish Redemptorists.

In 1882, the St Stephen's Green institution of the Catholic University officially changed its name and became University College. It opened its doors for the 1882-83 academic year with the appointment of the Rev. John Egan, professor of English (later Bishop of Waterford), as president. In association with the School of Medicine, University College now embarked on a new career, preparing students for the examinations and degrees of the Royal University of Ireland. In 1883, the bishops entrusted the management of University College to the Society of Jesus. The teaching staff of the former Catholic University continued to act under the new administration and included some of Newman's foundation professors.

The Royal University of Ireland was a non-denominational, purely examining body. It did not have the power to teach but was a degree-awarding institution modelled on the lines of the University of London. The RUI could confer degrees in Arts, Medicine, Law, Engineering, Music and Science, thus making recognised degrees and fellowships available to University College for the first time.

The senate which became the RUI's governing body was established at the beginning of 1881. Composed of an equal number of Catholics and Protestants, it had the power to appoint a number of Fellows who were not only examiners but also teaching professors. The RUI senate met at Earlsfort Terrace several times a year and all awards, results and recommendations had to be referred to, and confirmed by, this ruling body.

In October 1881, a year after its establishment, the RUI's senate submitted outlines and details of required accommodation, as no permanent site for the RUI had been built or indeed selected. The senate's list included requirements for examination rooms, offices, waiting and cloak rooms, laboratories plus equipment, a small museum together with a preparatory room, coffee rooms etc. A note suggested that

> it will be necessary to have two separate entrances (one for males and one for females) to the Examination portion of the Buildings.

The report concluded:

> We also desire to express our opinion that with a view to the convenience of students attending the examinations and their accommodation during the period of attendance, it is expedient that the University Buildings should be situated within the city of Dublin, and we deem it most important that a site should be selected which would allow for considerable extension hereafter, when the University has fully developed.[2]

The Exhibition Palace building at Earlsfort Terrace was allocated to the RUI by the Board of Works in 1883 who carried out the conversion of the buildings. The senate of the RUI submitted a *Paper of Queries* to the Board, outlining specific questions relating to the conversion of the Exhibition Hall for university purposes, as well as to building on ground which was being used as a skating rink. James H. Owen (died 1891),[3] the Board of Works' advising assistant architect, believed that the demolition of the existing building would be sensible. He went further, adding that retaining the existing hall would

> involve the sacrifice of good arrangement, and its position on the site would seriously limit the scope of any architect in forming a design for the complete building.

The cost of converting the Exhibition Palace was estimated at £40,000 and the skating rink at £2,000. In Owen's opinion, the combined areas were too small for a university, and he suggested an alternative site on Mespil Road. (A sketch of this proposal can be seen in the National Archives, Dublin.[4]) In a significant memo, Owen argued:

> What would be the probable cost of requisite alterations, and what time would be required to complete them? This question seems to take it for granted that the present building may be adapted without additions. I think that it would be better to enquire as to what saving of outlay in building would be effected by utilising the existing Exhibition Buildings?[5]

Owen's advice was ignored. Instead, Edward Kavanagh, architect and chief draftsman of the Board of Works,[6] set about adapting the existing Palace Exhibition building. From a total of eleven tenders received, a bid of £29,250 from George Moyers & Co., Contractors of South Richmond Street, Dublin, was accepted in mid-1884. As only £25,315 was available from the Treasury, a £5,000 saving was made by changing the facing stone in the new façades.[7] Patterson and Kempster of 95 Lower Leeson Street, surveyors for the Board of Works, prepared a bill of quantities.

Extensive internal alterations were carried out to all floors. These included converting suitable offices for the RUI on the first floor together with the Chamber, also situated on the first floor which was where the RUI senate was to meet. On the ground floor, the Great Concert Hall now became known as the Great Hall and was the setting for many distinguished ceremonial occasions and conferrals. Here Honorary Doctor of Music degrees would be awarded by the RUI to Princess (later Queen) Alexandra in 1885, the Duchess of Connaught in 1903, and to the organist and music historian, William Grattan Flood (1859-1928), in 1907. Annie Patterson (1868-1934), a distinguished teacher and music authority and one of the founders of Féis Ceoil, was the Royal University's first official Doctor of Music and the first woman to achieve that distinction. However, as academic engagements involving the Great Hall were not too pressing throughout the academic year, the senate frequently let the venue for concerts and other events.

External alterations to the Exhibition Palace building saw the east block (Earlsfort Terrace side) being faced in Dungannon sandstone. Other external alternations included removing the three allegorical stone figures of Hibernia, Industry and Commerce from the main front pediment. The figures were 'to be very carefully taken down and removed to a place of safety upon the premises'. Once removed, they remained propped against a wall behind the building until well into the 1950s. In 1987, they were taken to the Millennium Garden in Dame Street were they may be seen today.

The Royal University, Earlsfort Terrace, which shows the addition of Edward Kavanagh's (1845-1901) campanile which was built to disguise the building's ventilation shaft.

Also included in the RUI building programme, and occupying the space between Hatch Street and the south end of the newly converted Exhibition Palace building, were the new laboratories for the RUI which are still in use today.

In order to disguise the building's ventilation shaft, a cunningly designed campanile, in the Italianate style by Edward Kavanagh, was also executed in Dungannon sandstone. This was built by the Dublin firm of George Moyers[8] at the north-east corner of the east block (facing Earlsfort Terrace). The clock dial and bells, the cost of which amounted to £35,[9] had originally come from the General Post Office and dated from 1818. They were fitted in March 1887 by Frengley Bros.

The Arts and Crafts Society of Ireland, founded in 1894 by the Earl of Mayo and a 'few enthusiastic pioneers... amateurs and connoisseurs weary of the time-worn conventions of the Irish designer',[10] held their first exhibition in the small Concert Hall at Earlsfort Terrace in 1895. A retrospective section of Irish art-craftsmanship was on display, together with a loan collection arranged by leading practitioners of the English Arts and Crafts Movement. Exhibits also included architectural drawings, examples of book binding,[11] lace, porcelain, wallpaper design etc.[12]

While the Evicted Tenants' Association was refused an application to hold a meeting in the Great Hall, a function to celebrate the tercentenary of the potato was permitted in 1896. The following year, Countess Cadogan, wife of the Viceroy, mounted an extensive exhibition of Irish textile manufactures both at Earlsfort Terrace and in London.[13]

A list (dated 1899) of those generally permitted to use the university buildings on occasions, in particular the Great Hall, illustrates how turn-of-the-century Dublin was greatly enjoying all types of music, ranging from John McCormack and Nellie Melba to the Dublin Musical Society, the Dublin Orchestral Society and the Royal Irish Academy of Music. The Royal Horticultural Society of Ireland also made use of the building, as did the Military Society of Ireland, the National Teachers' Association, the Arts and Crafts Society, the Féis Ceoil Committee, and the Technical Schools' Committee. The Civil Service Commissioners and the Intermediate Education Board held their examinations there each year in June.

On occasions, conferrals in the Great Hall would get out of hand. In keeping with the nationalist and reformist mood of the country between 1900 and 1907, the students were becoming more critical of the political and educational status quo. Such acts as the playing of 'God Save the King' at conferrals resulted in rowdy interruptions by students and the singing of 'God Save Ireland'. With the police in attendance from 1903 onwards, protests did not diminish but rather increased. At the 1905 ceremony, the organ gallery was occupied to prevent the playing of the English anthem.

The inadequacy of the facilities coupled with lack of adequate space at Earlsfort Terrace, was now becoming a major problem for the RUI. *A Handbook to the Dublin District*, 1908 remarked:

The laboratories and lecture halls of the College are taxed to their fullest capacity in providing for the absolute necessities of students preparing for the University examinations; and recently temporary buildings have been erected to accommodate rapidly increasing numbers.[14]

The National University of Ireland

At the beginning of the twentieth century, the demand began to grow for a national university, one which would reflect nationalist cultural attitudes and not merely be an institution which complied with the Catholic viewpoint. In 1907, Augustine Birrell became Ireland's Chief Secretary.[15] An extraordinary, enlightened man, he succeeded in producing a piece of legislation which would revolutionise the Irish university system.

A skilful diplomat, Birrell persuaded parliament to pass the Irish Universities Act (1908). Under its terms, the University of Dublin, together with Trinity College, was to be left untouched. Queen's College, Belfast, was to enjoy the status of a university in its own right. And a National University of Ireland (NUI) was to be created comprising three constituent colleges – the Queen's Colleges in Cork and Galway, and a 'new' college in Dublin. The nucleus of this Dublin-based 'new' college was the existing University College at Nos. 84, 85 and 86 St Stephen's Green, together with the Medical School at Cecilia Street. These would now become known as University College, Dublin – UCD.

The Bill had been skilfully guided through parliament by Birrell and received the support of both the Conservatives and Liberals, while the Irish party had also lent their approval. On 1 August 1908, the Irish Universities Act became law. This brought to a close the Royal University of Ireland at Earlsfort Terrace and saw the demise of the Jesuit-run University College based at 84, 85 and 86 St Stephen's Green. These premises became the first home of the newly established University College. The Dean of the Medical Faculty of UCD, Dr Denis J. Coffey, was appointed its first president. UCD was now a constituent college of the National University of Ireland. It would become a powerful institution moulded by modern ideological and practical influences.

UCD at Earlsfort Terrace

The last examinations of the Royal University of Ireland took place at Earlsfort Terrace in the autumn of 1909, and the 'old Royal', as it was fondly known, was officially dissolved on 31 October of that year. University College, Dublin, the chief beneficiary of the 1908 Irish Universities Act, received the somewhat dilapidated RUI buildings and the Earlsfort Terrace site, together with an initial building grant of £110,000 for expansion purposes. The RUI apparatus, furniture and around 6,000 reference books also became the property of the college. However, an Internal UCD report stated:

In view of the necessity that the new College should be well placed in the city of Dublin, the possession of the Earlsfort Terrace site was of great advantage. But from the first, the inadequacy of the buildings grant, in view of permanent requirements, was apparent. The older buildings on the site, dating from the Exhibition of 1865 were, in the main, a few large halls, wholly unsuitable for the requirements of a teaching College and, as it turned out to be, from their disposition and structure, incapable of adaptation. The more recent buildings on the site, erected as examination laboratories in 1886, could at best and after modification give very limited accommodation, so that in effect the sum of £110,000 was all that was available towards almost the whole material outfit of the buildings and equipment of the new College.[16]

The buildings at Earlsfort Terrace were now quite dilapidated and run down, with facilities inadequate to cope with the ever increasing number of students. The newly appointed President of UCD, Dr Coffey, together with the governing body, decided to make an approach to their neighbour, Edward Cecil Guinness,[17] to see if it might be possible to expand the existing Earlsfort Terrace site. At the beginning, Guinness was not keen to dispose of any parcel of ground. However, following a communication from Dr Coffey, dated 24 April 1911, in which it was made clear that the old Royal University at Earlsfort Terrace was to become 'the permanent site' of UCD, Guinness complied. He agreed to dispose of a portion of his land bordering on Hatch Street[18] and a section of his riding school[19] situated on the St Stephen's Green side of the Iveagh Gardens.

On 12 June 1911, UCD's governing body accepted Guinness' proposal and a unanimous resolution was passed, tendering 'our heartiest thanks to his Lordship for his generous proposal'.[20] The conditions attached included an understanding that this concession was to be final and that no further extension of Guinness' property could or would be granted in the future. In a subsequent letter, Guinness asked if it might be possible that his gift to the college be associated with the names of two of his most valued friends, Monsignor

The marble plaque which commemorates the gift of Edward Cecil Guinness, 1st Earl of Iveagh, to UCD, Earlsfort Terrace, in 1911.

Molloy and Father Healy. He would further appreciate it if the governing body of UCD would allow this association to be permanently commemorated in the form of a memorial tablet to be placed in the building at Earlsfort Terrace. The governing body agreed to his request 'with pleasure'. Today, this marble plaque, which carries the Guinness coat of arms at the top and the college arms at its base, may be seen inside the building at Earlsfort Terrace on the first floor outside the Council Chamber.[21]

UCD's governing body was also anxious to increase the existing Earlsfort Terrace site by purchasing additional ground at nearby Hatch Street. This, however, was proving difficult to acquire. The Hatch Street portion was owned by the Hely-Hutchinson family and had been let to the Dublin Exhibition Palace and Winter Garden Company. The family was unable to waive the covenant against conducting a college or school on this particular piece of ground unless a payment of £100 was received. All costs, including the stamp duty on deeds connected with this agreement made between the Hely-Hutchinson family and UCD, were generously met by Guinness.[22]

An 'Irish' Competition

Details and additions to the site at Earlsfort Terrace amounting to some 5½ acres had at last been finalised and an open competition was held for designs for the new college. *The Building News (London) Journal*, dated 7 June 1912, included the following notice:

UNIVERSITY COLLEGE, DUBLIN

The Governors of University College, Dublin invite Irish architects only to submit designs for new buildings to be erected on a site in Earlsfort Terrace, Dublin. Mr Henry T. Hare, FRIBA is to act as assessor, and has drawn up the conditions ....

The competition was, in fact, open only to those 'living and practising in Ireland'. Twenty-two sets of designs were submitted and eventually exhibited at Earlsfort Terrace. The winning design was by Rudolf Maximillian Butler (1872-1943) of Doolin & Butler, Dawson Street, Dublin.[23] He was formally appointed architect on 28 October 1912.

A contemporary caricature of Rudolf Maximillian Butler, later Professor of Architecture at UCD, appointed architect for the new University College at Earlsfort Terrace in 1912.

R.M. Butler's Design

Butler's proposed plan for University College at Earlsfort Terrace envisaged the construction of four long, classical blocks to surround the existing buildings. It would incorporate quadrangles with classrooms built around the perimeter and placed symmetrically on either side of the library which was on the main axis of the entrance hall. The east block (facing Earlsfort Terrace) would house Arts, Commerce and Administration. The south block, next to Hatch Street, would provide accommodation for Medicine; Physics and Chemistry would occupy the north wing. The west wing would be devoted to Engineering and Architecture, along with the remainder of the departments of Medicine and Science which did not already occupy the south and north wings. The central block would house the Library and Aula Maxima. The original old buildings on the site would be progressively demolished as each wing was completed and eventually, the Great Hall would be replaced by a new examination hall on the central axis.

The first steps in construction at Earlsfort Terrace were to take place in three stages – the removal of the old Royal University façade facing Earlsfort Terrace; the erection of the north wing for Physics and Chemistry; and the building of around three-quarters of the east (front) block (facing Earlsfort Terrace) for Arts and Administration. The east block would extend as far as the termination of the portico (south) of the Royal University. The actual construction of both blocks would amount to around forty per cent of the total required area of that envisaged in Butler's original plan. His completed scheme, with quadrangles incorporated for classrooms around the perimeter and placed symmetrically on either side of the library, was to have been built, with furnishings, at a cost of £220,000. However, due to shortage of funds, the intention was to complete almost half of the design which would in turn accommodate all the departments on a moderate scale. The time-frame envisaged for the three stages was estimated at 2½ years, providing work began in June 1914.

The east block, consisting of a central columnar block with two side wings and a projecting pavilion at each end, was executed. The order adopted for this, the front façade facing Earlsfort Terrace, was Greek Ionic, adapted from the Temple of Eleusis. The north block was also built. However, evidence of insufficient funding for Butler's plans remain to this day and may be seen in the jagged projecting stones to be found on the north front, a monument to the inadequacies of government finance at the time. The construction of the proposed quadrangle was suspended – and indeed never built. The remainder of

PROPOSED UNIVERSITY COLLEGE DUBLIN

ELEVATION to HATCH STREET

Proposed elevation for University College, Earlsfort Terrace. The main façade by R.M. Butler was reminiscent of James Gandon's Custom House, Dublin, with a rusticated central tower which was never built. (Courtesy of Gill & Macmillan)

Butler's proposed plans were never completed. As a result, the Great Hall survived, to be converted and incorporated into the National Concert Hall.

Butler's original designs for UCD at Earlsfort Terrace paid tribute to certain elements of eighteenth-century Dublin architecture, in particular to James Gandon (1743-1823) and his design for the Custom House. However, when executed, it stopped short of including features such as Gandon's rusticated central tower. Butler wrote:

Of the many fine buildings of Dublin, the Custom House was incomparably the best ... and it is doubtful if any city in Europe possessed so fine a building of its sort...[24]

Butler's comments and criticism regarding developments in architecture in Ireland at the beginning of the twentieth century are contained in leading articles of the period. Essentially a fighter, Butler possessed a forceful, colourful style which was expressed in a column entitled 'Topical Touches'[25] in which he aired his views about the emergence of a new style or a 'new architecture' in Ireland. He denounced the idea of devising a 'purely native style' which he believed to be impossible. In Butler's view, styles were never invented but represented a natural growth and 'arose from the natural habits and aspirations of the people'.[26]

In a leading article in 1925 entitled 'A Native Style of Architecture', Butler asked whether Ireland should revive its native architecture. Enthusiasts who wished to renew their links with Celtic art and the Irish Romanesque style were, in his view, people...

without any special knowledge of Irish or any other architecture... Other and more rabid enthusiasts would go even further than the Celtic ornament revivals; they would ornament our public buildings with round towers, with portals, copies from some ancient models, friezes of wolfhounds and harps, and swags of shamrock, with pediments adorned with sunbursts.[27]

Butler believed that the modern Irish architectural style should 'be a very simple style, bold and vigorous, but very refined... indeed, almost severe'.

The New College

Tenders for construction of the new college at Earlsfort Terrace were invited in November 1913 and twelve were received. All were above the maximum available grant and ranged between almost £112,000 and £127,000. The contract was awarded to the Dublin firm of G. & T. Crampton Ltd,[28] subject to the limitation of the contract to £90,000 or thereabouts. It was agreed that a smaller portion of the scheme than that which was set out in the original tender would be built and kept within the limits of the parliamentary grant.

The firm responsible for building University College at Earlsfort Terrace is still owned by the same family today and run by joint Managing Director, G. David Crampton.

It was established by George James Crampton (1851-1925) in 1879 and has a long and respected tradition of building in the city of Dublin. Originally, the firm's headquarters had been established on the site of Richard Turner's Hammersmith Ironworks at Ballsbridge,[29] beside Trinity College Botanic Garden. In 1891, G.J. Crampton moved to Pembroke Road, a site which the firm was to occupy for the next seventy-four years, ultimately changing its title during those intervening years several times to the name by which it is known today – G. & T. Crampton Holdings Ltd.[30]

The Bill of Quantities for the construction at Earlsfort Terrace, and compiled by Morris & Kavanagh, Quantity Surveyors,[31] was available to prospective contractors and makes interesting reading. Bill No. 1, for example, included an estimate for

facing the front and sides of the Buildings with Co. Wicklow Granite, with Portland stone columns, frieze and main cornice, and alternative estimates are to be given for all granite and for all limestone (Stradbally or other approved white) also for Granite with limestone columns etc.[32]

Construction problems began almost immediately. An underground passage was discovered which had to be filled in and supported. Flooding of the Aughamadock quarries at Stradbally, Co. Laois,[33] caused a delay in the supply of limestone. Crampton's workers, with many others, called a strike in 1916. And dramatic wartime inflation caused further difficulties. Finally, no increase in capital appeared to be forthcoming which would have been required to execute Butler's original designs.

However, progress was being made. February 1917 saw the north and east blocks nearing completion at a cost of almost £150,000. The tower of Edward Kavanagh's campanile had been dismantled and removed to the Royal

College of Science (now Government Buildings) in Merrion Street. From 1915, it served as a chimney flue until it was taken down around 1972. The bells and dials remained propped against a wall in the college grounds at Earlsfort Terrace until well into the 1930s.

By 20 July 1920, the cost of the buildings at Earlsfort Terrace had escalated to £153,000. Debts to the architect, contractors and the bank amounted to £37,000. It was estimated that the Engineering and Medical buildings, a library and hall, and railings and furnishings, would cost an additional £150,000.

Financial difficulties meant that work at Earlsfort Terrace ended in 1919. An attempt had been made to curb inflation with an agreement between the contractors and UCD being drawn up in January 1918 which was 'supplemental to an agreement dated 23 April 1914'.[34] This sought to call a halt to rising inflationary prices due to World War I and specified that

The contractors shall complete the works in all respects to the satisfaction of the Architect within twelve months from the date of the agreement.

By December 1920, UCD's governing body was urging the government for a clearance of the debt 'contracted by the erection of the college buildings'. They also requested that the contractors be paid in full. The government showed little sympathy, however, pointing out that the treasury was unable to contemplate making any grant to the college over and above that already granted under the Irish Universities Act, 1908. The college would have to meet its debts from its own resources.

On 17 May 1921, the governing body assigned £5,000 to Cramptons and £2,000 to the electrical contractors.[35] Further facilities for managing the debt were required from the bank, and these were granted. Financial problems were

Building work is completed at Earlsfort Terrace. (Courtesy of G. & T. Crampton Holdings Ltd)

alleviated to some extent when the Provisional Government of January 1922 adopted a sympathetic view towards UCD's financial plight. A letter from the secretary of the Ministry of Finance to the president of UCD, Dr Coffey, stated:

I am directed by the Minister of Finance to inform you that he has had under consideration representations made to him as to the financial position of UCD, particularly in regard to the building debt, and I am to state that, after careful review of the whole position, the Minister is willing to sanction a special non-recurrent grant of £10,000 provided that an undertaking is given on behalf of the College that the whole of this amount will be applied in discharge of outstanding accounts in respect of buildings.

Payment of the amount in question will be [made] immediately on receipt of an undertaking to this effect.

On receipt of this payment, the governing body was able to discharge its outstanding debt of £8,623 due to Cramptons and the balance of £1,376 for architect's fees.

On completion of the east front, those entering the college via the main doors found themselves in the main hall which connected two narrow corridors or wings. On the right of the main entrance was the porters' office with the administration's general office on the left. In direct line from the main entrance and just across the main hall was the Great Hall (now the National Concert Hall) which could seat up to 2,000. This was used for large functions, 'freshers' week' and conferrals.

Prior to the construction of the new buildings at Earlsfort Terrace, a hard-pressed UCD had been using the Great Hall of the old Royal University of Ireland for its own activities, to the exclusion of all non-college functions. However, it was the main hall which became a favourite meeting place for students. Flann O'Brien's *At Swim-Two-Birds* describes the scene:

The College is outwardly a rectangular plain building with a fine porch where the midday sun pours down in summer from the Donnybrook direction, heating the steps for the comfort of the students. The hallway inside is composed of large black and white squares arranged in the orthodox chessboard pattern, and the surrounding walls, done in an unpretentious cream wash, bear three rough smudges caused by the heels, buttocks and shoulders of the students.

The hall was crowded by students, some of them disporting themselves in a quiet civil manner. Modest girls bearing books filed in and out in the channels formed by the groups of boys. There was a hum of converse and much bustle and activity. A liveried attendant came out of a small office in the wall and pealed a shrill bell. This caused some dispersal, many of the boys extinguishing their cigarettes by manual manipulation and going up a circular stairway to the lecture-halls in a brave, arrogant way, some stopping on the stairs to call back to those still below a message of facetious or obscene import.[36]

Numbers Increased

Despite all the financial difficulties and other problems encountered with the construction at Earlsfort Terrace, accommodation, however limited, had been provided for the ever-increasing numbers of students entering the college – from 1,100 in 1917 to over 3,000 in 1944. Unable to complete Butler's original plans, students' facilities had been seriously jeopardised, a situation which became more acute as time went on. The students themselves were fully aware of this. As early as 2 December 1920, the Students' Representative Council had conveyed a resolution demanding the establishment of 'the long-promised Students' Union' which was read at a meeting of the governing body held on that date.

The 'Troubles' and the Civil War

UCD was guided through these difficult times by Dr Denis J. Coffey, President of the College from 1908 to 1940.[37] These years also saw a remarkable expansion in the numbers of students and in the importance and relevance of the college's work to the country. The president's report for 1920-1921 expresses this:

We look forward with confidence to the new era about to open for our country and to that interest in Irish education which will aim at full and adequate achievement in all the activities of our national life.

The college now became the stage for a decisive period of Irish history. Until 1916, the majority of both staff and students went no further than supporting the constitutional objective of Home Rule. Evidence for this can be seen at a Home Rule demonstration held on 31 March 1912 when members of UCD's governing body, together with professors and students, spoke from the 'University platform'. *The National Student* noted with pride that University College was now playing a full role in 'national life'.[38] In faculties such as Law, students were expected by their parents not only to qualify as lawyers but to go further – enter government, become cabinet ministers and thus take an active part in shaping and moulding their country.[39] Several staff members also played an active role. The formation of the Irish Volunteers at a public meeting held in the Rotunda and attended by a substantial body of students from University College was presided over by UCD Professor, Eoin MacNeill.

Events of Easter Week 1916 appear to have taken the college by surprise, despite the fact that several members of staff and students were involved. Professor MacNeill, now Chief of Staff of the Irish Volunteers, had revoked the general mobilisation on Easter Sunday but was unable to keep control over those who marched out on Monday. Placed under arrest, court-martialled, and found guilty of inciting to rebellion, he was sentenced to penal servitude for life. Thomas MacDonagh, an assistant in English in the university, a man who had played an active part with MacNeill in the Irish Volunteers and one of the signatories of the Proclamation of the Republic, was executed for his part in the insurrection. Several junior members of staff and students had also been active in the Rising. These included Louise Gavan Duffy (Education), a founder-member of Cumann na mBan who had occupied the General Post Office during Easter Week, and Joseph Sweeney (Engineering). In his letter of resignation to Prime Minister Asquith, Ireland's Chief Secretary, Augustine Birrell, whose hard work and tact had persuaded parliament to pass the Irish Universities Act in 1908, commented:

> A great band of prisoners has been made today and I hear that some of the instigators and inspirers of this mad revolt are taken. A great many young fools from the National University! are amongst them.

In the UCD President's report for 1916, scant reference was made to the events of Easter Week which was summarised in one bleak sentence:

> There occurred during the session the sad and tragic events of the rebellion in Dublin.[40]

The report also stated that the university had made its contribution to the Great War. Four hundred and fifty students, both past and present, had enlisted 'for noble service'.

In the autumn of that year, both country and college were now experiencing a swing of sympathy towards the men and women who had taken part in the events of Easter Week. *The National Student* carried tributes in favour of such figures as Thomas MacDonagh.[41] A year later, it went so far as to openly discuss the 'advantages which will accrue to the University from the establishment of an Irish Republic.'[42]

After the establishment of Dáil Éireann in January 1919, the 'Troubles' or Anglo-Irish War had plunged the country into turmoil. On several occasions during the next few years, Earlsfort Terrace was raided and searched by British forces, with several members of staff and students either sent to jail or forced to go on the run. Arrangements had to be made for lectures to be given by colleagues in the absence of jailed members of teaching staff such as Eileen McGrane (late Eileen McCarvill), Eoin MacNeill and Michael Hayes. Richard Mulcahy, who had been involved in the Rising of 1916, enrolled as a medical student in the College and in 1918 became Chief of Staff of the

In the midst of the politics of the time, events such as this Farewell Concert for American Soldier Students were held at UCD during the first summer of peace. (Special Collections, UCD, Dublin)

Volunteers. During the War of Independence, he operated from a small office in the Chemistry corridor at Earlsfort Terrace, a fact apparently unknown to British intelligence,[43] although Chemistry Professor, Hugh Ryan, students and porters were fully aware.

It would appear that both staff and students appreciated the difficult position in which their president, Dr Coffey, and the college authorities found themselves. It must have been with a great sense of relief that Dr Coffey heard that the Truce had been signed and that a settlement of Anglo-Irish relations was being negotiated. This is hinted at in his report for 1920-21.

We look forward with confidence to the new era about to open for our country and to that interest in Irish education which will aim at full and adequate achievement in all the activities of our national life. [44]

UCD was to be the stage for a decisive period of Irish history. The Truce which halted the War of Independence was followed by the Anglo-Irish Treaty negotiations in London. The arrangement made there on 6 December 1921 was subject to ratification by Dáil Éireann. The subsequent heated debate and eventual acceptance of the Treaty, on 7 January 1922, took place in the Council Chamber[45] at Earlsfort Terracce.[46] In spite of this, little indication of the high drama being played out at Earlsfort Terrace is indicated in the governing body's minutes which tended to concentrate on the less contentious facts of life.

The president reported that he had granted the use of a portion of the College buildings for the important meeting of Dáil Éireann now being held, and that he had instructed the servants in the College Lunch Room to provide tea for the members and officers of the Dáil. The action of the president was approved. It was decided to pay the women attendants in the Lunch Room £2 each

The Treaty Debate, December 1921, in the Council Chambers of UCD, Earlsfort Terrace. (Illustrated London News)

and the College porters £1 each for extra work in connection with these meetings.[47]

The Kevin Barry Memorial Window

The Council Chamber at UCD – now known as the Kevin Barry Room – is on the first floor above the centre entrance doorway and overlooks Earlsfort Terrace. The nationalist sympathies of UCD staff and students are expressed in a brilliantly coloured stained glass window. It was commissioned in 1933 and executed by illustrator and stained-glass artist, Richard J. King (1907-1974) of the Harry Clarke Stained Glass Studios. The window was commissioned to commemorate the tragic figure of eighteen-year-old Kevin Barry, a first-year medical student in the college[48] who was executed on 1 November 1920.[49] The day after the execution, the Earlsfort Terrace premises were searched and raided by the security forces.

subjects are carefully and symbolically linked throughout the eight panels. The head and shoulders of Kevin Barry appear in part of the panel devoted to Robert Emmet and the 1798 Rebellion, an effective device connecting Barry to other figures in Irish history.[51] Brilliant colours – reds, blues, greens and gold – glow in a work so plainly inspired by Harry Clarke, especially his *Eve of St Agnes*, executed between 1923-24 and now in the Hugh Lane Municipal Gallery, Dublin. The Kevin Barry Memorial Window, one of the few King commissions to carry his signature,[52] is a jewel-like treasure which richly enhances University College building at Earlsfort Terrace.

Following the Truce and the subsequent Treaty negotiations, student life began to return to some form of normality. University life saw conferrals in the Great Hall forming an integral part of its activities. Professor J. Semple describes one such ceremony, probably in the 1930s.

The Senators took their places in their robes of state on the great platform with seats rising in tiers, the Chancellor high in their midst, the secretaries at the sides, the recipients of the degrees in due order on the floor below, each in his or her appropriate gown and hood, their admiring families at the sides or in the fine galleries which have now disappeared.[53]

Two Sinn Fein members guarding the approach to the Council Chambers where the Treaty was being debated in December 1921. (Illustrated London News)

Richard J. King was born 7 July 1907 in Castlebar, Co. Mayo, the son of John J. King, a sergeant in the Royal Irish Constabulary. When the King family moved to Dublin in 1926, King entered the Dublin Metropolitan School of Art and studied illustration[50] and design under Austin Molloy, entering the firm of Clarke and Sons in 1928. When Harry Clarke died in 1931, King became manager and principal designer.

The Nationalist outlook prevalent in Ireland at the time is expressed in this Celtic Revival window which protests against British rule in Ireland. The political and historical

UCD's First Professors of Music

Following the establishment of UCD, a part-time chair of Music was created in February 1914 with the appointment of the Reverend Heinrich Bewerunge (1862-1923). Following this, Bewerunge had returned home for the summer of 1914 but the outbreak of war forced him to remain in Germany. When Bewerunge had not taken up his post by February 1915, it was decided to take legal advice on the matter. Since his country was at war with Britain, and thereby with Ireland, Bewerunge's German citizenship was called into question. Following legal opinion, UCD's governing body passed a resolution that, as Professor Bewerunge had failed to discharge his duties since July 1914, and the governing body had not had any communication from him, the Chair of Music was declared vacant. Despite the brevity of his tenure, Rev. Bewerunge had already set a high standard for his students – carrying out his duties, it was said, 'with Teutonic thoroughness'.

The second music professor at UCD was Yorkshire-born Charles Herbert Kitson (1874-1944). Kitson's first important post in Ireland was as organist of Dublin's Christ Church Cathedral, a role he held for seven years from 1913. He was appointed Professor of Music at UCD in 1916. Five years later, he returned to London to join the staff of the Royal College of Music while simultaneously becoming Professor of Music at Trinity College in Dublin. Kitson held this non-resident position, as it was then, until 1935. His *The Art of Counterpoint*, published in 1907 and reprinted in 1924, represented a pioneering appraisal of the subject.

Reverend Heinrich Bewerunge, who very briefly held the Chair of Music at UCD prior to the outbreak of World War I. (Central Catholic Library)

John Larchet

In 1921, Kitson was followed by one of his own students, John F. Larchet (1884-1967), a man who would have a lasting influence on music in his native city and throughout the country. A pupil of Michele Esposito, Larchet was senior professor of harmony and composition at the Royal Irish Academy of Music from 1920 to 1955 and Professor of Music at UCD from 1921 to 1958. Thus a generation of Irish musicians, composers and music-lovers owes its education in one form or another to his work.

John F. Larchet was born in the Dublin suburb of Sandymount. Part of an already musical family of French ancestry, his early education came through the Marist Fathers in Leeson Street. As UCD was without a chair of music, Larchet undertook his degree course at Trinity College, Dublin, graduating in 1913 and obtaining his doctorate two years later. 1913 was also the year in which he married Madeleine Moore, a musician who was one of the finest all-round accompanists of her day.

Dr Larchet conducted many programmes for the Dublin Philharmonic Society, the Dublin Amateur Orchestral Society and the UCD choir. In 1923, he was appointed music adviser to the army where he introduced 'philharmonic pitch' – the one used previously was a semi-tone too high.

John Larchet's work as director of music examinations in secondary schools brought him throughout the state and in this position, he managed to raise the general standard of music education and training. His greatest achievement came with the acceptance of music as part of UCD's BA Honours course. He also managed to convince the university authorities to extend its travelling scholarship scheme to music students and this became available to them

Dr John Larchet became UCD's Professor of Music in 1921 and would influence an entire generation of Irish music and musicians. (NUI)

Order of Commendatore of the Italian Republic in 1958. He was keenly interested in, and dedicated to, the idea of a Concert Hall for Dublin and was active in the work of the Music Association of Ireland and its offshoot, Concert and Assembly Hall Ltd.

Due to his other activities, John F. Larchet found little time for composition but a legacy of songs, with some short choral and orchestral pieces, is marked by his own personal charm. Dr Larchet himself stated that one of his life's aims had been

> *to encourage students to adapt the native musical idiom to modern harmonic development and thus create a school of composers which would be truly evocative of the Irish spirit.*

in 1951. The first recipient, Anthony Hughes, would later succeed Dr Larchet as Professor of Music at UCD.

In a remarkably busy musical life, Dr Larchet also found time to act as president of the Dublin Grand Opera Society (DGOS), for which he was decorated with the

John and Madeleine Larchet's two daughters – Síle, harp, and Maire, viola – also contributed significantly to the musical life of Dublin. As members of the National Symphony Orchestra for many years, their appearances at the National Concert Hall covered a diverse range of music. Their engineer and horn-playing brother, Gerard, is a regular devotee of the NCH. As a member of her father's BMus. class, Síle Larchet-Cuthbert remembers him

> *as a gifted and brilliant teacher, with such an ability to communicate his love of and enthusiasm for music, that we seemed to understand with remarkable clarity what the composers were actually saying!*

Anthony Hughes

Professor Larchet was followed in UCD by his pupil, Anthony Hughes (b.1928). Another man of considerable influence on music in Ireland, Hughes received his early education from the Christian Brothers in Dublin's Synge Street. His musical studies took him to the RIAM where

Aerial view of UCD, Iveagh Gardens, and the surrounding city in 1931. (Army Flying Corps)

his professors were Dina Copeman, piano, George Hewson, organ, and Larchet himself, harmony and counterpoint.

Obtaining his first-class honours BMus. degree from UCD in 1949, Hughes was the first music graduate to receive a travelling scholarship from the college. Appointed assistant to Larchet in 1955, the year in which he was awarded his doctorate, Anthony Hughes assumed the chair of music on Dr Larchet's retirement in 1959. He subsequently oversaw the transfer of the music department from Newman House to Belfield in 1980 and is now its Professor Emeritus.

Among Larchet's and Hughes' students and assistants at UCD were Seóirse Bodley and Gerard Gillen, both of whom would have important roles in the National Concert Hall. Before UCD's move to Belfield, those who later had some connection with the NCH were pianists John O'Conor and Miceal O'Rourke, and conductors such as Cait Cooper, Gearoid Grant, William Halpin, Eimear Ó Broin and Colman Pearce, who directed the opening concert of the NCH in 1981. Composers who studied with Larchet or Hughes and whose music has been heard in the NCH include Gerald Barry, Seóirse Bodley, Frank Corcoran and Raymond Deane.

Space Is Critical

During his seven years (1943-1950) as head of UCD's School of Architecture, Professor Joseph V. Downes had been involved in drawing up plans for expansion of the existing UCD site at Earlsfort Terrace and the Iveagh Gardens. His own department was operating at a distinct disadvantage, as is highlighted in a letter from Downes to the president of UCD, Dr Michael Tierney, dated 29 July 1948.

The front façade of UCD, decorated for the Eucharistic Congress in 1932. (Central Catholic Library)

My Fourth Year students at present work on a screened-off portion of the gallery of the 'Museum'. It is the worst of a very bad lot of studios. It is cold, draughty and noisy. During the cold spell in the Spring of 1947 it had a temperature of 4 above freezing (actually recorded) when it had to be closed for nearly four weeks. It is separated from the open air by a timber screen and drawings pinned on this so-called wall have been seen to flutter like washing on a line on a windy day. Lecturing in this studio is usually impossible on account of noise from various external sources.[54]

It was Professor Downes who first drew up plans for locating the UCD campus at Stillorgan Road, and these he presented on 30 September 1948. Downes' plans were based on the assumption that the college could avail of Belfield, Stillorgan, and two adjoining properties as a suitable site for the new college buildings and sports grounds. However, it was some time before these lands were acquired in total by

Pressure of space and lack of equipment at UCD: two cartoons from Dublin Opinion in 1959.
(Top) 'We may have to abandon our first chemistry course — someone has broken the beaker.'
(Bottom) The Minister for Education presents UCD President, Dr Michael Tierney, with a shoehorn, enabling him to get another 500 students into the university.

UCD, a task which was undertaken by the UCD Buildings Committee between 1952 and 1965.

For the time being, the situation regarding space and conditions at Earlsfort Terrace continued to deteriorate. *Dublin Opinion* (1959) satirised the situation in a cartoon which depicted the Minister for Education presenting Dr Michael Tierney with a shoehorn to enable him to get another four or five hundred students into the college.[55]

As in the days of the 'old Royal', the Great Hall (now the National Concert Hall) was used for UCD conferral ceremonies and concerts. With the outbreak of World War II in 1939, and with a State of Emergency declared in Ireland, UCD President, Dr Coffey decided that the organ in the Great Hall could be a security risk and ordered it to be dismantled. Its pipes were carried outside and piled near the gymnasium, only to be removed, by degrees, by unscrupulous citizens. During the war, the Great Hall itself was used for storing turf and other goods. The post-war years saw the college reactivating the space for examination purposes. However, as an examination hall during this period, the Great Hall was particularly noted and remembered by students for its intense cold and draughts during the winter!

Rumbles of Revolt

Throughout its history, the Great Hall had also become the stage for a number of protest meetings and teach-ins, one of which took place in November 1968. In response to what students saw as the inadequacy of government grants, the USI (Union of Students Ireland) threatened direct and militant action which included disrupting the normal course of college life. On Friday 15 November, around 3,000 students from both UCD and TCD crowded into the Great Hall (much to the dismay of the

July 1959: The conferring of degrees in the Great Hall at Earlsfort Terrace. (UCD and its Building Plans)

authorities who felt such a large number was dangerous because of the hazards of fire and panic) to hear a panel of speakers discuss a possible merger between both universities. After a USI grants' march to the Dáil on 3 February 1971, students on their return from Kildare Street decided spontaneously to occupy the Great Hall in protest at what they looked upon as a 'sell-out' by USI and the Students' Representative Council (SRC).

UCD remained at Earlsfort Terrace for some fifty years, with the college property remaining largely unchanged throughout that period. On 31 March 1960, Dáil Éireann ratified the recommendation that University College should transfer from Earlsfort Terrace to Belfield and the plan for a new campus was set in place. Today, only the Medical, Architecture and Engineering[56] faculties remain at Earlsfort Terrace.

Throughout the 'University Era' at Earlsfort Terrace, the capitol's musical tradition continued as turn-of-the-century Dublin played host to some of the world's most renowned musicians.

*Maxim Vengerov (violin) giving
a master-class at the NCH.
(Photo: Eugene Langan)*

CHAPTER 6
CONTINUING A MUSICAL TRADITION

Performing in the Great Hall

Once the Royal University of Ireland was installed in the premises of the 1865 Exhibition at Earlsfort Terrace, many of the extraneous events which had taken place there had either ceased or were accommodated at the Rotunda. The RUI authorities were selective in letting their Great Hall to outside bodies, although the Dublin Musical Society, through the influence of Joseph Robinson, had managed to persuade them of the educational nature of its programmes. The Royal Irish Academy of Music was also allowed in. Otherwise, a fairly strict ban was imposed.

Before the axe fell, Cramer Woods managed to present Zelia Trebelli with Signor Foli, Ovide Musin, violin, and the pianist/composer Wilhelm Ganz on 9 and 10 February 1883. Trebelli was described as the 'matchless contralto', and on the second evening, the 'audience flowed over on to the orchestra [platform]'.

The DMS made its first appearance on 2 April under their new University landlords with Gounod's *The Redemption*. Bessie Herbert, Elizabeth Scott-Fennell and Charles Santley were among the soloists. But the box office organisation was called into question in *The Freeman's Journal* review the following day.

The arrangements at the place for payment of admission to the area were very bad and insufficient with a great deal of struggling, pushing, torn clothing, loss of temper and disappointment generally. We trust that this will be remedied against the next concert.

On 18 May, Dr Steeven's Hospital benefited from a concert which involved the RIAM. Perhaps the most interesting thing about this concert was Michele Esposito's first appearance in Earlsfort Terrace. In music by Beethoven, Brahms and himself, he had 'distinct power, precision and digital facility and appropriate emphasis, getting two recalls'. Esposito would soon be one of the most forceful personalities on the Irish music scene.

Michele Esposito, from a painting by Sarah Cecilia Harrison. (Courtesy RIAM)

Following the DMS' Mendelssohn, *Athalie*, and Schumann's *Paradise and the Peri* on 21 May, *The Freeman's Journal* commented on the concert venue situation in Dublin – which may seem strange when at least three were operational at the time. Suggesting that a large, purpose-built hall was needed, the writer maintained:

> *It would be an opportunity of enlarging the scope of concerts in... making room for that large section of the people who have considerable musical taste but who are not in the position to pay much money for the privilege of hearing classical works adequately performed. Were there a building which would afford accommodation to those who could pay a shilling for an area or gallery ticket a large audience would be secured from among the less wealthy classes and the Dublin Musical Society would benefit... However if we cannot have what we like we must do with what we have.*

The orchestra of the Royal Irish Academy of Music, greatly influenced by Joseph Robinson, brought music to Dublin for many years.

The writer went on to express the hope that the senate of the Royal University would continue to see the educational value of the concerts and persevere in making its hall available.

Joseph Robinson's fascination with Mendelssohn brought a revival of *Elijah* in January 1887 with his *Hymn of Praise* in March; *Athalie*, *Psalm 114* (the first Dublin performance) and the unfinished opera *Loreley* were performed in May. A review drew attention to the fact that Mendelssohn had been a friend of the conductor, that the hall of the RUI had been tastefully redecorated, and that the audience assembled was thoroughly representative and entitled to express an informed musical opinion.

While the DMS concert on 6 December 1888 was billed as its 'last', and with a presentation made to Joseph Robinson, the Society continued unabated for a good deal longer. Robinson's last concert finally came on 4 December 1890 with Mendelssohn's *St Paul* which involved over 350 performers.

The beautiful and pathetic solos came out in exquisite contrast to the choruses. Mr Henry Piercy sang the tenor music with admirable spirit and finish and gave 'Be thou faithful unto death' so finely that the audience encored (however not repeated). Soprano Miss Edith Montgomery made the audience thrill with her rendering of 'Jerusalem, thou hast killed my prophets'. Mr Plunket Greene sang the bass solos with great power and in the best style. Miss Fanny Emerson in the contralto music was excellent also.

Joseph Smith and the DMS

By this time, the fortunes of the DMS were in the hands of Joseph Smith, a highly regarded musician and, among other things, an examiner in music and professor at the Royal University. Over the next few months he would change the DMS repertoire, shifting its emphasis from Robinson's previous preferences. This may or may not have been wise. While Dublin audiences of the day appear to have been catholic in their choice of opera, they might not have been all that enthusiastic about sampling unfamiliar choral music. Yet Smith's first concert with the DMS on 27 May 1890 in the Irish premiere of Berlioz's *The Damnation of Faust* found not a vacant seat in the house.

Smith's adventurous side emerged on 12 March 1891 with Dvorak's *Stabat Mater* and with a combination of Sullivan's *The Golden Legend* and Act III of Wagner's

Tannhauser on 26 May. Apparently the concert had not started until 8.20pm and, as reported, it

was not over until 11.40pm. As a result people left the room whilst the performance of Wagner's music was going on. A feature not to be forgotten was the ovation bestowed on Mr Joseph Robinson who, on entering the room as a simple member of the audience, was received with hearty applause.

1891 was the year of Mozart's centenary and on 3 December, the DMS devoted its energies to selections from *Don Giovanni* and *Le Nozze di Figaro*, *The Magic Flute* Overture and the *Twelfth Mass*, a piece then considered to have been by Mozart. The review in *The Freeman's Journal* commented that the choir had been augmented for this concert; with a band of sixty-six, there were about 400 performers. The orchestra, led by R.M. Levey, had fourteen first violins, among whom were some ladies, twelve seconds, and eight violas, cellos and double-basses. The choir, not up to standard, was at times 'flat'.

There appears to have been some wrangling within the DMS as a Special General Meeting was called at the RUI on 19 February 1892 for the purpose of disbanding the Society. The DMS was wound up, but within three weeks, it had been reconstituted with the formation of a new committee at another Special Meeting.

Smith repeated Sullivan's *The Golden Legend* in May 1892 at the RUI, joining it with Gounod's motet *Gallia*. The 'book of words' pointed out that the committee had experienced difficulty in obtaining Sullivan's permission to perform the work as the composer did not wish the piece to become hackneyed! The band, augmented by members of the Hallé, was exceedingly large and allegedly the best that had been heard at the Society's concerts for some time.

While the following year found Nellie Melba at Leinster Hall on 7 and 11 February, Joseph Smith and the DMS were at the Royal University on 13 February with Verdi's *Messa da Requiem* (or, as it was announced, *Manzoni Requiem*). At an RIAM concert at the RUI in June, there was a band of over ninety players, including some RIAM professors, most of whom probably repaired to Leinster Hall in November 1893 where the Polish pianist, composer and statesman, Ignace Paderewski (1860-1941), gave two recitals. The review stated:

On Saturday every leading musician, professional and amateur, in Dublin were present, and some of them were permitted after the multitude had dispersed, regretfully since there was no more to hear, to pay personal respects to the eminent artist whose marvellous power and gifts had entranced them.

Taking advantage of the occasion, an advertisement for Pigott's later claimed:

Paderewski said 'Play only on an Erard whenever available'.

On 25 March 1896, the DMS celebrated the fiftieth anniversary of *Elijah* with Charles Santley as the Prophet at the Royal University, while Smith's promotion of Sullivan's music continued with *The Light of the World* on 6 May. Smith's performance, it was said, marked 'an epoch in the history of the Institution'. Sullivan was originally scheduled to conduct but a letter was read out offering 'a genuine expression of regret as well as an apology from him'. There was general praise for this biblical piece. The pre-concert advertisement advised that 'tramcars to Rathmines and Donnybrook and an additional service to Westland Row' would run after the event.

The DMS held its AGM later in May 1896 at the RUI. The meeting heralded a new departure for Joseph Smith

and the DMS as they took a considerable risk in partly turning their attention away from choral music by proposing a series of orchestral concerts. Taken for granted now, these were virtually non-existent in the 1890s. The senate of the RUI was eventually convinced of the merits of the proposition and placed the Great Hall at Smith's disposal. The first DMS orchestral concert took place there on 11 November 1896. Conducted by Joseph Smith, the main work was Beethoven's Fifth Symphony, with the lengthy programme including the Overtures *William Tell* and *Der Freischütz* with Meyerbeer's *Coronation March* and Johann Strauss' *Blue Danube* Waltz. A review promoted the theory that this

new departure for the Society [was] to advance the popularity of orchestral music in our city... not for gain to the Society but for the benefit of musical advancement and education... [The audience] was very large and reflected great credit on the orchestra.

The DMS celebrated its own coming of age and Queen Victoria's golden jubilee in May with a varied programme, including Beethoven's *Engadi*, Mendelssohn's *Hear my Prayer* and Handel's *Zadok the Priest*. A congratulatory report stated:

The DMS is now twenty-one and the Society has prospered as to be able to maintain its position as the leading choral society in the country...

The Feis Ceoil

This important anniversary year also heralded the birth of Feis Ceoil. For over a century, it has been the fertile breeding ground for many of the country's established artists – indeed there is hardly one who has not been a first prize-winner of its competitions. Because of the educational nature of its portfolios, Feis Ceoil's ideals were entertained by the RUI senate, and a number of its initial competitions were held at Earlsfort Terrace; its first concerts took place at the RUI during May 1897. Among the new music by Irish composers heard for the first time was Augusta Holmes' symphonic poem, *Irlande*, and Michele Esposito's cantata *Deirdre*.

Michele Esposito and the RUI

The Dublin Musical Society's first programme for 1899 found the composer, Hubert Parry (1848-1918), conducting his own *King Saul* which had been premiered during the Leeds Festival of 1894. One of the few occasions on which the Great Hall's acoustics were called into question, the reviewer noted that the work

> *represented the modern school of English musical composition... the audience, we regret to say, was inadequate, and there were echoes in the Hall which injured the performance in the ears of many hearers.*

The Society revived *Elijah* once again in May with a full band, a chorus of 400 and an audience of 'considerable magnitude'. Their last concert of the century, on 20 December 1899, was *Messiah* conducted by Joseph Smith and with Fanny Moody, Muriel Foster, Charles Saunders and Charles Manners. For some reason, the audience was not as large as for previous *Messiah* gatherings and as if foretelling fate, Dr Smith was much praised for his work with the Society.

Without further ado, the venerable Dublin Musical Society virtually came to an end. It took part in two

Grand Miscellaneous Concerts in November 1901, in two Grand Coronation Concerts for Edward VII in April 1902 with Clara Butt and her husband Kennerly Rumford, and another two Grand Miscellaneous Concerts in the following November, all at the RUI. After this, the Society was unceremoniously committed to history.

The DMS would be replaced by various other choral groups as new figures appeared on the musical horizon. Some would pass quickly from memory. Others, like the Culwick Choral Society which is still active today, would enjoy somewhat more permanent positions. But from 1899 onwards, the focus of attention at the RUI would be in an orchestral context. At its helm was the Italian expatriate Michele Esposito (1855-1929).

Born in Castellammare near Naples, Esposito won a scholarship to the Naples Conservatory where he studied piano and composition. He moved to Paris in 1878 where he came under the influence of Saint-Saëns and began his career as concert pianist and teacher. As Saint-Saëns advised him to make a name for himself outside the French capital and then return, Esposito came to Dublin in 1882 to fill a teaching post at the RIAM. He never returned to France, remaining in Dublin until 1928 when he went back to Italy. He died in Florence in 1929. While his impact on the RIAM, where he founded his unique piano school, was enormous, Esposito managed to influence almost every aspect of musical life in Dublin.

In addition to his involvement with the Dublin Orchestral Society, Esposito was responsible for the establishment of the Royal Dublin Society chamber music recitals which, until shortly after the foundation of the state, were held in the hall of Leinster House, now the meeting chamber of Dáil Éireann. A man of extraordinary energy, he regularly appeared as either solo performer or in ensembles at these recitals. In 1897, he was one of the prime movers in the organisation of Feis Ceoil and saw it reaching beyond its original ideas of promoting Irish music. Esposito's compositions, which cover a range of genres, include the cantata *Deirdre*, and a short opera, *The Tinker and the Fairy*, completed in 1903 to a libretto of Douglas Hyde. Esposito's piano music has been kept alive by Feis Ceoil through the special competition in his honour and by some recent recordings by the Dublin-born Paris-based musician Micéal O'Rourke.

The Dublin Orchestral Society

Early in 1899, following the extraordinary success of the Hallé Orchestra's visits to Dublin throughout the previous years, a number of prominent individuals, mainly connected with the RIAM, decided Dublin needed its own orchestra and set about doing something about it. The city already had its compliment of good professional players, most of whom were engaged in the theatres or in the police and military bands. There was also a ready supply of very competent amateurs, while the RIAM had its own accomplished professors and teachers and a goodly number of excellent student musicians among the ranks of its orchestra. Esposito, a man of energy and authority, became the leading light of the venture and the Dublin Orchestral Society (DOS) came into being with its first committee meeting taking place on 27 January 1899. No doubt waving the educational card, the senate of the Royal University was approached with the request that some DOS concerts should take place in Earlsfort Terrace. Recognising the seriousness of the intent and the eminence of the people involved, the senate gave its blessing to the new endeavour and fifty-four music stands were ordered from a firm in Camden Row.

Adelio Viani, Senior Professor of Singing with the Royal Irish Academy of Music.

The first DOS concert took place in the Royal University's Great Hall on 1 March 1899 under the baton of Esposito and with Harry Charles, a senior student of the RIAM, as soloist in Mendelssohn's *Serenade and Allegro giocoso* – the same piece which Charles Hallé played on his orchestra's first visit to Dublin in 1878. The symphony was Mozart's 40th and the rest of the programme comprised the overtures *Iphigenia in Aulis* (Gluck), *Egmont* (Beethoven) and *Faust* (Wagner), along with Bizet's First *L'Arlésienne Suite*. The attendance was limited, the hall being too great for the orchestra, and the audience too small to do it justice. The quality of the performances exceeded expectations, however, and Esposito was seen as the absolute master of the forces under his command.

Throughout 1900, Esposito continued with his band of stalwarts, playing the Schumann Piano Concerto himself on 9 April 1900 at the Royal University. This was the week of Queen Victoria's visit to Dublin and while she did not attend the DOS concert, she did grace the Royal University with her presence on 11 April when she viewed

The National Concert Hall today. (Photo: Eugene Langan)

Members of the First Board of the National Concert Hall. Standing from left: Noel Coade, Donnie Potter, John Ruddock, Gerard Victory, Fred O'Callaghan, Seóirse Bodley, Richard Stokes. Seated from left: Moira Pyne, Bernadette Greevy, Fred O'Donovan (chair), Dame Ruth King, Veronica Dunne.

The National Symphony Orchestra playing in the Main Auditorium of the National Concert Hall. (Photo: RTÉ)

The old music room in Iveagh House, where chamber music was played in the 18th century.

At the reception to mark the dedication of the new Steinway piano: John O'Conor, one of Ireland's distinguished pianists, with Lochlainn Quinn of Glen Dimplex, the sponsors, and NCH Chairman, Annraoi Ó Beolláin. (Photo: Frank Fennell Photography)

The Kenneth Jones organ and the piano in the present-day NCH. (Photo: Eugene Langan)

Designed and built by Kenneth Jones, the magnificent NCH organ was installed in 1991. (Photo: Frank Fennell Photography)

President Mary McAleese enjoys the colour of an ESB/NCH Open Day on a warm summer day in 1998. (Photo: Frank Fennell Photography)

Children gather on the front steps of the NCH in anticipation of an Open Day. (Photo: Frank Fennell Photography)

Composer Fergus Johnston communicates a passion for music to another generation. (Photo: Frank Fennell Photography)

Members of a youth orchestra discuss their NCH performance. (Photo: Frank Fennell Photography)

A Gospel choir performs in the Iveagh Gardens, an event which would have merited the approval of Benjamin Lee Guinness. (Photo: Frank Fennell Photography)

Cellist Steven Isserlis, one of many musicians who participate in master-classes at the National Concert Hall, passes his expertise on to an aspiring young musician. (Photos: Ray McManus Associates)

John McCormack singing in Dublin with conductor Fritz Brasé. A gold-medal-winner at the Feis Ceoil in 1902, he was said to be the greatest lyric tenor of his day.

the Great Spring Daffodil Show mounted by the Royal Irish Horticultural Society in her honour.

The season's most important event at the Royal University was on 28 August when Nellie Melba was part of a Grand Concert in aid of the Soldiers' and Sailors' Help Society. Given in the presence of the Lord Lieutenant and Lady Cadogen, the supporting artists included the Countess of Limerick, piano, and Joseph O'Mara, tenor. The hall was filled to overflowing and Melba, who did not overtax herself in the programme, was principally heard in the Mad Scene from Donizetti's *Lucia di Lammermoor* with Frederick Griffith, flute, and Theodore Flint, piano.

A portion of the long, flowery review is worth quoting.

The exquisitely ornate passages came to the ear with a purity and a fluency that could scarcely be excelled, rippling or vigorous, soft or virile as the artiste wished and the grand florid run ended up with a display of vocal gymnastics of such graceful agility that we cannot remember ever hearing anything like it even from Melba. The blending of voice and flute in the delicious scale passages leading to the climax were so perfect one didn't know which deserved the greater praise, the singer or the instrumentalist...

Gracefully acknowledging the audience appreciation, Melba then sat down at the piano and accompanied herself in an 'encore' selection. This did not receive the reviewer's approval as it 'justified the time honoured rule that a prima donna should never accompany herself'. However, Joseph O'Mara 'proved himself a consummate artiste at the zenith of his powers', and the Countess of Limerick 'exhibited a good deal of executed skill in a pianoforte solo by Chopin'.

The Hallé Orchestra made yet another call to the Rotunda on 12 and 13 November 1900. Schumann's *Rhenish* Symphony and Beethoven's Seventh were the main works under Richter but the reviewer appeared to be a little anxious that

the musical fare provided was so excellent that it might challenge comparison with the most cherished experiences of the majority of those present.

A DOS concert the following week, with the baritone Denis O'Sullivan (whom a Feis Ceoil competition commemorates) as soloist, posed the question as to whether Dublin wanted and would be willing to support its own resident orchestra. The response, in the negative, was slow in coming so the DOS adventurously and ambitiously struggled on.

The Hallé must have had a particular preference for Dublin as they were back in March 1901, again at the Rotunda, not Earlsfort Terrace. The lengthy programme included Siegfried's Funeral Music from Wagner's *Götterdammerung*, heard for the first time in Ireland, as a tribute to the late Queen Victoria. It also contained Dvorak's *New World* Symphony and Elgar's *Enigma* Variations, which was receiving its Irish premiere. *The Irish Times'* review was interesting.

Regarding the Elgar, it was felt that the audience might be pardoned if they did not appreciate the design of the composer in 'picturing' his friends in the composition. In hands less capable than the Hallé, in parts, it might have become a confused medley. Here and there an attractive melody relieved the dullness of the whole.

The Hallé's second concert was less ambitious in scale but contained Wagner's *Rienzi* Overture, *Siegfried Idyll* and *Kaiser March*, as well as Beethoven's Eighth Symphony and Tchaikovsky's Overture *Romeo and Juliet*. Eight years later, Esposito and the DOS would programme Tchaikovsky's *Pathétique* and Elgar's *Enigma* in the same concert.

While Tchaikovsky's *Nutcracker* Suite had been aired by the DOS on a number of occasions, the orchestra ventured on to his B flat minor Piano Concerto on 11 December 1901. This first Dublin performance was given by local pianist, Annie Lord, for which her fee, like the other DOS soloists, was two guineas. One of Esposito's most talented pupils, she introduced many works by Debussy and Ravel to Ireland and gave the first Dublin performance of Saint-Saëns' Fifth Piano Concerto at a DOS concert at the Royal University on 26 January 1905. The review referred to its *andante* as 'barbaric and gaudy to a degree better fitted the Brocken than the concert room'.

Around this time, the name of Clyde Twelvetrees (1875-1956) was beginning to appear on the the DOS soloists' roster. Cello professor with the RIAM, he also taught at Manchester's Royal Northern College of Music and played in the Hallé Orchestra. He was the cellist of a remarkable piano trio of RIAM professors, along with Achille Simonetti and Esposito, which flourished in Dublin in the years before World War I. It was said (by Esposito's daughter, Bianca) that both Esposito and Hamilton Harty judged Twelvetrees to be as fine a cello player as any world celebrity of his time, not excluding the great Casals, and that his modesty and reserved sensitivity had led him to choose the less spectacular but more serious career.

While audiences for the DOS were enthusiastic, they rarely reached the Royal University's full capacity. Their concert at the RUI on 6 April 1903, the Tuesday of Holy Week, was sparsely filled. It was certainly undemanding with Grieg's First *Peer Gynt Suite*, Bruch's G minor Violin Concerto with Adolf Wilhelmj, Wagner's *Siegfried Idyll* and Beethoven's Fifth Symphony. Indeed the Beethoven 'held the audience spellbound' but the reviewer in *The Irish Times* considered the concert a test case of the musical taste of Dublin.

It has been applied and failed. After this concert the Dublin Orchestral Society, as such, ceases to exist. We do not believe our resident orchestra should be allowed to disappear.

That the DOS did continue to exist at all is a remarkable feat. But realising the need to build his audience, Esposito inaugurated a series of short Sunday afternoon concerts in the Antient Concert Rooms where, at times, solo items would be inserted between the orchestral numbers. These proved highly successful but, the longer concerts at the Royal University, while artistically more distinguished, may have been eventually financially ruinous. Still, the DOS continued to be the flagship of local orchestral music-making in Dublin until 1914. When the Royal University closed its doors to outside lettings in 1910, the DOS continued to use the ACR, the unsuitable Gaiety Theatre and occasionally the more acoustically favourable Theatre Royal. Its eventual demise in 1914 left a serious vacuum in Dublin's musical activity.

The activities of Feis Ceoil, despite the conciseness of the actual competition period, continued to make their presence felt and found accommodation at the Royal University during the 1900s. Not only were its prize-winners' concerts held there but many of its larger choral and orchestral competitions took place in the Great Hall.

John McCormack was one of the greatest lyric tenors of his day. Touring Australia with Nellie Melba in 1911, he was made a Papal Count in 1928 in recognition of his generosity to Catholic charities.

The Royal University was also the venue for the Feis' Grand Concerts. The RIAM Students' Concerts continued to use Earlsfort Terrace while both the newly formed Dublin Philharmonic Society (DPS), under Charles Marchant of St Patrick's Cathedral and the Dublin Oratorio Society (DOrS), under Vincent O'Brien of the Pro-Cathedral, were also given permission for concerts at the Royal University.

The first appearance of the DOrS in the Great Hall was on 20 December 1906 with *Messiah*. O'Brien's soloists were Clementine de Vere, Marian Broom, John Child and Charles McGrath. The performance 'drew a large gathering to the Royal University Hall and all sections were crowded and many had to content themselves with standing room'. In May, Gounod's *The Redemption* and Rossini's *Stabat Mater* gained compliments for the Society's 'rich voices and strong singing'. In the following November, the DOrS returned to the Royal University for *Elijah*. Given its regularity in the previous decade, this proved less popular than *Messiah* and elicited this comment from *The Irish Times*:

> There was a considerable number of empty seats – among them conspicuously those reserved for Royal University Senators, from

which, presumably it is to be inferred that Oratorio is not an engrossing study with those grave and learned fathers.

Messiah was repeated on 19 December 1907.

In May 1908, the DOrS took part in the Balfe Centenary programme at the Royal University. Vincent O'Brien again conducted, with soloists Amy Charles and Joseph O'Mara. As usual, Arthur Darley, a distinguished teacher, recitalist and collector of Irish folk music, led Vincent O'Brien's orchestra. Amy Castles was joined by the tenor Henry Beaumont at the Royal University on 3 November 1908 for the DOrS concert of the Grail Scene from Wagner's *Parsifal* (heard in Dublin for the first time), Gounod's *Gallia* and O'Brien's *Easter Hymn*. The DOrS again gave the pre-Christmas *Messiah* on 22 December in Earlsfort Terrace. The lady soloists were Agnes Treacy and Mary Durkin, while the bass was the well-known English artist Robert Radford. The tenor, in his only recorded appearance at the Great Hall, was John McCormack who 'distinguished every theme he sang'.

The Dublin Philharmonic Society commemorated the Mendelssohn centenary with his *Hymn of Praise* and a selection of his shorter choral pieces at the Royal University on 3 February 1909, adding his operatic fragment *Loreley* to Haydn's *The Creation* the following month. Like the DOrS which, with O'Brien at its helm, would mount the Irish premiere of Elgar's *The Dream of Gerontius* at the Theatre Royal on 11 April 1911, they would soon require another premises to present their concerts.

Quite soon, the face of Dublin, Ireland and Europe would alter forever and a 'terrible beauty' would be born. The Great Hall of the Royal University of Ireland would gradually fall into disrepair. The Rotunda and the Antient Concert Rooms would become picture houses.

CHAPTER 7
THE SEARCH FOR A NATIONAL CONCERT HALL

The State Finds its Musical Feet

In the Ireland of the 1920s, it is not surprising that the government of the day had more on its mind than a concert hall. The state was still in its infancy and more or less finding its feet with the simple welfare of its citizens at heart. However, there were those who felt the nation required some kind of broader artistic outlet. A national broadcasting service had been established in 1926 and with it, a small group of musicians, three at first and then four, were employed. The initial band of warriors comprised violinist Terry O'Connor, Rosalind Dowse, viola, and Terry's sister Viola O'Connor, cello, with pianist Kitty O'Doherty (later O'Callaghan) who would become the station's official accompanist.

By June 1926, this quartet had increased to a septet, known as the Station Orchestra, and had grown to nineteen by 1933. With Vincent O'Brien as Radio Éireann's director of music and conductor, the orchestral personnel gradually rose to twenty-eight in 1937. O'Brien usually conducted but occasionally other musicians would be handed the baton. Among these were Michael Bowles, James Doyle, Arthur Duff and Dermot O'Hara from the Army School of Music and Walter O'Donnell of the BBC in Belfast. Bowles eventually succeeded O'Brien as Radio Éireann's director of music and principal conductor of the

The original 2RN Orchestra in the late 1920s.

Station Orchestra, by this time called the Radio Éireann Orchestra (RÉO). Initially seconded from the Department of Defence, he retired from the army in 1944 to be fully employed in the broadcasting service. A charismatic figure, Bowles took the orchestra from its cramped and microphone-bound studio confines out into the open.

The RÉO broadcast from studios in Dublin's Henry Street. From 1941, Bowles organised public concerts for the RÉO at Dublin's Mansion House (seating capacity around 800) and the larger 1,200-seat Gaiety Theatre.

Vincent O'Brien (1871-1945), Radio Éireann's first director of music.

The popularity of these concerts meant a transfer to the Capitol Theatre which could comfortably accommodate approximately 1,800. 1948 saw the enlargement of the RÉO, forming the Radio Éireann Symphony Orchestra (RÉSO) of some sixty-six players, and the establishment of a smaller body, the Radio Éireann Light Orchestra (RÉLO), comprising twenty-two musicians. The introduction of a national television service added the word *telefís* to the orchestras' titles in 1963. The RTÉSO, with its numbers at almost full symphonic strength, became the National Symphony Orchestra of Ireland in 1990. The RTÉLO, with its personnel numbering forty, had its name changed to the RTÉ Concert Orchestra in 1979.

Concert Hall Proposals

But what of plans for a state concert hall? On 10 May 1934, a letter appeared in the *Daily Express* from one Mr R. Stephen Williams deploring the fact that Feis Ceoil, the music festival established in 1897, was without a proper hall to hold its competitions.

> *Dublin has a concert season among the first half-dozen outside London. Dublin has no concert hall... Every year a half-hearted discussion takes place about the advisability of having one, but nothing is done... It is my dismal experience that, apart from a faithful few, the Irish do not care about music.*

The Irish National Music League (INML) took up the cudgels. One of its aims was 'to promote good music at popular prices'; they had already organised a series of concerts in 1933. In a letter sent to P.J. Little, parliamentary secretary to Éamon de Valera, President of the Council (as the head of government was then called), the league pointed out that the Theatre Royal was now a cinema. They were not asking the government to build a new hall but to provide financial assistance. Their letter claimed further that the Mansion House was too small and did not lend itself to

> *the production of good performances at reasonable prices... the smaller the audience the higher the prices of admission... if the expense of producing the performance had to be covered.*

The letter went on to request a meeting between de Valera and members of the INML, and this took place on 15 June 1934. De Valera advised the deputation to form a committee and come back to the government with proposals.

Some months later, in October 1934, the highly respected Hamilton Harty, then conductor of the Hallé Orchestra and one of Ireland's leading musical exports, wrote to de Valera requesting a meeting on the establishment of a first-class orchestra and the building of a concert hall in Dublin. Harty wished to be of service to his country and, as he believed funds could be obtained from expatriate sources in the United States, he expressed his willingness

Sir Hamilton Harty (1879-1941), the Irish-born conductor of the Hallé Orchestra.

to raise the issue on his next visit to America. The response indicated de Valera's interest in the conductor's ideas. In ensuing correspondence, Harty suggested that as he would be in Belfast, he would come to Dublin to meet de Valera. Their meeting took place on 17 October 1934.

Harty proposed a main hall of 3,500 seats, with a downward adjustment to 1,500 by closing the balconies; the hall would be equipped with an organ. His plans also envisaged two smaller halls to seat 800 and 500 respectively. The total cost would be in the region of £240,000, with running costs of around £4,000 per year. Harty proposed a number of sites:

- The south side of St Stephen's Green (Iveagh Gardens was not actually mentioned but this is where he may have had in mind)

- The Rotunda Gardens

- Mountjoy Square, with decaying Georgian edifices on Dublin's north side

- The Round Room, which would need to be demolished, of the Mansion House

- 'The Pound' opposite the Chapel Royal in Dublin Castle

Correspondence between Harty, de Valera and Maurice Moynihan, Secretary of the Department of the President, continued for the remainder of 1934 and extended through 1935. When Harty and de Valera met again on 6 January 1936, the Rotunda seemed to be the most likely venue for a concert hall. In addition to its long connection with music in Dublin, de Valera was also aware of its connections with the national movement: Parnell had addressed meetings there, many Fenian gatherings had taken place, and the premises had also housed other national assemblies of various kinds.

However, even before Harty's second meeting with de Valera, there had been rumblings from the Minister for Finance, Seán McEntee, who was firmly opposed to the general idea of a concert hall. In a note to the President of the Council in the early days of 1936, McEntee wrote:

The percentage of the public in Dublin likely to be attracted to good music to an extent which, taking an average over the year, would be moved to attend public performances is very small and drawn mainly from the members of the Royal Dublin Society. This class, however, is falling off.

Realising there might well be some opposition to his plans, Hamilton Harty had an interview with *The Irish Times* which appeared on 6 January 1936. In it, he made a strong plea for a symphony orchestra for Dublin. For this, Harty maintained that a hall was essential, as an orchestra could not function properly without one. He also wrote this memorandum to de Valera following their meeting on 6 January 1936.

> *If it could be arranged, the Concert Hall in Earlsfort Terrace – now part of the National University [UCD] – is admirably suited to orchestral concerts. It was originally designed for that purpose and, if not absolutely necessary to the work of the University, it might return to its original use, especially if brought up to date as regards seating, platform design and other similar details.*

Harty felt a new building, with a main hall and smaller halls, was the only answer. Regarding the orchestra, Harty suggested the United States' system of two concerts per week – one 'classical', one 'popular'. The symphony orchestra must have at least fifty-six to sixty players. Harty went on:

> *Looking at the problem from a broad point of view, is it not justifiable and desirable to provide the people with some means of escaping from the everlasting Cinema, with all that implies in its vulgarity and stupefying influence...The symphony orchestra would mean an opportunity for embryo composers and conductors, in providing a platform for singers and instrumentalists and proving to the world that Ireland is still the country of music she was in past days.*

The Rotunda Again

Harty's pleas may not have had any affect on the Minister for Finance, Seán McEntee. But in a letter to de Valera dated 10 January 1936, McEntee dealt with the hall situation. The Rotunda's current tenant, McEntee proposed, might act as manager of the hall and the company formed might also manage the symphony orchestra and its conductor-in-chief. Further, it might be asked to involve itself in:

> *the encouragement and development of instrumental talent in Saorstat Éireann by providing facilities for aspirants to positions in the orchestra to train and practise.*

Despite his initial opposition, and in fairness to him, Seán McEntee sought the advice of some of the senior officials in his own and other government departments. But perhaps hoping to extricate himself, McEntee suggested that the Minister for Posts and Telegraphs should be involved, not the Minister for Finance.

In October 1936, one of the government officials, H.P. Boland, quite unofficially, prepared a memorandum on the subject of a concert hall which favoured refurbishing the Rotunda.

Matters became acute when Vincent O'Brien, who was due to retire as conductor of the Radio Éireann Orchestra, let it be known that he was anxious to arrange the broadcasting of a series of symphony concerts. These would involve extra musicians and an 'outside' venue as the existing accommodation was inadequate. Strange as it may seem, this resulted in an interdepartmental government committee being set up to investigate the entire situation. Their report was presented to de Valera in March 1937 and set out the current situation, especially the costs involved.

For a concert hall, the committee favoured the Rotunda. The idea of schools' concerts was promoted as a desirable option. The Rotunda was also seen as suitable for Irish-language drama along with Irish plays, exhibitions, dances, traditional singing and physical exercise displays. However, it felt audience interest would need stimulation. The Dublin Philharmonic Society was again cited as a resourceful body but was deprived of funds. Like Seán McEntee, the committee felt that the hall should not be government-owned and recommended that a company in which the government would be a share-holder should be set up to undertake its operation.

In April 1937, a memorandum from notable Irish citizens was addressed to de Valera. In their opinion, the Rotunda could be bought for £20,000 with an additional £6,000 for refurbishment. The state should provide the funding. They pointed out that public monies were already going to the Royal Irish Academy, the Royal Irish Academy of Music, the Royal Hibernian Academy, the Abbey Theatre and the zoo. The state already recognised the principle that 'personal' as opposed to 'mechanical' performances for public entertainment should be encouraged – something which the Entertainment Tax Bill had established. The memorandum suggested that a cinematograph should not be allowed in the Rotunda, the acoustics of which were cited as excellent.

As H.P. Boland considered the matter to be urgent, he suggested that de Valera meet a deputation of the memorandum's signatories. This took place on 19 May 1937, with de Valera meeting Boland, Hubert Briscoe, Con Curran (Registrar of the High Court), Conor Maguire (President of the High Court), and Dermod O Brien (President of the Hibernian Academy). Although de Valera was keen on the idea, he was occupied with more urgent matters of state. With the outbreak of hostilities in Europe and the declaration of a 'State of Emergency' in Ireland, the concert hall project, no matter how worthy, was forced onto the back burner.

The Capitol Theatre

Odd as it may seem, though, on 17 February 1942, the subject of a concert hall suddenly boiled over again. The Capitol Theatre in Dublin's South Prince's Street, beside the General Post Office in O'Connell Street, had come up

for sale. A memorandum was submitted to the government by the Minister for Posts and Telegraphs, P.J. Little, on the question of the

Acquisition of premises in Dublin for public performances of the Broadcasting Services and the purposes of a State Opera House.

Little put forward suggestions which would give the public the opportunity to attend broadcast performances of high-class orchestral music, oratorio etc. He pointed out further that a public concert hall would be an important adjunct of the Radio Éireann Orchestra's studio performances. Recognising that live performances raised

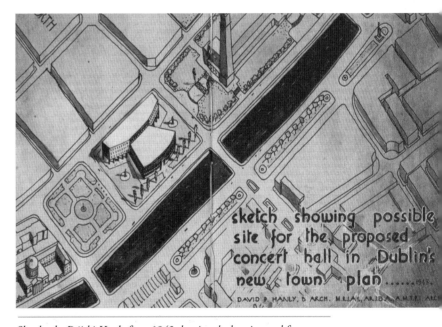

Sketches by Dáithí Hanly from 1942 showing the location and front elevation of a proposed concert hall on the River Liffey..

the public's interest in musical matters, Radio Éireann had been trying to develop such events. However, they were hampered in their efforts by the absence of both adequate studio accommodation and a suitable hall.

A site in Dublin's Exchequer Street was also being contemplated for a concert hall, with a new broadcasting

Sketch by Dáithí Hanly from 1942 showing the front elevation of a proposed concert hall.

studio and office accommodation. But once again, 'The Emergency' and the resultant difficulties in finding building materials meant that this was not feasible. The solution lay in finding an existing hall of suitable position and size which could be adapted at a reasonable cost.

The Capitol was now deemed far more suitable than the Rotunda or, indeed, any other premises. The Minister for Posts and Telegraphs, P.J. Little, went on to say that he had learned that

> ... it [the Capitol] could be purchased for £90,000. No effort had been made by government to place Dublin on the same footing, in relation to music, as the principal cities of other countries. In this respect Dublin is very backward as compared with even English provincial centres. For musical performances of a higher type it has ordinarily been dependent on companies and artists imported, chiefly from Great Britain, but now due to the times there has been a revival of local musical talent and of public interest but after hostilities cease, the earlier position will revive. The development of a national musical culture was needed... The Royal Dublin

Society people do not attend due to that venue [the Mansion House] lacking status but [they] would come to a suitable hall.

Little proposed that a board of trustees, nominated by the Minister for Posts and Telegraphs, would have use of the theatre for broadcasting purposes. Mr Little considered his plan to be a good one. But as many a one before and since, the Minister for Finance threw cold water on the idea, pronouncing that he could not support the scheme due to the expenditure involved.

J.F. Larchet, professor of music at UCD and a fairly influential figure, had his sensitive ear to the ground and now entered the fray. On 13 February 1942, he was quoted in the national press as saying:

> Dublin is bursting with talent and artistic energy... a solemn duty of all of us [is] not to allow our cultural future to pass from our grasp.

The concert hall matter reached the cabinet at its meeting on 17 February 1942 when it was decided that an effort should be made to extend the option on the purchase of the Capitol and that various government departments should examine the matter further. The Commission for Public Works did an evaluation but their principal architect, James M. Fairweather, was not enthusiastic. He argued that the façade of the theatre, which also housed the La Scala ballroom and extended sideways to Middle Abbey Street behind Eason's book store, had little architectural merit. He maintained that the theatre was 'acoustically satisfactory but the stage is too small for operatic works of any magnitude'. Fairweather was against the project. Even if recast, the Capitol would be suitable only for 'cinema, concerts and possibly operas with small casts'.

As Minister for Posts and Telegraphs, P.J. Little was undeterred. The matter continued for some time, with

The charismatic Michael Bowles (1909-1995) conducting in the Capitol Theatre.

Eason's being offered alterations to their premises which would enable structural work to be done on the theatre. There was protracted correspondence between the Departments of Finance, Posts and Telegraphs, the Office of Public Works and the Solicitors, Gerald Byrne of 7 Ormond Quay.

On 6 June 1942, P.J Little approved the Capitol scheme in principle. Another detailed report on the theatre was compiled with very special attention given to a State Opera House. It was suggested that its scope of activity, besides concerts, would now include Shakespeare plays. Feis Ceoil could be held there, as well as the Oireachtas (the Irish-language music festival), historical pageants and lectures. Films of Irish interest and of an educational and cultural character could be shown but commercial films would be excluded. The proposed Radio Chorus would be available to it and the organ of the Chapel Royal in Dublin Castle should be transferred there. A board would run it, with fees to its members of £100 per person per annum, with something additional for the chairman.

The Commission of Public Works was called in to quantify costs. £126,000 was suggested, and the Minister for Posts and Telegraphs strongly recommended the purchase. However, the Minister for Finance was not convinced about the Capitol plan and proposed that the scheme be rejected. He felt that the

...national economy [is] passing through a grave and dangerous crisis; supplies of various essential commodities are scarce; the standard of living of the poorer classes of the country has suffered a serious reduction.

P.J. Little, closely associated with concert hall plans for many years.

Still, the matter did not end. On 20 August 1942, the government told the Minister for Posts and Telegraphs to enter into negotiations with the proprietors of the Capitol, but with an authorised limit of £65,000. However, Minister Little required clarification on a number of points and the business again became protracted. Eventually the option on the purchase lapsed and the Capitol plan passed into oblivion. The idea of a national concert hall would not be considered again for another four years, by which time Europe and Ireland were beginning to recover from the effects of World War II.

P.J. (Paddy) Little (1884-1963) had nurtured his ideas quietly as he observed the continuing growth and appreciation of classical music in the country. A highly cultured man, he had been educated at Clongowes and was a graduate of University College, Dublin. He had also studied philosophy in Munich before World War I where

he availed of every opportunity to attend operas and concerts, including a number conducted by Gustav Mahler. Back in Ireland, Little was seen regularly at the theatre and at many musical gatherings and was totally supportive of Michael Bowles in his efforts to organise public concerts and in expanding the Radio Éireann Orchestra; both hoped that it would reach full symphonic strength in due course. Indeed, Little hoped that a symphony orchestra, besides that of Radio Éireann and with a major international figure as it principal conductor, could be established in Dublin. This, he believed, would reap many benefits, not least of raising Dublin and the country's status on a global cultural scene.

The Rotunda Reconsidered

Then, in January 1946, the concert hall idea again sprang into life when Minister Little realised the lease on the Rotunda was due for renewal. He raised the issue with the government, and a cabinet committee was appointed and asked to report to government. This time, Minister for Finance, Seán McEntee, seemed keen and on 19 February 1946, the cabinet agreed to investigate matters further, while imposing a rent figure not exceeding £2,000 per annum. The Minister for Posts and Telegraphs would be the responsible agent. (In an interesting aside, this committee also recommended the establishment of a National Arts Centre managed by a board corresponding to the Arts Council of Great Britain. This would eventually lead to the founding, in 1951, of An Comhairle Ealaíon – The Arts Council.)

Using his good offices, Little obtained an agreement from the governors of the Rotunda Hospital for a 250-year lease. The Capitol and Allied Theatres happened to be the

The RÉO in rehearsal in the Phoenix Hall in the 1950s.

holders of the lease and they now sought compensation of £30,000 for the release of their interest, which also covered the Gate Theatre and the adjacent dance hall, both of which they had sublet.

The Commissioners for Public Works was authorised to buy out all the interests in the property on the best possible terms so as 'to permit the construction of a concert hall with accommodation for 2,000 people'. One of their leading architects would prepare plans and propose a system for maintaining the buildings. The designs should fit in with those of the Rotunda's own architect. The hall must be acoustically perfect, with a first-class organ, and a platform installed which would be suitable for one hundred musicians and a choir of 200. It should be operated by a board of some twenty, or even more, with representatives suggested from universities of Cork, Galway and Belfast.

Raymond McGrath (1903-1977), the Australian-born architect who was then a member of the staff of the Office of Public Works, was allotted the task of producing a suitable design. His initial sketch plans were ready by May 1946. By January 1947, McGrath had prepared measured drawings ready for departmental examination. These were placed on public display but once again, matters became protracted and the urgency which had rekindled the entire debate on the Rotunda abated.

In a general election in the spring of 1948, the Fianna Fáil government was ousted from office and an inter-party coalition took over the reins. At this time the country was experiencing a particularly virulent strain of tuberculosis and the Minister for Health, Dr Noel Browne, demanded substantial financial assistance in building new sanatoria and modernising many older hospitals to accommodate an increasing number of patients. The government acceded to Minister Browne's demands but this led to retrenchment in other departments. Among several early decisions was one against proceeding with the Rotunda project. The new Minister for Posts and Telegraphs, James Everett, also forbade the funding of Radio Éireann public concerts which would now be confined to the Phoenix Hall in Dame Court, into which its orchestra had moved in 1946. On 8 July 1948, negotiations with the Rotunda were terminated and some £124 paid to its legal and technical advisers. It would take another four years for the question of the Rotunda to raise its head again.

In 1952, *An Tóstal* (an assembly, pageant or a hosting of tribes), a country-wide festival of various artistic endeavours, was being planned for the following year. A proposal from the Arts Council, of which P.J. Little was now chairman, was submitted to government, outlining the need for suitable accommodation in Dublin for holding some of its events. The Rotunda was again mentioned as worthy of consideration as yet another of its five-year leases was due to expire in October 1952.

In September 1952, letters passed between the Department of Industry and Commerce and the Taoiseach. The claim that *An Tóstal* could fail if the Rotunda was not acquired was dismissed, as was Bord Fáilte's suitability as the body to administer the event. Dr R.J. Hayes, Director of the National Library, along with other members of the Arts Council, proposed: that the Commissioner of Public Works should take charge of the matter and arrange for the Rotunda to be leased to the Arts Council; or that the Arts Council itself should lease the premises with money made available to it for that purpose. It now transpired that:

the concert hall designed for the Rotunda site in 1947 by the Office of Public Works Architect is for orchestral and choral music... its acoustic would not be satisfactory for speech or talking films.

Still, it was decided to ask the Minister for Education to re-examine the Rotunda situation and to advise on what action, if any, should be taken on a site other than the Rotunda. While this was going on, the government learned that:

A committee of persons interested in providing a concert hall for Dublin [has] selected, if not actually acquired, a site beside the Franciscan Church on Merchants' Quay.

If the latter was certain, it would be 'unwise and wasteful of government to forestall this private project' which would be financed in part by subscriptions to be raised by the promoting committee. Probably to the relief of many government officials, this was cited as a reason against acquiring the Rotunda.

Then a further twist occurred. On 28 November 1952, the Arts Council Chairman, P.J. Little, wrote to Maurice Moynihan of the Department of the Taoiseach, saying that Alexander Bayne, managing director of the Irish Assurance Company Ltd, had offered £75,000 to the Arts Council for the purpose of acquiring the Rotunda as a concert hall. On 5 December 1952, the government agreed to guarantee the principal and interest costs of a lease by the Irish Assurance Company. The Commissioner for Public Works was to act as agent for the Arts Council and this was agreed by the Council on 9 December 1952.

A Concert and Assembly Hall

On 18 December 1952, a piece in the *Irish Press* announced the formation of 'Concert and Assembly Hall Ltd' (CAH), with Mabel Olive Smith, Alexander Wallace Bayne, Peter Kennedy, Augustus Percival Reynolds, Edgar Martin Deale, Lord Moyne and Michael Scott on its board. Concert and Assembly Hall Ltd had been incorporated on 8 December 1952 and was an interesting offshoot of the Music Association of Ireland (MAI), a voluntary body set up in 1948. The MAI council members had included: Olive Smith, a formidable woman passionate about music and its teaching; Brian Boydell, professor of music in Trinity College; and Edgar Deale, a lawyer and composer. Their principal aim was the building of a concert hall and conference centre in Dublin. With exceptionally limited resources, CAH had examined a number of sites in the Dublin area in some detail. These included:

- Blessington Basin – on the north side of Dublin at the top of Blessington Street. Dublin Corporation ruled this site to be totally unsuitable.

- Merchants' Quay – on the south bank of the River Liffey. The capital sum needed for this site was deemed excessive.

- High Street – adjacent to Christ Church Cathedral. Dublin Corporation, which was not against the CAH proposals, had itself proposed two sites in this area for a concert hall.

- The Mendicity Institute on Usher's Island – farther up the River Liffey from the Merchants' Quay site. This too was considered unsuitable.

- Greenmount Oil Works – on Harold's Cross Road, also on the south side of the city. Like the Mendicity Institute, it was dismissed as unsuitable.

- The High School in Harcourt Street, near St Stephen's Green (now Garda Headquarters). This needed a £60,000 capital outlay.

- The grounds of Montrose House – on Stillorgan Road beyond Donnybrook Church and now the home of Radio Telefís Éireann.

The Rotunda, once so highly favoured, was not even considered. The idea of remodelling it into a modern concert hall had finally disappeared.

Prior to Éamon de Valera's re-election as Taoiseach following the general election of 1953, Mabel Olive Smith had contacted him, stating CAH's case and wondering if he had any plans to revive a concert hall project if returned to power. After de Valera reassumed office, Mrs Smith speedily contacted him, setting out the proposed sites but emphasising the suitability of the one at Montrose.

Montrose was originally a private house standing on twenty-three acres. It had been purchased by the state for University College, Dublin but the college's sports' fields were, in fact, on the grounds of Ardmore House, some short distance away from Montrose on the other side of Stillorgan Road. This land had been acquired in 1947 by the Commission for Public Works as a site for Radio Éireann. However, it now seemed a sensible idea to exchange Montrose for Ardmore and the adjacent Belfield as the proposed site for University College and leave Montrose to Radio Éireann. CAH would require just three acres and Radio Éireann was quite sympathetic to this plan. After all, it would eventually be needing a more permanent home for its symphony orchestra, but felt three acres was the maximum area it could concede and hoped CAH might do with something less.

CAH were pleased to accept this situation and the government, believing this could be an answer to a constantly nagging question, again asked Raymond McGrath, then chief architect of the OPW, to draw up plans for this site. This he did and the initial drafts were ready by the end of 1953.

But 1954 brought another change of government with a man not particularly interested in concert halls, J.A. Costello, as Taoiseach. Despite this, Costello did meet a deputation of Olive Smith, Alexander Bayne and Edgar Deale in November that year. They set out CAH's plans – a large hall to seat 2,000 and a smaller one with a capacity of 500, with various rooms and accommodations. The estimated cost was £650,000. Concert and Assembly Hall Ltd pointed out that they wanted:

a government guarantee to enable the bulk of the money to be obtained on the most advantageous terms possible and thereby to reduce the annual charge against revenue for the interest and sinking fund of the loan... We contemplate that the concert and assembly hall must be constructed and managed without Government subsidy.

Having an independent spirit, Olive Smith wanted the hall to operate without any political interference. Costello asked for written proposals but insisted that the government could not guarantee funds.

When Mrs Smith realised that the Arts Council agreed with CAH's proposals, and as three months had elapsed since her letter to the Taoiseach on 24 December 1954, she demanded a response from Mr Costello. He had forwarded her letter to the Minister for Finance for his comments but these had not been forthcoming. In fact, Mr Costello indicated that the matter did not warrant any speedy reply with the remark: 'No need to remind the Minister for Finance for the present' on Mrs Smith's

second letter. Naturally, nothing happened – apart from a brief note to CAH in June 1955 in which the Taoiseach said he planned to discuss the situation with the Minister for Education.

Yet a number of ideas were being floated. The *Irish Independent* reported that the Town Planning Committee of Dublin Corporation had decided on the Nicholas Street/High Street site for a concert hall as its own new offices would be located elsewhere (the controversial Wood Quay blocks now being the monument to this decision). Neither had J.F. Larchet been silent. In a speech to the Engineers' Association, he stated that

the nation's interests would be better served by the provision of a suitable concert hall than by large scale reconstruction of roads.

In August 1955, he and P.J. Little met the Taoiseach with a proposition which now returned to the Capitol Theatre. It seemed the entire building could be bought for £175,000, or £135,000 without its restaurant. Costello was unimpressed, and a further letter to him from Olive Smith dated 12 December 1955 intimated that Concert and Assembly Hall Ltd had accepted the Corporation's idea of Christ Church Place. £50,000 of the total cost of £500,000 would be raised from the public. The balance could be raised by the issue of stock guaranteed by the government.

On 14 May 1956, five months after her initial contact, the Department of Finance finally wrote to Mrs Smith, saying money was unavailable for any such project at the moment. Olive Smith expressed her disappointment and various newspaper articles pleaded her cause for a concert hall. All fell on deaf ears. Even Éamon de Valera's return to office did nothing to assist the concert hall's case. Furthermore, in 1958, a personal proposal from Edgar Deale of the CAH board, reminding de

Valera that a concert hall might be a fitting memorial to the patriot, Theobald Wolfe Tone, the bicentenary of whose birth would be celebrated in 1963, brought the response that

he [de Valera] felt it was inadvisable to combine a Wolfe Tone memorial with a concert hall.

Fund-Raising

In the meantime, CAH decided to battle on and began organising a number of fund-raising concerts with eminent performers such as the Spanish soprano, Victoria de los Angeles, Swedish tenor Nicolai Gedda, and the young Russian pianist, Vladimir Ashkenazy. But profits generated from these events were minimal. In 1958, the arrival of the Hungarian conductor, Tibor Paul, for a concert with the Radio Éireann Symphony Orchestra, led to a number of later engagements and his eventual appointment as principal conductor and director of music at Radio Éireann. He deplored the lack of a concert hall in Dublin and aligned himself to Concert and Assembly Hall's cause.

A fund-raising concert launching the national appeal for a concert hall was organised for 15 January 1960 and Olive Smith took the initiative of inviting Éamon de Valera, who by this time was Ireland's president. The Taoiseach, Seán Lemass, also attended the event which took place in Dublin's Theatre Royal.

As a venue, the Theatre Royal may not have been the wisest choice. It had a 3,500-plus capacity, and the theatre was hardly full. Still, the concert had drummed up sufficient interest for the national press to engage public debate. In her letter of thanks for his attendance, Mrs Smith told Mr Lemass that £1,000 had been raised and

As a young pianist, Vladimir Ashkenazy took part in fund-raising concerts for Ireland's concert hall.

that the Dublin music loving public had clearly demonstrated their desire for a concert hall.

By this time, members of the Dáil were being lobbied to raise the concert hall situation. As a result, Declan Costello, TD, asked the Taoiseach a question in the Dáil, enquiring

...whether the Government are in favour of the proposals to erect a concert hall in Dublin. Whether they propose to give financial assistance to build a concert hall and, if so, when and if he will make a statement on the matter.

The Department of Industry and Commerce agreed to take the question. In reply, its minister, Jack Lynch, said:

I have indicated to the promoters of the concert hall project that I am interested in the proposal and they have promised to

let me have a statement indicating how the erection and operation of the hall might be financed. Until then I cannot say whether it will be possible for the government to assist the project in any way.

The ball was now back in CAH's court.

The Royal Dublin Society

The Royal Dublin Society, however, put a spoke in the CAH wheel. It had plans to extend its own hall in Ballsbridge and was seeking government support through a grant or interest-free loan. The RDS also indicated it was against CAH's plans for a completely new hall which it felt would cost in the region of £750,000, as against the £330,000 for the RDS. However, in October 1960, the Dáil and Seanad Éireann agreed to approve £125,000 for a hall (or ⅓ of the cost, if less) on the understanding that Concert and Assembly Hall Ltd would find the balance of the £750,000 it required.

While this looked rather hopeless for Concert and Assembly Hall Ltd, the group decided to continue its fund-raising and, with the assistance of Tibor Paul, organised another series of events. These included a sold-out 'Concert Hall Fortnight' in which all Beethoven symphonies and concerti were performed under the baton of Paul, with international and local artists, at Dublin's Olympia Theatre in March 1961. Another series of concerts took place in April 1962.

Negotiations, to which CAH had an input, continued between the RDS and the government, and on 9 March 1962, the Society eventually proposed to give a site to CAH... provided the RDS controlled it. A meeting took

Raymond McGrath in typical pose. This photograph is in the possession of his daughter Jenny (Mrs Donal O'Donovan). It forms the frontispiece of 'God's Architect: A life of Raymond McGrath' by Donal O'Donovan (Kilbride Books, Bray 1995)

place between the government and RDS officials in which the government offered the services of its OPW architect, Raymond McGrath, to assist with design and planning. By 13 April 1962, the government approved of assisting the RDS 'towards the provision of a conference and concert hall at Ballsbridge'.

Plans Undeterred

On 31 May 1962, the RDS was informed that the government would offer it a grant not exceeding £100,000, subject to Dáil approval. Concert and Assembly Hall Ltd and Bord Fáilte would be given an opportunity to comment on the plans.

CAH's response came through a letter from Olive Smith to the Taoiseach, Seán Lemass on 11 July 1962. She expressed her sorrow that the RDS idea was only a 'make-do' hall and stated that she would submit a CAH document to him outlining a scheme embodying the various estimates.

Sir George Mahon, Chairman of the Music Association of Ireland's Council, also wrote to Lemass about the RDS proposals. And on 17 July 1962, Mrs Smith again wrote to the Taoiseach, saying that CAH preferred either the Nicholas Street/High Street or the Montrose site and was seeking a meeting with him. This was arranged for 29 August 1962 when it was learned that Concert and Assembly Hall Ltd was being reconstructed as a charitable trust. CAH still preferred Montrose and had been in touch independently with Radio Telefís Éireann. The government favoured Dublin Corporation's involvement as, after all, it had offered the project a free site. So for a while, the focus of attention turned to the Corporation, with Mrs Smith quickly dispatching a letter to the principal officer of the Corporation's Finance Committee setting out CAH's proposals and seeking a meeting with him. Negotiations between CAH, the Corporation and the government ensued, and on 10 December 1962, the government informed Dublin Corporation it must prepare to give Concert and Assembly Hall Ltd £100,000, provided CAH could: arrange the balance required for the hall; provide sources for any additional costs; furnish estimates of revenue and expenditure to assess their suitability to operate a project of such magnitude; and refund the grant if the hall ceased to be a concert hall within thirty years.

All previous offers of loan guarantees from central government were thereby withdrawn.

Once again, the matter lay firmly in the hands of CAH but the case seemed hopeless. Things became even worse when Dublin Corporation decided on essential road-widening in the general High Street/Christ Church area and the site ear-marked for the concert hall vanished under tarmacadam. Possibly due to a certain remorse because of its previous commitment to CAH, a totally obscure site on Dublin's Haddington Road was offered to CAH as an alternative. CAH agreed – but money still had to found.

JFK Memorial

Events took an unusual turn on St Cecilia's Day 1963 in Dallas, Texas, with the assassination of the President of the United States, John F. Kennedy. In the ensuing months, the government discussed plans for a lasting memorial and petitioned the Arts Council for ideas. They suggested a concert hall cum conference centre. The idea was accepted, and an all-party committee was set up under the chairmanship of the Minister for Finance, Dr Patrick Hillery, to advance and shape the project. In January 1964, the government made a statement to the effect that the entire costs of building the hall would come from state funds. On 12 March 1964, Raymond McGrath was officially appointed its architect.

Dublin Corporation's Town Planning Officer was now asked to suggest sites for the committee's consideration. Several of these were very restricted in area while others involved so many interests that acquisition would be very slow. On balance, the committee decided that the Haddington Road site had obvious advantages, one of these being the complementary facilities which the nearby RDS could offer when the JFK memorial building was being used for international conferences. It was then suggested that the new National Library, which was to have been sited on Morehampton Road, should be incorporated in the Haddington Road complex of buildings making it, to some degree, a cultural centre on a 14½ acre site.

It might be interesting to note some of the other ideas floated to commemorate the late US president. Among them were a swimming pool of Olympic standards, an open-air sculpture park within Iveagh Gardens, the completion of the JFK Stadium in Santry, and a Kennedy Memorial Exhibition Hall with a permanent exhibition of Kennedy memorabilia and other items of US/Irish interest.

Plans For Haddington Road

Raymond McGrath, now principal architect of the OPW, maintained that the hall could be designed by the OPW on the basis of the experience gained in the plan of the proposed Rotunda Concert Hall. In this case, however, there should be a local consulting architect, perhaps Michael Scott, and maybe an eminent US architect such as Philip Johnson who had done consulting work on the Lincoln Centre in New York. McGrath felt the committee should visit the Liederhalle in Stuttgart and the Philharmonie in Berlin, so a number of halls abroad were visited by McGrath and John E. Lyons, a staff engineer of the OPW's broadcasting section.

Re-examining McGrath's extensive designs for the Rotunda complex from 1947, it was determined that the proposed hall should be modest, with a seating capacity of 1,600 to 1,800. There would be provision for a platform for an orchestra, choir and organ. A small ancillary hall of approximately 350 seats was also proposed. These would be halls for music, with facilities for radio and television broadcasting. They should be buildings of

simple dignity with a beautiful and adequately equipped interior embellished by the tributes of Irish artists to the memory of a great American President.

Detailed drawings and acoustic designs and calculations were prepared, and in March 1964, Raymond McGrath announced his preferred team: Ove Arup and Partners, Structural Consultants; J. A. Kenny and Partners, Mechanical Consultants; Desmond MacGreevy and Associates, Quantity Surveyors; and Dr Lothar Cremer, Acoustic Consultant, who acted for the Philharmonie in Berlin. On 15 October 1964, these suggestions were approved by the committee.

By this time, it was planned to have the hall ready by 1968. The National Library was also planned for Northumberland Road, adjacent to the hall. But the Stationery Office, already located in inferior premises on the same site, would first have to be demolished and relocated.

It now transpired that the owners of some of the houses in Northumberland Road, which would have to be purchased and then demolished, were seeking exorbitant prices for the properties while others were unwilling to sell. However, on 16 November 1964, the Minister for Finance, Dr James Ryan, stated that plans must go ahead as soon as possible. By December 1964, McGrath estimated the cost of the hall to be in the region of £1,250,000 but believed £1,800,000 to be nearer the eventual mark. The cost of the National Library would be a further £1,260,000.

Organ Design

On 10 December 1964, Professor Ralph Downes of the Royal College of Music, London, and Brompton Oratory, was appointed organ consultant by Minister for Finance, Dr James Ryan. The plans were for a major instrument in the large hall and a chamber organ in the recital hall. Downes made seven proposals on the capabilities, character, integrity and balance (a variety of registers to fit performances of different types, including 'light music'), employing the best materials. It would be a four-manual instrument. Downes suggested specifications and possible organ builders.

Plans continued apace in 1965 but by March of that year, the hall costs had risen to £2,500,000. Six houses on Northumberland Road had been purchased but nine others were needed, with another two a possibility.

Plans Announced

On 9 March 1965, an up-beat Taoiseach, Seán Lemass, hosted a reception which announced details of the hall for the Haddington Road/Northumberland Road site as prepared by Raymond McGrath. The main auditorium would have seating for 1,840, with ramped floor, balconies and boxes. The orchestra floor and pit would be adjustable. The choir seating for 200 would be fixed, and a public address and simultaneous translation system would be incorporated. The plans included rooms for conductor, soloists, artists and managers, as well as a musicians' buffet. Also envisaged were eleven instrument and two choir practise rooms, assembly rooms, radio and television control and recording rooms, and a reception lobby for distinguished guests.

The minor hall promised seating for 464 persons, 332 on a level floor and 132 in the balcony. It would also enjoy a simultaneous translation system, have a conductor's and soloists' rooms as well as a green room, buffet, separate instrumental and choral rehearsal rooms, and three tuning rooms. Details of the foyers, maintenance quarters, management accommodation, restaurants and buffets,

conference suites and toilet facilities were set out, as were the sketches for the exhibition areas which would include a Kennedy Room for personal papers and mementoes. McGrath's drawings were circulated to the press and these appeared in the national papers.

Just six weeks later, when the projected costs had risen to £2,750,000, the first sounds of alarm were heard. The committee sought modifications but Raymond McGrath was seeking extra staff for his office as, with its present establishment, he could not be ready to go to tender before 1968.

Further Difficulties

At the end of April 1965, the secretary to the Minister for Finance wrote to the Secretary of the OPW, urging due economy on the project. The 1966-67 estimates indicated expenditure of £77,000 and the completion date now looked more like 1971, even 1973. Changes were continually taking place. The decision to remove the Stationery Office from the old military barracks was still outstanding by February 1966 when Jim Gibbons, Parliamentary Secretary to the Minister for Finance, wrote to his minister, Jack Lynch, seeking a discussion on the hall. Cash problems were becoming evident and construction at Haddington Road/Northumberland Road now seemed unlikely to commence before 1968-69 at the earliest.

When the Dáil committee met on 24 February 1966, Minister for Finance, Jack Lynch, told the gathering that while there was no question of postponement, limitations on capital expenditure had to be understood. There was also a shortage of planning staff, difficulties over property acquisition, and the whole matter of the relocation of the Stationery Office. As two of the houses on the Haddington Road/Northumberland Road corner had been vandalised, they would have to be

The John F. Kennedy Memorial Hall as it would have looked in the Phoenix Park, Dublin. The Phoenix Park site, mooted in 1967, was one of several porposals considered by the goverment. This perspective drawing, made by Raymond McGrath, is in the possession of Norman McGrath, his son, who is an architectural photographer in New York. The photograph of the drawing was taken by Norman Mcgrath.

pulled down. Due to the many delays now being experienced, Seán Dunne, TD, suggested that the committee should consider a site in the Phoenix Park.

Had the death knell sounded for the Haddington Road site, indeed for the hall itself? If it had, Raymond McGrath had not heard it and continued his work. In addition, there were changes within the government; Jack Lynch was now Taoiseach, succeeding Seán Lemass in 1966. Charles J. Haughey took over as Minister for Finance and chairman of the all-party committee administering the hall's planning.

By February 1967, McGrath began to realise that the Phoenix Park idea might have 'considerable attractions' as a site and would be the best possible solution to the present problem.

The Focus Shifts

The Phoenix Park proposals were mentioned in Dáil Questions and Oral Answers during July 1967. The Phoenix Park idea had also been raised by the Royal Institute of Architects in Ireland, which was somewhat alarmed by the suggesion of a new building in the park. Its president, Wilfred Cantwell, contacted Raymond McGrath who responded by letter on 5 September 1967.

Some take the view that the Phoenix Park should be prepared as a kind of glorious cow-pasture... [But] the Philharmonie in Berlin is in the Tiergarten, and the Meistersingerhalle in Nurnberg is in the Volkspark.

Three other sites were also mentioned around this time: the Model Schools in Marlboro' Street opposite the Pro-Cathedral; Bachelors' Walk on the north side of the River Liffey; and an area between Dame Street and Wellington Quay on the south side of the River, part of the now fashionable Temple Bar.

But the Phoenix Park site already had some planning work done on it and the OPW saw merit in it. Charles Haughey agreed with the idea but realised that public objections would arise as some would see their recreational facilities being restricted. A plan to take down the Wellington Monument was thought unwise, although it was envisioned that the hall should be built between it and the Citadel Pond. There was also a Dublin Corporation proposal to run a road through the park at that point.

The Architectural Association of Ireland, which was opposed to the park location, called a public meeting at the Mansion House. Its chairman was Jack Dowling of RTÉ, and the meeting was addressed by Joe McCullough, consulting engineer and secretary to the National Trust; Wilfred Cantwell, president of the RIAI; Charles Acton, music critic of *The Irish Times*; and Patrick Delaney, architect and town planning consultant and *Irish Times'* correspondent. The meeting found little favour with the Phoenix Park plan.

Other Sites

Government estimates for 1968-69 suggested £53,500 as a reasonable figure for spending on the hall in that financial year. *The Irish Times* of 17 September 1968

reported that the OPW had confirmed that 'work on the planning of the hall was proceeding'. Sites at the King's Hospital School in Blackhall Place and the very attractive St Anne's Park in Raheny were now gaining ground. Charles Haughey, who was himself keen on the St Anne's Park proposal, asked for a report on this site. On 31 October 1968, Raymond McGrath gave some examples of the difficulties which might arise at St Anne's. He also cited the rarity of meetings of the committee, the last of which had been on 15 June 1967. McGrath was also experiencing personnel problems in his office at the OPW, but he did make and submit plans for St Anne's as Haughey had requested.

With questions from a number of Dáil deputies receiving evasive answers, Raymond McGrath realised that his original plans for the Haddington Road/Northumberland Road hall may have been over-ambitious for the current climate. On 30 January 1969, he wrote to Minister Haughey stating, among other things, that the cost of the hall had been reduced to £2,500,000 due to a reduction of site works. He was seeking ministerial approval to proceed with invitations to tender in accordance with the programme now submitted.

The matter rolled on indecisively until, on 22 August 1969, Noel Lemass, Parliamentary Secretary to the Minister for Finance, wrote to Charles Haughey, proposing that the state contribution to the hall be limited to £750,000/£1,000,000. The rest of the costs would have to be financed by a special committee who would be given a site, the plans and the exchequer contribution. Noel Lemass suggested that large numbers of wealthy patrons of the arts would be keen to subscribe and that these need not be confined to Ireland. A special committee could comprise representatives from bodies such as CIE, Bord Fáilte, Aer Lingus and Radio Telefís Éireann, as well as large industrial firms, insurance companies and cultural associations. This novel idea did not gain much ground, however.

Noel Lemass was now a member of the hall's inter-party committee, along with Minister for Education, Pádraig Faulkner. The following month, the *Evening Herald* carried a piece on the hall, reporting that work was beginning on the Haddington Road site and showing a picture of a Northumberland Road house being prepared for demolition. But this was wishful thinking. The estimates suggested for 1970-71 proposed £301,700. The total estimated cost had risen to £2,764,500. And the matter rolled on.

Evasiveness

By May 1970, George Colley had become Minister for Finance. He, too, was evasive in answers to Dáil questions on a concert hall. Raymond McGrath wrote to him on 20 May, putting forward his views on the current situation. McGrath, who by this time had retired from the OPW although his services had been retained, wondered about the tendering stage of the hall. He explained that the five remaining staff in his office had been reassigned to other duties on 13 May 1970 and the closure of the office would soon have effects on public opinion. McGrath continued to emphasise that Dublin needed the hall and the country needed a conference centre. He estimated the cost of the hall was now £3,540,000, the figure which Minister Colley presented to the Dáil two months later.

On being asked if the minister would consider abandoning plans for the new concert hall and instead purchase the Capitol Cinema – the long-forgotten project of 1942 and now proposed for demolition – Noel Lemass responded that he would bring the

suggestion to the all-party committee. In an interesting piece in *The Irish Press*, Aidan Marsh drew attention to the fact that Michele Esposito had looked for a hall for Dublin in 1908 and that Edward Martyn had offered £10,000 to the Corporation if they found a further £40,000 for its construction – and this was the time of the Rotunda, the Antient Concert Rooms and the Great Hall of the Royal University. Raymond McGrath sent a hand-written letter to the Taoiseach, Jack Lynch, along the lines of his letter to George Colley. It showed an element of deep frustration and regret. Here was an eminent and respected architect who had been involved with concert hall projects for thirty years – and nothing had ever gone further than the drawing board and scale models.

Questions continued to be asked in Dáil Éireann, particularly from members of the all-party committee which had not met for some time. Nothing positive resulted from these.

The futility of the committee members' position had a small side-effect when the entrepreneur, Noel Pearson, organised a concert with Elmer Bernstein and Henry Mancini in October 1970. Pearson's aim was

> *of gathering funds for the concert hall seeing that, to all intents and purposes, the idea of a national hall has become dormant.*

The profits from Pearson's concert were offered to the Minister for Finance but Pearson was advised to place the cash on deposit until work commenced.

And still matters dragged on. Dr Noel Browne, anxious about a committee meeting and wondering whether work would ever begin on the hall, again raised the issue in the Dáil on 28 January 1971. He said:

We can take it the scheme is being shelved. Kennedy is dead.

Minister Colley replied:

If that is what the Deputy wishes to say, I cannot prevent him.

In March 1971, the tenacious Raymond McGrath made new proposals to build the hall, without any ancillary buildings. For these, Desmond MacGreevy, the still retained quantity surveyor, provided a revised figure of £2,494,384, updating this to £2,684,699 for 1971 inflation.

The committee which met in May 1971 consisted of Minister for Finance Colley and Minister for Education Faulkner, with Dáil deputies Noel Browne, Ray Bourke, Liam Cosgrave, Maurice Dockrell, Noel Lemass and David Thornley. It also included Raymond McGrath, C. Farrell, chairman of the Office of Public Works and A. O'Beirne of the Department of Finance. It confirmed the Phoenix Park as a suitable site. The park plans, drawn up by McGrath, were to be put to the government. But if they aroused public opposition, the committee would meet – yet again – to reconsider the question of Haddington Road.

The following year, 1972, passed without much heed to the hall but interest was reactivated in 1973 when attention turned away from the Phoenix Park towards the RDS in Ballsbridge. Although this ground had been covered before, it now had a slightly different twist. On 3 January 1973, Noel Lemass wrote to Minister George Colley telling of a meeting with Maurice Dockrell, Dáithi Hanly, former City Architect, and Raymond McGrath. The outcome was to urge the government to support an RDS proposal in its efforts to acquire the Masonic Girls' School next to its own premises in Ballsbridge which was then for sale by tender. The JFK Hall could now become part of the RDS' own development project. Noel Lemass told Minister Colley that he, too, had held confidential discussions with RDS representatives.

A Return to the RDS

Ten months later, following a fair amount of dialogue, a meeting at Minister Colley's invitation was held, with RDS chairman Professor James Meenan, RDS secretary W.E. Wylie, and J.R. Whitty of the Department of Finance. Colley said the 'cost of the JFK Hall was out of the question in the present financial situation'. However, as an alternative, the state would help the RDS with its proposals. The meeting retraced the ground of the 1960s' RDS suggestions and how they had come to nothing. Meenan agreed to bring the matter to the RDS music committee, prior to placing the proposal before the RDS council on 25 October 1973. The OPW would be asked to collaborate if the RDS agreed. This was favourably received by the RDS council, but the OPW had looked at the RDS members' hall in the 1960s and now felt a feasibility study would be worthwhile unless, to quote Oscar Leach who had undertaken that earlier study, 'all were prepared to regard the existing [RDS] hall as no more than a site and a very restricted site at that'.

While it may very well have been worth a try, this scheme also passed into oblivion. And besides, in its own wisdom, Dublin Corporation had zoned the Beggars' Bush/Haddington Road area as residential in its development plan. New offices for government departments would have to be located elsewhere. The John F. Kennedy Memorial Hall, wherever it might be, would not be there. However, while all these discussions had been going on with the RDS, yet another scheme was emerging which, after thirty long years, would have a happy and successful conclusion.

CHAPTER 8
THE NATIONAL CONCERT HALL AT EARLSFORT TERRACE

A Change of Plan

In 1934, land on Dublin's Stillorgan Road had been purchased for UCD sports fields. In 1960, the government also agreed to build a new campus for UCD on a portion of this land, a project which would lead to the majority of UCD's departments leaving Earlsfort Terrace. This took time to evolve but by 1970, the college faculties were preparing to abandon the inner city. The transfer was gradual – indeed thirty years on, it is still incomplete, with Medicine and Engineering still firmly *in situ* in the old location.

In February 1972, Radio Telefís Éireann (RTÉ) cast a shrewd eye on Earlsfort Terrace. Since 1963, its symphony orchestra had been renting the far from attractive St Francis Xavier Hall in Dublin's Sherrard Street. From there, the orchestra broadcast its regular studio concerts, usually before a live audience and for whom admission was free. Realising its musicians deserved better working conditions, RTÉ was on the look-out for a more desirable home for the orchestra. Seeing the opportunities of Earlsfort Terrace, RTÉ contacted the Office of Public Works regarding the future of UCD's Examination Hall once the move to Belfield was complete. The OPW's Oscar Leach, having

an exceptional grasp of the technical criteria following his long and arduous undertakings with Raymond McGrath, was asked for a preliminary assessment. His report was cautious – much needed to be done.

There were problems with reverberation, ventilation, the floor, the glass roof, noise penetration and echo. Even without a new balcony, he estimated the cost of conversion at £205,000. Matters went a step higher in March 1972 when RTÉ chairman Dónall Ó Moráin wrote to Minister for Finance, George Colley, reiterating RTÉ's contact with the OPW and quoting a figure of under £250,000 for conversion. The hall would have a stage for an orchestra of one hundred, space for a choir of 200 and accommodation for an audience of 1,000 which could be increased by 350 with the restoration of the balcony. There was an element of urgency in the letter. Ó Moráin felt the college authorities would be accommodating but the minister would have to 'move very quickly' as others had 'got wind of the word' that the hall was available.

A feasibility study which proposed that the Great Hall be used as a concert hall for RTÉ broadcasts was issued in November 1972. More or less on the lines of Leach's earlier report, it put the cost at between £415,000 and £442,000, depending on the scheme adopted.

Discussions between the departments of Finance and Education and the Higher Education Authority, UCD and the OPW were suggested; J.R. Whitty of Finance pursued the matter. Also cautious, he queried the costs involved in converting the Great Hall.

Two years after the initial RTÉ contact with the OPW, the all-party committee reconvened, after a three-year lapse, on 17 April 1974. With Fine Gael now leading the government, it consisted of Minister for Finance Richie Ryan as chairman, with Senator Noel Browne, and Dáil deputies Maurice Dockrell, David Thornley, Ray MacSharry, John Wilson and Sean Moore; F.H. Kenny represented the Department of Finance. The OPW was represented by Con Farrell, Gerry McNicholl and Raymond McGrath. Expressing his pleasure at Raymond McGrath's presence, Richie Ryan hoped that the committee would not be too disappointed with the decision the government felt obliged to take. The latest estimates for building the John F. Kennedy Memorial Hall were £6,500,000. As it would take two years for work to commence, a further escalation of cost was certain. This expenditure, according to Ryan, could not be justified at the present juncture. The Great Hall would be handed over to the state by UCD under the arrangements involving the college's move to Belfield. The government would allocate £700,000 for the immediate conversion of the Great Hall into a concert hall.

The majority of the committee took the view that, although the hall might provide an adequate solution to the problem of a suitable home for the RTÉSO, it fell short of the standards required of a national concert hall. Writing to Minister Ryan on 26 April 1974, Raymond McGrath also expressed his displeasure and stated that he believed the idea of converting the Great Hall was misguided. He pointed out all its flaws and the continued occupancy of some UCD departments. In his view, it had no architectural value except that it provided four walls. The adaptation, as far as McGrath was concerned, would be a 'make-shift project'.

Richie Ryan Remembers

Almost thirty years later, Richie Ryan recalled the events of 1974.

In these days of national budget surplus, many will have difficulty in understanding how, in the 1970s, the Exchequer's limited funds could not meet all competing demands... Nonetheless, I realised there was a pressing need for a concert hall for the performing arts, particularly the RTÉ symphony orchestra, and I was determined to provide it.

One thing was clear. If the only solution was the proposed John F. Kennedy Memorial Hall, another generation or longer would pass before there would be any concert hall. A more modest solution costing less would have to be found. Hence I asked the Office of Public Works to examine the possibility of upgrading or adapting some existing halls. The Earlsfort Terrace premises offered the best answer, and with UCD's move to Belfield, this could be undertaken right away...

I might mention that I was somewhat perplexed at the OPW recommendation of Earlsfort Terrace as I recalled the derelict condition of the hall when I was a student at UCD from 1946 to 1949. It was used to store turf, and pigeons flew in and out and roosted there. When it was floored and re-roofed to permit its use as an examination hall, the idea arose to have the RTÉSO play there. This proposal was abandoned shortly before the intended performance because of fears about the stability of the roof during the concert.

At government level, when I made the proposal, some ministerial colleagues wanted the money involved to be spent

The Great Hall finally comes to life as the National Concert Hall, An Ceoláras Náisiúnta. (Frank Fennell Photography)

instead on their pet projects. With the strong support of the Taoiseach, Liam Cosgrave, however, I won the day...

Then a press conference followed to announce the decision... I will never forget it. It was the most hostile and vicious press conference I ever experienced. The previous forty years of promises made no impression. The know-alls were not interested in my contention that, as the 'Kennedy Hall Dream' could not be achieved for a long time, it was better to accept a compromise which would give Dublin a good hall in Earlsfort Terrace within reasonable time. The funny thing is, had I done nothing I would not have attracted so much abuse. All the critics have since apologised and expressed their admiration of what was achieved.

[In the end] The Board of Works did a magnificent job. Great credit is due to the entire OPW team... The earlier drawings were for a tiered stadium but it was right to alter the plans to provide balconies. While it would be nice to accommodate larger audiences for celebrity occasions... I believe its size is just right... There is an additional advantage in that there are still possibilities of further expansion on the site to improve facilities for performers and audiences. Its location is almost ideal, being accessible to more people than the proposed location of the Kennedy Hall in Phoenix Park.

Understandably there was disappointment, which I shared, that the original Kennedy Hall did not go ahead. Nobody regretted that more than its designer, 'God's Architect' Raymond McGrath. Another disappointed man was my friend and regular concert-goer, Maurice Dockrell. Both he and Liam Cosgrave were members of the all-party Kennedy

Memorial Committee but Liam supported the Earlsfort Terrace decision as the only one possible... The fact that it was a compromise does not take away from its remarkable success. I received a postcard from Liam Cosgrave a couple of days after the opening of the Concert Hall. In a typical cryptic message, he said: 'I see the culture vultures are now claiming credit for the concert hall. The credit is yours for the greatest musical event since the harp was played in Tara's Halls!' I don't deserve any credit but I am glad that I had the common sense to give it the go-ahead. What began as a compromise can stand proudly on its own merits.

The Plan Proceeds

As Richie Ryan stated, the press conference on 9 May 1974 brought adverse reaction. Mrs Olive Smith declared:

This whole project is ridiculous. Even the Gaiety Theatre, which holds 30% more people than this scheme, is far too small for modern concert audiences, classical or pop.

The Music Association of Ireland, through Professor Brian Boydell, said the idea of Earlsfort Terrace was selling the nation's birthrights for 'a mess of potage'. However, Michael Bowles, former director of music in the old Radio Éireann and then active as composer and arranger, was in favour:

Better to make use of facilities that we now have than engage in another ten years of idealistic conversation.

Minister Ryan established a steering committee in December 1974 with its members including Richard Stokes of the Department of the Taoiseach, P. Feeney of the Department of Finance, Oliver Maloney, assistant director general of RTÉ, and Gerry McNicholl, John

Allen and Noel de Chenu of the OPW. Anxious about the hall's management, RTÉ stated its preference of taking charge of it themselves. Two concerts per week involving five days' rehearsal – space for which might be required – were envisaged. George Waters, RTÉ's director of engineering, thought seating for between 1,300 and 1,500 would be more desirable than the 900 proposed, but the OPW believed that installing a balcony would cause acoustic difficulties. Richard Stokes was against RTÉ's management of the hall and in fact suggested a two-tier system, with the government nominating a committee to deal with the overall administration.

Positive steps were at last being taken, with the OPW carrying out a detailed study which considered taking in the adjoining Denis J. Coffey lecture hall, now part of the artists' room.

The Arts Council, perhaps somewhat peeved that they might not be involved, requested information, and Richard Stokes, a member of that body, was asked to liaise on the progress of Earlsfort Terrace. The employment of a quantity surveyor, mechanical and electrical engineers also arose, as did the matter of an acoustician. In November 1975, the committee chose Vilhelm Lassen Jordan of Denmark who was invited to an interview in Dublin. Seamus Monahan of Dublin's Northbrook Road was officially appointed as quantity surveyor, with Varming, Mulcahy and Reilly suggested as mechanical and electrical consultants. Almost immediately, fears of delays were expressed should UCD be slow in its departure. Some members of the committee visited halls in London and Berlin but the Department of Finance was against too many persons travelling on the grounds of costs and restraints.

The OPW architects' report, setting out different designs, was to be ready by January 1976, with the OPW's Michael

O'Doherty stressing the importance of the acoustic expert's input. O'Doherty also emphasised the need to obtain the ancillary areas around the Great Hall from UCD. Feasibility studies would be ready by the end of 1975, the scheme design by July 1976, and the working drawings by December 1976. Acoustician Vilhelm Jordan came to Dublin in early January 1976 and spoke favourably on the hall's potential. The report from the OPW's design team was presented in March, along with a model and various drawings. The cost was now in the region of £1,379,000, including £207,000 for additional unforeseen works.

After the Minister for Finance had accepted the design report, the preparation of documents necessary to bring the project to tender began. Some additional space, a portion of the Medical School, was required from UCD, but it now looked as if the Great Hall would not be relinquished until the end of 1978. UCD believed its School of Architecture could be moved but problems with the Medical School presented difficulties.

The Architecture Faculty would transfer to Belfield by the end of 1979 and work on the concert hall itself, whatever about its ancillary areas, could proceed. In February 1977, the cost of the hall still stood at £1,379,000 and the aim was to go to tender by June of that year. Michael O'Doherty visited halls in Oslo and Copenhagen. He also met Vilhelm Jordan who expressed his pleasure with the acoustic tests on the model he had built and planned to display in Dublin Castle. The invitation to tender appeared in the national press on 15 June 1977. By this time, the cost had risen to £1,800,000.

The seven tenders received by the closing date came from:

E. Stone – £1,924,000
O'Connor and Baily Ltd – £1,938,000
Cunningham Bros. – £1,943,000
G. and T. Crampton – £1,950,000
John Smith – £1,950,000
W. and J. Bolger – £2,054,000
Cooney Jennings – £2,102,000

The quantity surveyors, Seamus Monahan and Co., supported the Crampton bid but that of E. Stone, recommended by Michael O'Doherty, was accepted. Although a slight discrepancy had been found in their tender, it was considered insignificant. Their revised figure stood at £1,965,433. The permission of the Department of Finance, with George Colley once again its minister, was sought on that figure.

The question of the hall's management came up for discussion towards the end of 1977. RTÉ believed they were the best people for the job but understood that public money was involved and that the Arts Council would be seeking an input. Indeed, in August 1977, Dinah Molloy, the Arts Council's music officer, visited a number of English halls. Her report stressed the vital and most urgent importance of proper management and financial planning structures being put in place at once.

Work Begins

In January 1978, the OPW received a ninety-nine-year lease of stipulated areas of UCD. Stones accepted a contract to build, subject to the guarantee of an insurance bond. When this could not be obtained, they asked to be relieved of their contract and the next two lowest tenders were examined in some detail. Both decided that, as their other commitments had now altered, they no longer wished to be considered. Crampton's tender was then re-examined and the Minister for Finance approved their revised figure of £1,992,035 on 9 May 1978. Ten days later, the contract was signed and, almost immediately, work began on the Great Hall.

Composer Seóirse Bodley. A member of the NCH's first Board of Management, his work Ceol *was commissioned by RTÉ and played at the State Opening of An Ceoláras Náisúinta.*

Discussions continued with UCD on the difficulties experienced with the building work at Earlsfort Terrace and by May 1979, Seamus Monahan and Co. gave the cost of the building at £2,531,815. On 3 October, the committee heard a progress report from Michael O'Doherty and the idea of commissioning a piece of music for the opening concert was raised, with Seóirse Bodley's name to the fore. It was also mentioned that there would be large areas available for decoration and art work with, perhaps, a permanent exhibition which would be discussed with James White of the National Gallery and the painter Louis le Brocquy.

Occasionally, the unforeseen made an appearance. The School of Architecture's darkroom caused a problem as its location under the Great Hall had been overlooked. Neither its move nor the provision of amplification had been included in the estimates. Anxious about concerts by the Chieftains, the internationally renowned Irish

traditional music group, and the work of composer Roger Doyle, a sound system was raised by the Arts Council's new music officer, Marion Creely. More seriously, a cement strike almost brought work to a halt in April 1980.

At this time, Richard Stokes asked for permission to advertise for a concert hall manager and, quite importantly, the possibility of including an organ in the hall. Perhaps prompted by this, Gerard Gillen, professor of music in Maynooth College and organist of Dublin's Pro-Cathedral, wrote to the Taoiseach, Charles J. Haughey, about installing a pipe organ. The Taoiseach responded that, having passed Mr Gillen's letter to the committee, they found the idea an unwarranted and unnecessary expense. Haughey promised to communicate Gillen's suggestions to the board of management which he intended appointing.

In June 1980, although building work was proceeding apace, the committee learned that the building programme was behind schedule and an opening date of 9 April 1981 was deemed as being too early. Testing and tuning could not take place before 25 May 1981.

The First Manager

The administration of the hall now became an extremely pressing issue. The position of general manager was advertised in the national press and one of the applicants was the manager of the New Irish Chamber Orchestra, Lindsay Armstrong. Some months elapsed before he was offered the position in the days before Christmas 1980. (Armstrong's wife is the pianist and harpsichord player, Gillian Smith, the daughter of Lyall and Olive Smith, the long-term protagonist for a concert hall in Dublin.)

The National Concert Hall was then a building site, although the planned opening was scheduled for May

1981. Armstrong saw the futility of this as there was little infrastructure in place. He was immediately anxious about the musicians' off-stage facilities, the booking-office arrangements and the lack of a board of directors. However, realising the impossibility of operating without some back-up, he appointed Anne Cant-FitzPatrick as his secretary. Armstrong did a short familiarisation course at the Fairfields Hall in Croydon, outside London, and plunged into the task of running the NCH.

The First Board

It was some months before the Taoiseach, Charles Haughey, appointed the board of directors or, as it turned out, the board of management. It was led by the then chairman of RTÉ, Fred O'Donovan, and consisted of an interesting cross-section of musical endeavours. It included Noel Coade of the Irish Federation of Musicians and Colonel Fred O'Callaghan, head of the Army School of Music. Gerard Victory, RTÉ's director of music, represented that body, with Moira Pyne and John Ruddock respectively on behalf of the Cork International Choral Festival and Limerick Music Association. It also involved the eminent singing teacher, Veronica Dunne of Dublin's College of Music; the distinguished alto Bernadette Greevy; Dame Ruth King of London's Royal Academy of Music and Britain's National Youth Orchestra, then living in Dublin; the composer Seóirse Bodley; Donald Potter, chairman of the Dublin Grand Opera Society; and Richard Stokes, head of Arts and Culture Division at the Department of the Taoiseach and a member of the Arts Council.

Dublin-born Fred O'Donovan, co-founder and Group Managing Director of the Eamon Andrews Studios, had directed innumerable television shows and films in Ireland and the United States. His Gaiety Theatre productions

were lavish – the musical *Annie* broke all box-office records and his *Juno and the Paycock* and *Man and Superman* were landmarks in the theatre's history. Fred O'Donovan also directed all of the 'Frank Patterson and Friends' shows at New York's Carnegie Hall.

At the first board meeting, held on 21 March 1981 in the Department of the Taoiseach – there was no space available in Earlsfort Terrace – Fred O'Donovan insisted on the establishment of three committees to take charge of management, artistic selection and patrons. Salaries and fees were considered; back-stage and front-of-house staff were to be employed immediately and advertisements placed in the press for booking office personnel. As a result, James Potter was appointed back-stage manager; the late Dick Levins, services manager; John Dunne, house manager; with Mary Lehane in charge of the box office. It was decided that the new National Concert Hall

The distinguished alto, Bernadette Greevy, has been closely involved with many events at the NCH. A soloist at the State Opening, she also served on two boards of the National Concert Hall.

would open on 9 September 1981, despite the opposition of both the general manager and Gerard Victory who believed the 'back-room' areas for the orchestra would be too unfinished. The first meeting directed that artistic booking could begin at once and that conference bookings might be accepted in principle. An acoustic test would be held towards the end of May, to which music critics would be invited in private capacities.

However, it would soon be obvious that, despite the respect which the chairman and general manager had for each other's views, their ideas on the running of the hall came from different perspectives and would, in the long run, become incompatible. Both were under exceptional pressure of work over the coming months and both saw the opening of the National Concert Hall on schedule, on 9 September 1981, as imperative. However, when the position of director of the RIAM presented itself, Armstrong was the successful candidate and resigned his NCH post in October 1981.

As building work on the Great Hall continued under the guidance of principal architect Noel de Chenu, project architect Michael O'Doherty and site architect Alan Smith, the board's sub-committees were particularly active in planning for the opening concerts and future events. Some of the initial work on engaging artists had already been undertaken by Dinah Molloy-Thompson, formerly music officer of the Arts Council, but then living in London having engaged herself in concert promotion following her marriage to Eric Thompson of the British Arts Council. When Ruth King's sub-committee took over the task of artist engagement, they were greatly assisted by her knowledge of and influence in Britain's musical circles, as well as with agents and impresarios.

The patrons' sub-committee was also active in its proposals for developing a Friends and Patrons Scheme.

Veronica Dunne has served with distinction on a number of Boards of Management and was particularly influential in raising funds for the NCH pipe organ.

They also examined the possibility of displaying works of art and commissioning pieces for permanent exhibition. The matters of day-to-day management were naturally for the management sub-committee, and among its responsibilities was rent from RTÉ; the importance of the RTÉSO to the hall's viability could not be over-stressed. Fred O'Donovan's twin hats, as Chairman of the RTÉ Authority and Chairman of the National Concert Hall board, had to be worn with equal skill.

An interesting matter was raised by Donald Potter as early as April 1981 – the installation of an organ. The board was receptive to the idea but, having recourse to the ruling of the earlier steering committee, decided the matter could not be carried any further. The financial implications would need careful examination as would the changes in the hall's specifications and any ensuing acoustic difficulties. Within a short space of time, Veronica Dunne would raise the issue again and while a conclusive decision might not be reached, neither would the matter be shelved. Gerard Gillen and Kenneth Jones, Ireland's well-established and internationally respected organ-builder, strongly expressed their opinions on the need for a pipe organ within the hall.

A Test Concert

As the opening day drew near, it was decided to hold an experimental concert for the purpose of acoustic tests in the presence of an audience. This took place on 8 July 1981 with the RTÉSO under its principal conductor, Colman Pearce. The invited audience was confined to the stalls as the balcony was still unfinished and the critics were permitted to express their opinions. My own review of the test concert appeared in the *Evening Press* the following day.

> *While the peripherals and adjuncts foyer, cloakrooms, bars, artists' rooms and facilities are as yet incomplete, the auditorium is almost ready for its paying customers. Last night's invited gathering found a bright and airy spaciousness awaiting them. Pastel shades of green and white with some gold leaf adornments predominate. At the moment, twelve acoustic discs hang from the ceiling above the platform. Black acoustic panels contrast with the green but it is a pity to find some nasty looking speakers protruding from the walls. Lighting above the audience was initially very strong but this was agreeably dimmed during the music.*
>
> *Seating, also green and with plain backs, is good. Rather straight, it gives a comfort more Spartan than luxurious...*
>
> *The test concert was preceded by the hall's general manager, Lindsay Armstrong, emitting twenty retorts from a pair of pistols at pre-determined intervals and in different directions. The hall's acoustic expert, Denmark's Dr Vilhelm Jordan, was*

on hand to monitor these aural assaults and the orchestral sound provided by the RTÉSO, under Colman Pearce, which followed. This consisted of three works – Beethoven's Coriolanus Overture, Bruch's G minor Violin Concerto and Brahms' Symphony No. 2. The result was revelatory. I can safely say the RTÉSO has not been 'heard' in Dublin before. The opening chords of the Beethoven reverberated like magic. Then one noticed the actual depth of the violin tone which followed. While lower woodwind emerged clearly, it was strange that the deeper strings did not. It was one of the disappointments of the hall that from neither seat I took did I hear violas, celli or basses distinctly when playing with the full body of strings. They were constantly covered by their higher sisters.

Full orchestral sound was, however, very solid and the hall did accept this without smudging detail. Clarity in concerted passages was good – given the reservations about the lower strings. Woodwind seems to get singular and lovely exposure. This was noticeable in the Bruch where Audrey Park's solo work was unblemished and abundantly clear. In the Brahms, the brass were nicely mellow and again the prominence of the woodwind was to be welcomed.

Colman Pearce has conducted many important works at the National Concert Hall.

Audrey Park (1936-1994) – the much-loved Leader of the RTÉSO.

A New Era

One thing was plain. The hall did (and will) show every imperfection, however minute. The musicians will already have reached this conclusion. The slightest deviation in intonation is highlighted to a fine degree. Coarseness, if there be any, will be more evident and woolly, fluffy playing will be recognisable for what it is. Another thing is certain – An Ceoláras Náisiúnta is a challenge to our musicians and audiences...

Six weeks later, the National Concert Hall, although not quite ready and with odd lengths of tapestry judiciously placed here and there to cover the blemishes, welcomed its first concert-goers.

The State Opening of An Ceoláras Náisiúnta which took place on 9 September 1981 was performed by Úachtaran na hÉireann, Dr Patrick Hillery, who, as Minister for Finance in 1964, had served on the first committee of the proposed John F. Kennedy Memorial Hall. Possibly akin to the opening of the Exhibition Palace in 1865, but with fewer titled persons present, it was another glittering occasion. The attendance included Charles J. Haughey, leader of the opposition, and former Taoisigh Liam Cosgrave and Jack Lynch as well as many members of the diplomatic corps. Seen live on RTÉ, the opening was also screened by the BBC, Belgian television and the television services of the Soviet Union. It was broadcast by state radios in Belgium, Spain and Yugoslavia and beyond Europe in Australia, Indonesia, Sri Lanka and the United States.

The *Irish Times'* music critic, Charles Acton, commented:

> *Acoustically I can report that the improvement compared with the tests last July is dramatic. It is also a place where listening to music is a festive, important affair, quite apart from the glitter of a state opening.*

The chosen music was Beethoven's Ninth Symphony and RTÉ's commissioned *Ceol* (Symphony No. 3) by Dublin-born composer, Seóirse Bodley. This was entirely fitting, as Bodley was the most senior of our working composers to have taken his degrees from the Music department of UCD. His *Ceol* was a large-scale work which involved the RTÉ Singers, RTÉ Chorus, the boy choristers of St Patrick's Cathedral and Our Lady's Choral Society. Opening-night soloists were Violet Twomey, soprano; Bernadette Greevy, alto; Louis Browne, tenor; William Young, bass; and Aindreas Ó Gallchoir, narrator. The specially written text of *Ceol*, which explored the nature of music and its relationship to its listeners, came from the pen of Brendan Kennelly, one of the country's leading poets who also held the chair of Modern Literature at Trinity College. The piece, which included audience participation in the final (tenth) section of its three movements, was well received. Repeated the following evening during the first Gala Concert, *Ceol* has not been heard since.

The Chieftains had the honour of giving a traditional Irish music concert in their own inimitable way on 11 September, while the first solo 'classical' recital was given by one of the pianists of the younger generation, John O'Conor. His programme on 12 September included the premiere of the Second Piano Sonata by Raymond Deane which had been specially commissioned by the Performing Rights Society. The first chamber music event came on 15 September with RTÉ's Cork-based Academica String Quartet in Bartók's Fourth Quartet and Beethoven's Op. 132. Final decorations continued before the RTÉSO gave its second concert, a European Broadcasting Union event, on 24 September. This drew together a French-Canadian conductor Pierre Morin, a Danish cellist Hans Jorgen Jensen, and Yugoslav, English and German composers. The next public event was on 30 September when the Dublin Concert Band, under the baton of Co. Kerry musician Robert Houlihan, held the platform.

The first recitals by visiting artists occupied the hall on 3 and 4 October when soprano Galina Vishnevskaya made her first Irish appearance, with her husband Mstislav Rostropovich being heard here for the first time in the role of accompanist.

The initial season continued, as it could only do, with a series of 'firsts'. The RTÉSO's initial subscription concert took place on 4 October with its former principal conductor Albert Rosen (1924-1997) in charge for Seán Ó Riada's short orchestral essay, *The Banks of Sullane,* Rakhmaninov's *Paganini Rhapsody* with the Cypriot pianist Tirimo, and Bruckner's Sixth Symphony. Frank Patterson (1938-2000) made his NCH debut with his pianist wife, Eily O'Grady, on 6 October, while the New Irish Chamber Orchestra was in the hall for the first time on 11 October under the baton of János Fürst, with Bernadette Greevy as soloist.

As 1981 marked the centenary of Bartók's birth, it was fitting that the first opera heard in the NCH should be his *Duke Bluebeard's Castle* on 11 October. Coupled with Mozart's *Jupiter* Symphony, its concert performance was sung by Hungarians Klara Tokacs and Laslzo Polgar under Colman Pearce. The RTÉ Concert Orchestra (RTÉCO), based in the Montrose Studios, travelled to Earlsfort

Frank Patterson (1938-2000) made his NCH debut in 1981 with his pianist wife, Eily O'Grady.

Terrace on 16 October with Albert Rosen and Dublin pianist John Gibson. The accolade of the first visiting ensemble went to the Ulster Orchestra on 18 October with Bryden Thomson, then its principal conductor, on the rostrum with Bernadette Greevy heard in the Berlioz song cycle, *Nuits d'été.*

Visitors in November 1981 included the violinists Stephane Grapelli and Yehudi Menuhin, and the tenor Dennis O'Neill. December offered the Russian pianist Emil Gilels with his daughter Elena in an all-Schubert programme. The Spanish soprano, Montserrat Caballé, presented by the Dublin Grand Opera Society with its conductor Napoleone Annovazzi as her accompanist, also graced the platform.

Another Dublin-born pianist, Veronica McSwiney, made her NCH debut with the RTÉSO in November while the

band concert on the 21st – the Irish Transport and General Workers' Union and the Christian Brothers' School, Westland Row – shared the baton between RTÉ clarinet player John Finucane and James Cavanagh, then assistant house manager of the NCH.

Our Lady's Choral Society made two further appearances with Beethoven's *Missa Solemnis* on 20 November and Handel's *Messiah*, the choir's perennial favourite, on 18 December. Both were conducted by Proinnsías Ó Duinn who, as principal conductor of the RTÉCO since 1975, has become one of the most frequent artists on the NCH platform.

Within three months, the National Concert Hall had firmly established itself as the country's premiere music venue with many of its events enjoying almost full occupancy. It also set the standard which the chairman and board had sought to achieve.

Pianist Veronica McSwiney.

A New Manager

Lindsay Armstrong's departure shortly after the hall's opening meant his managerial position had to be filled quickly. The choice fell to the long-established RTÉ staff member, Frank Murphy. He had joined the Radio Éireann Orchestra from school as a horn player on the instigation of Michael Bowles, then the orchestra's conductor. He was the first civilian to enter the brass section as, up to that time, its duties had been discharged by members of the Army No. 1 Band. Moving to the RÉ Light (later Concert) Orchestra on its formation in 1948, Murphy eventually became its manager in which capacity he also guided the orchestra in its national and overseas engagements. He had also worked with Fred O'Donovan on a number of projects, including acting as manager on an extensive and highly successful tour of the United States by the Garda Choir and Band.

Frank Murphy had an extraordinary facility for getting things done by finding the right people in the right place at the right time. This legendary capacity for knowing people often meant turning the inconceivable into reality; indeed it is through this charisma that the magnificent Waterford glass chandelier, designed by Timothy O'Halloran and which hangs over the John Field Room, and the two smaller ones which adorn the board room, came to be presented to the NCH by Waterford Glass in 1985. Murphy's earlier relationship with Fred O'Donovan was probably to the advantage of both and to the running of the hall.

The hall was now up and running and, as its staffing levels came within the remit and restrictions of the civil service, it was one of the earliest tasks of the board to work within these limitations. To this end, Dolores Ferran was appointed the NCH's first finance officer.

A Piano, Friends and Visitors

The purchase of a Steinway grand piano was one of the board's early decisions. The assistance of Ruth King was again a valuable asset as she elicited the help of the eminent English pianist, Clifford Curzon, in testing and choosing a suitable instrument. It would have its own technician, and its use would be largely restricted to the NCH's own promotions.

The idea of a Friends and Patrons scheme was continuously discussed and in due course, a suitable plan emerged. Among the benefits accruing would be an annual concert. One of the most unusual of these came in November 1986 with the visit of the US Marine Band from the White House in Washington DC – an event marking only the second occasion on which the band had played outside the United States.

The First Year

The first event of the year, on 2 January 1982, had the Irish Youth Orchestra establishing a tradition of ending its post-Christmas course with an NCH concert, usually in the first few days of the New Year. It was conducted by Hugh Maguire, the Irish violinist and teacher who, in 1970, had masterminded its formation with Olive Smith.

Ten days later brought 'the concert that never was'. The biennial Dublin Festival of 20th Century Music, run by the Music Association of Ireland, had the work of the controversial German composer, Karlheinz Stockhausen, as its main attraction. The composer was engaged to conduct the RTÉSO in a performance of his *Inori* on 12 January. As it happened, Dublin was hit by an unprecedented snowstorm and an ensuing spell of severe weather brought the city to a standstill. Some members of the orchestra found themselves unable to reach the NCH, leading the composer/conductor to a state of exasperation. Frictions also arose between Stockhausen and the musicians, which led to industrial relations problems. The result was the concert's cancellation, but with Herr Stockhausen on hand to introduce a commercial recording performance, with the participation of dancers, of *Inori*. The receptive gathering was nonetheless disappointed.

Later in the year found the distinguished singers, baritone Robert Merrill, tenors Robert White, Carlo Bergonzi and Giuseppe di Stefano, and the sitar-player Ravi Shankar on the NCH platform. The year also commemorated a number of centenaries which embraced literature, music and politics. James Joyce was honoured in an RTÉSO concert in February with part of his *Finnegans Wake* set to music by the English composer, Humphrey Searle, and narrated by Anna Manahan. There was a new piece, *Six Epiphanies of an Author*, by Gerard Victory; Colman Pearce included a *Ulysses* extract, in Matyas Seiber's setting, in an RTÉSO concert in June. The year celebrated the 250th anniversary of Haydn's birth, the bicentenary of John Field and Stravinsky's centenary. The former's music was spread strategically throughout the period, while the seven John Field Piano Concertos were heard in four concerts from the New Irish Chamber Orchestra, with John O'Conor under Nicholas Kraemer during May. The main Stravinsky event was on 16 June with his *Capriccio*, the ballet *Jeu de Cartes* and the Symphony in Three Movements from Colman Pearce, the RTÉSO and Irish pianist Miceál O'Rourke.

Concerts on 17 March and 24 October celebrated the centenary of patriot, parliamentarian and president, Éamon de Valera. The first programme brought another great Irish actress, Siobhán McKenna, to the NCH in the

Belfast-born flautist, James Galway, in the NCH ante-room. (Photo: Eugene Langan)

company of Bernadette Greevy and violinist Geraldine O'Grady. The second, produced by Fred O'Donovan, had soprano Mary Sheridan de Bruin and pianist/composer Bernard Geary, Frank Patterson and Eily O'Grady, the Inis Eagla Dancers and the Third Day Chorale.

Among other notable events of 1982 was the seventy-fifth birthday of the doyen of Irish pianists, Charles Lynch (1906-1984) who appeared on 15 March. There were visits of the Israel (February) and Moscow Piano Trios (October) and a four-recital series by the Takacs String Quartet in July. The Irish 'Ring', a trio of operas – *The Lily of Killarney, The Bohemian Girl* and *Maritana* – had concert performances from RTÉ and the Glasnevin Musical Society. A variety of soloists performed during May and June, while folk music held sway for a week in February with a Five Nations Folk Festival. The Chieftains returned in July in the company of the Chinese song and dance troupe, Tianjin, previewing the group's immensely successful tour of China.

In June, for a Haydn commemoration as part of the Dublin International Organ Festival, Gerard Gillen played on a small instrument brought in for the occasion. Built by Kenneth Jones, the organ highlighted the deficiency in the NCH's own fabric. (The instrument is now in the Catholic church in Newcastle, Co. Down.) The year also launched the RTÉCO's 'Music for Fun' concerts for young people in November and ended on a frivolous note with a televised RTÉSO New Year's Eve extravaganza. Produced by Anne Makower, there was an array of artists, including the twenty-six members of the Dublin Horn Club and NCH secretary Anne FitzPatrick. *Umbrage*, a specially commissioned piece for mixed

soloists and orchestra by James Wilson, took a number of Dublin music critics onto the NCH platform. In unaccustomed roles were Fanny Feehan, Mary MacGoris, John Honohan, Ian Fox, James Maguire and the author. However, our efforts went without review even by our senior colleague, Charles Acton, who had declined to join our gallant endeavours.

During the year, the board of management continued its deliberations on a number of diverse issues, from the material needs of the hall to the physical needs of its staff. Other issues arose such as the display of works of art and the naming of the rooms adjoining and adjacent to the auditorium. The extended foyer area was named in honour of the tenor, John McCormack (1884-1945), while John Field (1782-1837), the creator of the nocturne,

The celebrated pianist, John O'Conor, under the watchful eye of composer John Field. (Photo: Eugene Langan)

Members of the Pittsburgh Symphony Orchestra on their visit to the NCH in 1999. (Photo: Eugene Langan)

was chosen for commemoration in the main bar and reception area. In time, this would serve as the temporary small recital arena. The travelling harpist/composer, Turlogh Carolan (1670-1738), was awarded the first floor room where board meetings and receptions are held.

A bust of John Field, commissioned by the OPW from Yann Renard Goulet (1914-2000) stands in his chamber – part of the Sculpture Room of the Exhibition Palace – while there are copies of McCormack memorabilia in the foyer area, given by his own family and the family of Vincent O'Brien, the singer's life-long friend, teacher and accompanist on his pre-World War I American and Australian tours. McCormack's portrait is the work of Leo Whelan. A small bust of the Irish prima donna, Margaret Burke Sheridan (1889-1958) is placed on the wall at the top of the stairs leading to the mezzanine. The idea of exhibitions in the Field and McCormack areas was realised through a series of thirty photographs by a Japanese artist held from 16 February to 8 March 1982. Richard Stokes was responsible for the first important travelling exhibition to be carried by the hall, consisting of forty paintings by the Australian artist, Sidney Nolan (1917-1992), which were shown in 1984.

Another exhibition was later arranged through the combined efforts of Richard Stokes, James White of the National Gallery, and Noel de Chenu of the OPW. They persuaded the businessman Vincent Ferguson to loan the NCH some thirty pieces from the collection in his offices in nearby Hatch Street. A painting of pianist Charles Lynch was presented to the hall by its artist, Thomas Ryan, who also gave a small portrait of composer, Seán Ó Riada. A number of paintings are now on permanent loan through the OPW and the Arts Council's State Collection Scheme.

Challenges Overcome

While the board and management had, by now, settled into the running of the NCH, they also made sure its public was being fed a nutritious diet of home-produced programmes as well as some of the best fare from the international circuit. In this latter category, 1983 saw a number of visiting orchestras coming to the hall, among them the BBC Philharmonic from Manchester for a concert in January and the Royal Liverpool Philharmonic which gave two concerts in July.

The German Bach Soloists under Helmut Winschermann made two appearances on 4 and 5 November but, despite the separate merits of these ensembles, it was the mainly Tchaikovsky programme from the USSR State Symphony Orchestra, conducted by Arvid Jansons and with Valery Klimov as soloist in the Violin Concerto, which generated the greatest advance excitement and retrospective adulation on 14 November. It may have been something akin to the Hallé's debut at the Exhibition Palace in 1878 as it showed orchestral playing in a sparkling perspective.

The excitement created by the USSR State Symphony Orchestra had hardly died away when the Helsinki Symphony Orchestra reached Earlsfort Terrace on 4 February 1984. With Paavo Berglund at its helm, Sibelius, by way of his enigmatic Seventh Symphony, came along with the Brahms Second Symphony and Liszt's Second Piano Concerto with Bernard d'Ascoli, the blind French musician, as soloist. The BBC Philharmonic returned for two further concerts in November.

European Music Year

Among the first board's many achievements was the challenge of the European Union's designation of 1985 as European Music Year. The National Concert Hall rose to the occasion in various ways.

It began with board member Bernadette Greevy putting her own experience and helpfulness to good use with a series of master-classes for young singers in the first week of January. Later that month, the Italian tenor Giuseppe di Stefano returned to Dublin for a shared recital with his protégé, soprano Monika Curth, and the young tenor

Mstislav Rostropovich, with his baton instead of his cello at the National Concert Hall.

Mario Malagnini. They were followed in February by the NCH's own promotion of the Swedish soprano, Elizabeth Söderström, and the English soprano Rosalind Plowright in March.

The first orchestral visitors came from London on 16 February when Mark Elder conducted the BBC Symphony in Tippett's Second Symphony and Brahms' Second Piano Concerto with Peter Donohoe. The Vienna Philharmonic fulfilled all expectations with their concert on 28 March. On its first visit to Dublin, and with a programme of Mozart's Symphony No. 29, Stravinsky's 1919 *Firebird* Suite and the First Symphony of Brahms, the orchestra was directed by Lorin Maazel. This conductor was back at the NCH on 17 August with the Pittsburgh Symphony when the concert was devoted to *Don Juan* by Richard Strauss, Stravinsky's Symphony in Three Movements and the Berlioz *Fantastic* Symphony.

Prionnsías Ó Duinn, Principal Conductor of the RTÉ Concert Orchestra.

Almost sated by these magnificent performers, the icing on the cake was provided by the National Symphony Orchestra of Washington on 28 September. This brought the return of Mstislav Rostropovich, with his baton instead of his cello, for a programme of Beethoven's Fourth Symphony and Shostakovich's Fifth.

A New Board

The NCH's first board of management completed its highly successful tour of duty in March 1986 with the appointment of the second board seeing a number of significant changes. Lewis Clohessy, then director of the prestigious Dublin Theatre Festival and previously chief executive of An Táisce, took over the role of chairman.

From the first board, only Veronica Dunne, Donald Potter and John Ruddock remained to offer a continuity of expression. Of the eight new members, Aideen Lane was much involved in music in Co. Wicklow, while American-

born composer Jane O'Leary, living in Galway, was an influential and committed figure in music-making in that city. Jim Aiken was a highly successful concert and artistic promoter outside the classical field. RTÉ was represented by Jane Carty, its senior music producer who had a life-long interest in promoting young people in music and whose 'Musician of the Future' competitions had been established in the mid 1970s.

Business was represented by Patrick Brennan and Mairtín McCullough. Brennan had been secretary of Aer Lingus, while McCullough came from McCullough Pigott, Dublin's premier music store. The Pigott connection was a carry-over from the cellist and music-publisher of the 1820s, Samuel Pigott.

Patrick Buckley represented the Department of the Taoiseach, to which the NCH was responsible. Another significant appointment was that of Gerard Gillen, professor of music at Maynooth College and titular organist of Dublin's Pro-Cathedral. The second board was later increased by three – the architect Patrick Campbell who was also a prominent performing member of the Rathmines and Rathgar Musical Society; Paul McGuinness, the manager of the rock group U2; and Liam McKinney, a Co. Longford constituency colleague of the Minister of State for Arts and Culture, Ted Nealon.

The first board had made several contacts with UCD regarding extra space but the college authorities, while sympathetic, could not see any immediate solution to either its own or the NCH's difficulties. Thus the second board broached the subject with Belfield. Their response understood the problems in Earlsfort Terrace but, without government funding, nothing could be done about moving the Engineering Library to allow an extension beyond the John Field Room wall. Attempts were also made to have summer concerts in the Iveagh Gardens but, while negotiations with the Department of Foreign Affairs and the OPW were hopeful, conditions in Northern Ireland were such that Iveagh House and its adjoining gardens were placed on a high-level security alert. The idea of concerts had to be abandoned.

Staffing at the NCH had been gradually increasing throughout its various departments, but other changes also took place. Finance officer Dolores Ferran decided to vacate her position and was replaced by John Nolan who still retains the hall's demanding treasury portfolio. Laurie Cearr, public relations officer for RTÉ's music department, had worked tirelessly for the hall's promotion during the exhausting period preceding and following the September 1981 opening. The ensuing years found Ms Cearr seconded to Earlsfort Terrace from RTÉ, but she has now returned to her parent authority.

Dublin's Millennium

As the first board had the European Music Year during its term of office, the second found planning for Dublin's Millennium Year on its agenda almost from the outset. With the input and co-operation of many, not least the invaluable support of RTÉ, the NCH housed a plethora of interesting events. In fact, it was the NCH which led Dublin City into its millennium in 1988 with a New Year's Eve concert from the RTÉSO conducted by Proinnsías Ó Duinn, and *Thresholds*, a commissioned piece by Raymond Deane. In conferring a number of honorary doctorates celebrating the millennium year, Trinity College chose Mstislav Rostropovich as a recipient. The cellist returned to Dublin for the occasion with the Ulster Orchestra, which he also directed.

The BBC Symphony returned on 9 April when Marek Janowski conducted an evening of Wagner, reminiscent of

the old DOS concerts under Esposito in the Royal University, and the Brahms Fourth Symphony. Its Manchester and Glasgow sisters had three concerts between them with the BBC Philharmonic under the baton of Sergiu Commissiona on 9 – 10 May. The BBC Scottish Symphony, with George Hurst in control, offered Britten's 'Sea Interludes' from *Peter Grimes*, some of Mahler's *Das Knaben Wunderhorn* songs with mezzo Christine Cairns, and Beethoven's *Eroica* on 26 November.

Two other orchestras crossed the Iron Curtain to celebrate Dublin's thousandth birthday. Antoni Wit conducted the Polish National Radio Symphony in Beethoven's Violin Concerto with Konstanty Kulka and Sibelius' Fifth Symphony on 24 October. Then on 13 November, the Moscow Radio Symphony arrived in Earlsfort Terrace with Nikolai Demidenko as soloist in Rakhmaninov's Second Piano Concerto. With Vladimir Fedoseyev on the rostrum, Tchaikovsky's *Sleeping Beauty* Suite and the Mussorgsky/Ravel *Pictures at an Exhibition* made for stunning colour.

As principal conductor of the RTÉSO, János Fürst had a number of concerts during the year, beginning with Mahler's Second Symphony on 8 January with RTÉ's Philharmonic Choir and soloists Sheila Armstrong and Bernadette Greevy. Continuing a Mahler cycle, Fürst conducted the Seventh Symphony on 4 March and on 29 April, he gave the first Irish (concert) performance of Richard Strauss' *Elektra* to a shamefully half-empty house. Not to be outdone, the Irish Chamber Orchestra invited Yehudi Menuhin to conduct its concert on 21 November when a former pupil, Dublin cellist Daire Fitzgerald, played one of the Haydn concertos.

Premiered in 1984, Gerard Victory's *Ultima Rerum*, introduced by the composer, had a welcome second performance on 16 March 1988 from Colman Pearce,

*Violinist Isaac Stern relaxes during the 1994 Celebrity Concert Series.
(The Irish Times)*

while John Buckley spoke about his First Symphony prior to its premiere under Albert Rosen on 3 June. Shaun Davey was one of the soloists in his own *Granuaille* and *The Brendan Voyage* on 14 August with the RTÉCO under Proinnsías Ó Duinn, with vocalist Rita Connolly and Liam Ó Floinn, pipes. Perhaps drawing inspiration from the Dublin International Organ Festival which the organists of the city's three cathedrals – John Dexter, Gerard Gillen and Peter Sweeney – devised in the late 1970s, John O'Conor and a number of like-minded enthusiasts including Ann Fuller, a lady of commanding ability, came up with the idea of an international piano competition for Dublin. Using his considerable persuasive powers, O'Conor drew a powerful committee around him but, more importantly, enlisted the financial support of a number of influential bodies, not least Guinness Peat

Aviation. Besides enjoying the essential backing of RTÉ and assistance from its PRO, Laurie Cearr, the GPA Dublin International Piano Competition moved from an embryonic state to reality.

Following extensive preliminary organisation, the first of these triennial events took place at the NCH in May 1988. To public acclaim, the first prize went to Frenchman Philippe Cassard who, while returning to Dublin on many occasions, has also marked out a considerable career for himself in Europe and elsewhere.

City of Culture

With the success of the millennium year behind them, the second board turned its attention to planning the NCH's contribution to Dublin 1991 – European City of Culture. The result was dynamic. It was interesting that the first concert of the year – the Lucan Concert Band with the

Canticle of St Mary and West County Choir – should have a very senior civil servant, Michael Grant, as its accompanist. Grant had been involved in the amateur music scene for many years and indeed had appeared on the NCH platforms in a number of guises.

The first fruits of a recently signed contract between RTÉ and the Naxos/Marco Polo recording company were harvested on 13 January when Richard Bonynge, the Australian conductor and husband of *prima donna* Joan Sutherland, took the stage to direct a concert performance of Balfe's opera, *The Bohemian Girl*, immediately prior to its Naxos recording. The title role was sung by American soprano, Nova Thomas, with New Zealander Patrick Power as Thaddeus.

The first of the year's visiting orchestras was the Bucharest Philharmonic on 8 May. In this Friends of the NCH gala, Horia Andreescu conducted and the soloist in the Brahms Concerto was Japanese violinist, Hideko Udagawa. Following the success of their 1990 concert, the New Jersey Symphony returned on 15 July. Again with Hugh Wolff on the podium, an American programme included Gershwin's Piano Concerto with Christopher O'Riley, and Stephen Albert's symphonic poem, *Riverrun*, inspired by James Joyce.

The same mid-September week brought orchestras three and four in two concerts each. In retrospect, this was bad planning as even the Czech Philharmonic's Dvořák programmes were not totally filled on the 16th and 17th; the Scottish Chamber Orchestra's mixed and esoteric agendas on the 18th and 19th mustered only selective interest. The Czechs, conducted by Libor Pesek, coupled Dvořák's Seventh Symphony and Violin Concerto (Miriam Fried) and the *New World* with the Piano Concerto (Garrick Ohlsson).

The Scottish concerts mixed classical and contemporary works. Conducted by Paul Daniel, the first juxtaposed

Mozart's *Paris* and Haydn's *London* Symphonies with Edward McGuire's *Riverside*, which involved the folk group, the Whistlebinkies, and Richard Rodney Bennett's Percussion Concerto with Evelyn Glennie. The second concert had Mozart versus Peter Maxwell Davies, who also directed. Dublin pianist John O'Conor played the C minor K 491 Concerto, while Glasgow cellist William Conway was the soloist in Davies' *Strathclyde* Concerto No. 2. The composer/conductor's *Orkney Wedding, with Sunrise* saw piper George MacIlwham back on the NCH platform.

The fifth orchestra of 1991 was the London Mozart Players, directed by the pianist/conductor Howard Shelley, while the last came from the Hamburg-based North German Radio. Under Michel Tabachnik, Richard Strauss' tone poem *Also sprach Zarathustra* brought this sequence of unusual concerts to a resounding conclusion.

A Dream Realised

While the first board of management felt the NCH should be self-financing, the second believed that extra government funding should be sought. It also looked for and achieved an increase in commercial sponsorship. The second board also brought about the purchase of a new Steinway. With the advent of the first GPA Dublin International Piano Competition in 1988, John O'Conor, its director, persuaded the board of the necessity of finding the wherewithal, which it duly did.

Shortly after coming to office, the board set out to attain another goal – the installation of an organ. It is only fair to point out that the NCH's first board did make an effort to position an instrument in the NCH and in December 1984, an electronic Dutch instrument was actually used in the hall. However, Gerard Gillen's opinion of it was

Philippe Cassard, winner of the first GPA Dublin International Piano Competition, rehearses at the NCH.

unfavourable. Ultimately, the instrument was returned to the organ's agent and never mentioned again.

To promote the real thing, a launch was held in the hall to which representatives of a number of commercial and financial institutions and some private individuals were invited. The cost of an organ and its installation were estimated to be in the region of £600,000 and it was hoped to attract pledges, subscriptions and donations from the assembled guests. This proved fairly successful, although it was basically left to the offices of Patrick Dowling, a deputy chief executive of the Allied Irish Banks, to devise a scheme of guarantee, donation and subscription against which the bank would initially underwrite £350,000. Contact with Dowling, who in turn called in the assistance of the entrepreneur, Dermot

Desmond, had come through the efforts of NCH general manager, Frank Murphy, and from him to board member Veronica Dunne.

A small sub-committee was also set up to pursue the project which Patrick Dowling was invited to join. Along with Chairman Clohessy, Veronica Dunne and Gerard Gillen undertook a fund-raising tour to the United States. This was done in the wake of a government promotional visit by a number of TDs, including Ben Briscoe, a great devotee of the hall. While Briscoe did not actually seek funding, he was able to open doors which might have remained closed to the sub-committee on their visits to Dallas, Denver and Boston.

During the course of the visit, and through Veronica Dunne's own personal connections in Texas, she was able to contact an elderly lady, Mrs Lucy Owsley, the widow of the first United States Minister to Ireland. Mrs Owsley had been in Ireland before that time and remembered hearing the speeches of James Larkin during the 1913 general strike. She expressed an interest in assisting the organ cause and donated $27,000 to it through the Ireland Fund. She was later able to come to Dublin and experience the instrument first hand. The tour also brought $10,000, through trustees, from Dr A.J.F. O'Reilly of the Heinz Corporation. Other donations followed, including that of Time Warner Inc., through the efforts of Paul McGuinness, and eventually, £550,000 of the targeted £600,000 was gathered, leaving the state to finance the remainder.

The practical side of things was now set in motion. Tenders were invited and three firms were considered: Kenneth Jones of Bray, Co. Wicklow, whose reputation was particularly respected in Ireland and his work recognised in a number of Dublin churches, among them Christ Church Cathedral, the Carmelites', Whitefriar

Street and the Most Holy Redeemer in Bray; Marinssen's of Denmark who built the Bridgewater Hall organ in Manchester; and the well-established German organ-builders of Klais, based in Bonn. The choice fell to Kenneth Jones. It was Taoiseach Charles Haughey's wish to have the organ fully installed during Dublin's term as European City of Culture, and indeed the instrument was ready by September 1991.

The NCH Organ

Kenneth Jones wrote an introduction to his instrument around the time of the inauguration.

What is this new instrument, this pipe organ, which stands in the National Concert Hall? Most people never see inside a pipe organ, cannot be aware of what may be called its guts, and cannot be expected to know how it works or how it makes music.

So most people will describe a pipe organ as a large instrument, describe it by what they see and possibly by the sort of sounds it makes. But what is seen is only a fraction of the whole. What is not seen is much more interesting!

An abbreviated specification of the new concert organ which we have designed and made for Ireland's premier concert venue would describe it as having four manual keyboards and pedals, 52 speaking stops, 12 couplers (facilities which

Members of the National Chamber Choir take a break beneath Kenneth Jones' magnificent pipe organ. (Photo: Eugene Langan)

combine the resources available on the various keyboards and on the pedalboard), 4,045 pipes, tracker key-action, and electric stop-action with electric combination-action...

The organ is housed in a Renaissance-style organ-case which I designed to be in sympathy with the architecture of the hall, of solid timber throughout and with hand-carved decorative work. The visible pipes are of polished 75%/25% tin/lead, with 22-carat gold leaf on the mouths and on two central embossed pipes. The case is some eleven metres tall...

This organ is innovative in its tonal and technical design and is unique. Part of its ethos looks forward to the performance of and creation of new music – it would be a failure of opportunity and creativity if it were to be a more-or-less standard concert-hall organ.

The organ-case, designed by Kenneth Jones, was made in the firm's workshops in Bray and painted to a colour scheme chosen by the designer in consultation with the Office of Public Works. Hand-carved work was designed by Derek Riley and Kenneth Jones, executed by Derek Riley and Keith German, and painted, with glazing by Paddy Gordon and J.F. Keatinge & Sons. Kenneth Jones' team which worked on the creation of this organ consisted of Trevor Crowe (tonal evolution and voicing), David Maybury, Stephen Adams, Aidan Walsh, Susan Hemmens, Albert Archer, Keith O'Briain, Jean Walsh, Donal McKay, Scott Macnaughton, Ann Keogh, Kenneth Jones and many vacation-time students whose contribution was considerable.

As it happened, the second board of management did not see the organ's completion as its term had ended in March 1991. It did, of course, have the arrangements for the inauguration set in place, as well as the many concerts by visiting orchestras and soloists which enhanced the year considerably for Dublin's music-lovers.

Naturally, the instrument did not emerge overnight. To allow the building work to proceed, the main auditorium closed from 9 March to 21 April, reopening the next day with a recital by renowned mezzo, Ann Murray, accompanied by Stuart Bedford. Only then did the instrument reveal itself in all its glory. The inauguration concert on 28 September, with the programme repeated two days later, demonstrated the organ's extensive musical prowess.

The NCH organ was christened by the English musician, Peter Hurford, with music by Purcell, Mozart, Schumann, Alain and J.S. Bach whose E flat Prelude and Fugue, with its three-fold thematic scheme, ran a gamut of multifaceted contrast. After the interval, Gerard Gillen, a blissfully happy man following his and so many others' years of persuasive activity, joined the NSO and Proinnsías Ó Duinn in Saint-Saëns' Third 'Organ' Symphony. I described the performance as 'a luscious excess' but added that its festive brilliance was the perfect end to a truly gala occasion. The pipe dream was now a reality.

A series of celebrity organ recitals, spread over several weeks, began with America's extrovert Carlo Curley and ended with Ireland's Peter Sweeney. The installation of the instrument led to two major NCH/RTÉ commissions for concertos from John Buckley and Ian Wilson. Both works were premiered by Peter Sweeney and the NSO.

The Third Board

The second board of management came under the remit of Taoiseach Garret FitzGerald, while the third, in 1991, was appointed by Charles J. Haughey. It was led by Annraoi Ó Beolláin who had extensive financial

Composer Gerard Victory (1921-1995). His epic Ultima Rerum *was premiered in March 1984.*

experience in a long business career. A school and university colleague of Haughey's, they had formed their own firm of chartered accountants and auditors in the early 1950s. When Haughey moved into politics, Annraoi Ó Beolláin remained in the old firm of Haughey Boland until 1991 when it merged with the larger firm of Deloitte and Haskin Sells. *An tUasail* Ó Beolláin, a silver medal-winner in Feis Ceoil for Amránaíocht, and who studied at the RIAM, was deeply interested in music, playing both viola and piano as well as singing.

The NCH's third board retained the services of Veronica Dunne and Donald Potter, so far the only ones to serve three chairmen. Jane O'Leary was also invited to continue, as were Jim Aiken and Patrick Buckley, while Bernadette Greevy was asked to return following her successful input to the first board. Of the new members,

Frank O'Rourke was former chief executive of the Bank of Ireland while Patrick Dowling, who had put so much effort into the organ sub-committee, was appointed as a fully fledged associate.

The RTÉ representative was the composer, John Kinsella, who had become head of music following the retirement of Gerard Victory. Shay Hennessy, from the entertainment world, was also a board member of the Irish Music Rights Organisation (IMRO), while Malachy P. Smith came from the business world. During the course of the board's five-year tenure, its numbers were increased by the inclusion of Eileen Gleeson and Ellen Gunning, both of whom had considerable experience in the advertising and public relations fields; Thomas Kennedy came from the fashionable outfitters, Alias Tom. As Patrick Buckley wished to engage in other duties, he was replaced by the return of Richard Stokes who had also served with distinction on the first board and who had recently taken early retirement from the Department of the Taoiseach.

New Director, New Procedures

When the general manager, Frank Murphy, indicated a desire to relinquish his position as general manager and assume other activities, and the house manager, John Dunne, also decided to retire in 1993, the board felt that the hall's management needed a complete structural change. The ESB, noted for its long-standing and diverse support for the arts in general and music in particular, agreed to sponsor a report which was undertaken by its manager of personnel services, Rory O'Donnell. One of its recommendations was for the appointment of a director who would be a chief executive and upon whom the board could rely.

The board accepted this counsel, dispensed with the internal sub-committees and speedily advertised for a Director/Chief Executive. The result was the selection of Judith Woodworth who assumed the role of director in 1993. A product of both Alexandra and Trinity Colleges in Dublin, she studied piano with the eminent Rhona Marshall at the RIAM, thereby reinforcing once again the link between Westland Row and Earlsfort Terrace.

Dublin-born, Judith Woodworth studied history and political science at Trinity which was paralleled with an involvement in musical activity at the college. She studied classical singing, was a member of the Trinity Singers and became well-known on the folk scene in addition to recording a number of recitals for RTÉ. On moving to London, she was employed initially by the

Dermot Egan, Chairman, and Judith Woodworth, Director of the NCH, on the concert hall steps. (Frank Fennell Photography)

renowned artists' agency, Ibbs and Tillett, before transferring to Harrison Parrott, another agency which manages the careers of many eminent musicians.

Woodworth became artistic director of the 'Music in Great Irish Houses' festival in 1981 and, upon returning to Ireland in 1986, set up her own agency and commenced as a concert promoter. Two years later, she began organising a very successful celebrity concert series at the NCH, bringing such artists as Anne-Sophie Mutter, Radu Lupu and Andras Schiff.

One interesting cultural connection for the NCH, which took place shortly after Judith Woodworth's appointment, was an Irish/Polish lecture/recital in March 1994. Given by Terry de Valera and pianist Dearbhla Collins, this dealt with the life and music of John Field and their corresponding influence on Frederic Chopin. This led to an unusual event in December 1994 when the NCH itself was the recipient of a commemorative John Field medal. Presented by the Chopin Society of Warsaw during a Friends of the NCH gala concert, it celebrated Irish/Polish cultural relations. The soloist with the Irish Chamber Orchestra in Chopin's Second and John Field's First Concertos was Irish pianist, Miceál O'Rourke. Judith Woodworth was also invited to visit Warsaw and Krakow, where she met the composer Krysztstof Penderecki. He presented her with one of his signed manuscripts which now hangs in the director's office in Earlsfort Terrace.

The Fourth Board

The board selected in 1991 ended its term in March 1996 when the fourth and current board of the NCH began its tenure of office. It is led with distinction by Dermot Egan, who had a long association with the arts and during his time with Allied Irish Banks (AIB) he was the executive responsible for the development of the prestigious AIB art collection. He is a founder-member of Cothú, the Business Council for the Arts and was their first chairman. (The organisation has recently changed its name to Business2Arts.)

Apart from the continuity of Malachy P. Smith from the previous group, the other board members came fresh to Earlsfort Terrace. The provincial representatives include Audrey Corbett from Galway, Aiveen Kearney from Cork and Joan Parker from Limerick. The board also includes RTÉ's director of music, Niall Doyle. For the first time, the NSO has a representative through its principal flautist, William Dowdall. Ann Fuller's outstanding service as administrator to the Dublin International Piano Competition and An Táisce has merited her position, while Marie-Louise O'Donnell's involvement in third-level education gives her a defining role. The public relations world has Pat Heneghan, with Fergus Johnston representing the composers' standpoint.

Education is embodied through Joan Hickey, a teacher with a special interest in training school choirs; Irene Nolan who is engaged in educational publishing; and Peter McEvoy, formerly programme officer for Irish aid to Lesotho and one-time deputy chief executive of Higher Education for Development Co-operation. The financial connection is maintained through John McNally, Chief Executive Corporate Banking and Financial Markets in Ulster Bank.

New Horizons

The present board recognises the inadequacy of the John Field Room, and one of Dermot Egan's main objectives since becoming chairman is the establishment of a second recital hall. It had been hoped that UCD might have evacuated its Medical Library within the Earlsfort Terrace

Two Minister for Arts, Heritage, Gaeltacht and the Islands – Michael D. Higgins and Síle de Valera – have been successful in increasing the arts funding which has benefited the National Concert Hall. Minister de Valera seen with Poet Brendan Kennelly (right) and Henry Lorton, Chief Executive of TSB bank, sponsors along with ACC Bank, of the NCH Millennium Calendar.

precincts but as this has not proved possible, the old gymnasium or tennis court building has now become central to the idea. This slate-floored structure, separate from and to the right of the complex, is currently under the control of UCD's Engineering Department as a testing workshop. It was handed over to the government as part of a bequest from the Guinness family.

The NCH chairman approached the Minister for Arts and Culture, Michael D. Higgins, and indeed the minister sought and obtained EU funding of £1,750,000 for conversion purposes. The OPW's architects have already drawn up plans for the hall and, although it has a glass roof, they believe it possible to make the building acoustically acceptable. An Bord Pleanála also found in favour of the redesignation of the building and Dublin Corporation granted planning permission once certain criteria had been fulfilled. However, the Real Tennis Association has raised objections which have led to a judicial review of the situation. This has been set for sometime in the year 2000. Meanwhile, the National Concert Hall, having developed its artistic policy for a new hall, is still without an adequate second recital-performance space.

Since 1993, the Grant-in-Aid from the Department of Arts, Heritage, Gaeltacht and the Islands has risen considerably. This is in line with other wide-ranging developments in the arts throughout the country since the establishment of a specific government department in 1992. Through their positions at the cabinet table, the successive ministers, Michael D. Higgins and Síle de Valera, have delivered huge increases in arts funding. The NCH has benefited accordingly. Additional state support to the NCH comes through the OPW under chairman Barry Murphy, assisted by Michael O'Doherty, Angela Rolfe and Klaus Unger. A major refurbishing of the hall is scheduled for 2003.

Other objectives of the board include the significant expansion of the hall's corporate support programme. The Friends of the NCH scheme is also being broadened and now covers visits by members to musical events in Ireland and overseas.

Education and Community Outreach

A major objective of the board was to establish a policy for Education and Community Outreach activities. The theory propelling this strategy was the development of a project that would encourage people, regardless of age, background or location, to see the National Concert Hall as a musical resource, thereby enriching their experience and enjoyment of music.

The programme, established in 1997, concentrates on three main areas – events in the hall; in regions of both the inner city and greater Dublin; and around the country. It is targeted at primary, post-primary, third level and adults of all ages. Musicians from the National Symphony Orchestra, the RTÉ Concert Orchestra, the National Chamber Choir, as well as a number of freelance musicians and composers, act as workshop facilitators.

The wide-ranging operation includes workshops encompassing music composition; music and visual art; music and dance and music performance. Master-classes for third-level performance students are given by visiting artists appearing at the hall. To date, these have involved Barry Douglas, Steven Isserlis and Maxim Vengerov. Music appreciation classes for adults and 'open' rehearsals by visiting orchestras are further elements of this campaign.

As part of 'In Tune' music residencies' policy, under an ESB/NCH co-sponsorship agreement, teams of

Members of the National Symphony Orchestra of Ireland wait in the wings before their performance at the National Concert Hall.

musicians have visited many different parts of Ireland. They undertake creative music composition workshops in schools as far afield as the Inishowen Peninsula in Co. Donegal and Tralee in Co. Kerry. This scheme also affords training sessions for primary and post-primary teachers, linking these with return visits by children and teachers to the National Concert Hall.

During June each year, the NCH hosts its Open Day. This highly popular day-long event, which embraces as many as a thousand performers, show-cases many professional musicians, amateur ensembles and young artists. These perform within the precincts of the hall

itself and in the adjoining Iveagh Gardens, thus emulating the musical activities experienced there during the Great Exhibition of 1865.

RTÉ at the NCH

RTÉ's contribution to the success of the NCH through the residency of the National Symphony Orchestra cannot be over-stressed. Since opening in 1981, the National Symphony Orchestra has given the vast bulk of the hall's symphony concerts. These have involved an enormous range of music from its permanent, guest and visiting conductors, some of whom have emphasised individual composers through specific cycles of their music. For example, during his term of office, Bryden Thomson

Members of the Royal Irish Academy of Music's Wind Ensemble perform in the Iveagh Gardens. (Photo: Eugene Langan)

(1928-1991) highlighted the work of Jean Sibelius, Carl Nielsen and the symphonies of Anton Bruckner, to which he coupled piano concertos by Mozart. János Fürst featured the work of Gustav Mahler, while in more recent times, Alexander Anissimov turned to the output of Sergey Rakhmaninov. The three Rakhmaninov symphonies, as well as a number of his other orchestral works, were commercially recorded at the NCH by Anissimov and the NSO for the highly successful Naxos label. Albert Rosen, who had a thirty-year involvement with the orchestra, excelled in the music of his Czech homeland and in those gigantic scores of the late nineteenth and early twentieth centuries.

The Irish conductors – Robert Houlihan, Eimear Ó Broin (now retired), Proinnsías Ó Duinn and Colman Pearce – have delivered an extensive repertoire to NCH audiences since 1981 and their interest in contemporary Irish music has meant a continuous championing of the country's ever-growing population of composers.

As part of its own development, the RTÉ Symphony Orchestra was transformed into the National Symphony of Ireland from 1 January 1990. While it had been this in all but name, its official strength increased to ninety-three and the first concert in its new format was under the baton of then principal conductor, George Hurst. The NSO's first soloist, in Schumann's Piano Concerto, was Hugh Tinney, an artist of insight and integrity.

The opening of the NCH added an unusual stimulus to the life of the RTÉ Concert Orchestra. Up to 1981, most of its endeavours had been studio-bound in Montrose but, under its permanent conductor Proinnsías Ó Duinn, who celebrates his silver jubilee in that position in the year 2000, and with a number of visiting conductors, it now engages itself in a varied array of public concerts. These offer music from the classical repertoire as well a range of lighter material from past and present and have generated a particular audience which might not otherwise attend the National Concert Hall.

The fiftieth birthdays of both RTÉ orchestras were celebrated in 1998. The NSO's gala concert, under principal conductor Kasper de Roo, had Russian soloists, the young pianist Ilya Itin and soprano Galina Gorchakova, and while the Concert Orchestra had its gala away from the NCH – in the O'Reilly Hall on the Belfield campus – an anniversary programme in the hall in October was devoted to George Gershwin (1898-1937). Conducted by Wayne Marshall, Kim Criswell was soloist.

Although based in Cork, the internationally renowned RTÉ Vanburgh String Quartet, like its predecessor the RTÉ Academica String Quartet, also makes regular sorties to the NCH. The group celebrated its tenth anniversary in 1995 with the cycle of Beethoven Quartets, while more recent programmes have included a series of piano quintets with Irish and visiting artists.

Since its formation in 1986 from the old RTÉ Choral Society, the RTÉ Philharmonic Choir, initially trained by Colin Mawby but now under Mark Duley, makes as many annual NCH appearances as the programme schedule demands.

RTÉ's 'Musician of the Future' and 'Young Musician of the Future' competitions, initiated in 1976 by Jane Carty, now take place in the NCH with the preliminary rounds held in the John Field Room and the final round with the NSO in the main auditorium. Involving instrumentalists, singers and composers and under the overall direction of Jane Carty, these follow nationwide auditions and bring the best of the country's young artists to the NCH. Many of the competition winners, not least soprano Cara O'Sullivan, pianist Hugh Tinney, violinist Maighread McCrann and accordion player Dermot Dunne, have become established international artists.

RTÉ, with an eye on the large commercial district surrounding the NCH, initiated a series of summer lunchtime concerts in May 1984 with extremely favourable results. Their success led to the idea being taken up by other outside promoters and by the NCH itself, and lunchtime concerts are now a regular and very popular addition to programming at the NCH.

Opera and Musicals

While not designed with opera in mind, the NCH has staged some successful full-scale productions. In 1989, the Dublin Grand Opera Society ran into problems with the Gaiety Theatre management and their spring season almost foundered. However, all was not lost as their artistic director, Michael McCaffrey, saved one production – Bellini's *Norma* – which was mounted with imaginative skill on the NCH platform and choir balcony. The cast was led by Suzanne Murphy, making a welcome return to the DGOS. Make-shift though the production may have been, it saved the day for the beleaguered DGOS and was greatly enjoyed by the packed houses at its three April performances.

On 3 and 4 November 1994, Isolda Operatic Productions presented a semi-staged production of Bizet's *Carmen*. The brains behind Isolda was Bernadette Greevy who undertook the title role, with the Canadian tenor, Paul Frey, as Don José. The conductor was Franz Paul Decker with whom Greevy continues to work at home and abroad. The production team included former NCH personnel – Fred O'Donovan as technical consultant and Frank Murphy as operations manager.

More recently, the Dublin-based Lyric Opera has been using the NCH for its productions. These have included *Il Trovatore, Lucia di Lammermoor, La Bohème, Madama Butterfly, Nabucco* and *Aida*. Lyric Opera musicals, *The King and I* and *Fiddler on the Roof,* were particularly successful in January and August 2000. The visiting Chishinau National Opera of Moldova has been presenting its touring productions at the NCH over the past three years to great popular appeal. On a somewhat smaller scale, the music students of the Dublin Institute of Technology have managed minor miracles with their productions of Handel's *Alcina,* Mozart's *La Clemenza di Tito,* Menotti's *Amahl and the Night Visitors* and Ravel's *L'Enfant et les Sortilèges.*

The long-established Glasnevin Musical Society and the Rathmines and Rathgar Musical Society use the NCH for several of their annual shows. Tastefully and cleverly staged, these give the impression of a full theatrical production without incurring the extensive related costs. The continued popularity of operatic concerts, many of

which are promoted by Barra Ó Tuama, bring a broad spectrum of international and local artists to the NCH in the type of programme which would not have been out of place in the Exhibition Palace.

Choral Societies

The opening of the NCH was an answer to a prayer for Dublin's choral societies. Having to 'make do' with various churches and other venues requiring the erection of special platforms and stages, and often with difficult acoustics, probably meant nightmare preparations before their concerts. Our Lady's Choral Society has given many memorable performances in the hall, including Elgar's *The Dream of Gerontius* and Verdi's *Requiem*. The choir's annual pre-Christmas *Messiah*, which in 1981 had one performance, is now given four times due to public demand. The oratorio's 250th anniversary was remembered by the men of Our Lady's Choral Society and the boys of the Palestrina Choir on 13 April 1992. Using forces similar to Handel's original in Fishamble Street, Cara O'Sullivan, Lynda Lee and Deirdre Cooling-Nolan were the ghosts of Susannah Cibber, Christina Avoglio and Mrs Maclaine.

Celebrating the fiftieth anniversary of its own foundation in 1945, through the instigation of Dublin's then Archbishop John Charles McQuaid and the efforts of Vincent O'Brien, Our Lady's brought the unusual juxtaposition of Elgar's oratorios, *The Apostles* and *The Kingdom*, on 10 and 11 February 1995. Rarely, if ever, are the two works heard in such close proximity and these performances were all to the society's credit. Proinnsías Ó Duinn conducted, with soloists Lynda Lee, Bernadette Greevy, Paul Charles Clarke, Frank O'Brien, Michael Pearce and Ian Caddy.

Visitors to the National Concert Hall – An Ceoláras Náisiúnta. (Frank Fennell Photography)

Among the other choral bodies to appear regularly at the NCH are the Guinness Choir, who premiered Gerard Victory's epic *Ultima Rerum* on 2 March 1984. This work of genius must rank as the most expansive piece to date by an Irish composer. Conducted by Colman Pearce, the first performance soloists were Virginia Kerr, Bernadette Greevy, Adrian Thompson and Peter McBrien. Fr John O'Brien's St James Choir, Colin Block's Dublin County Choir, the Culwick Choral Society which celebrated its centenary with Verdi's *Four Sacred Pieces* on 20 February 1998, the Tallaght Choral Society, the Galway Baroque Singers and the Dun Laoghaire Choral Society also frequent the hall. Some smaller groups including the three Dublin Cathedral Choirs, the Goethe Institute Choir, Ethna Barror's Lindsay Singers and Ite O'Donovan's Lassus Scholars and Piccolo Lassus are also welcome performers.

Artistic Milestones of the Fourth Board

The high-profile visits of the New York Philharmonic and Chicago Symphony Orchestras took place in August and September 1996. Making their first Irish visits, the New Yorkers were conducted by Kurt Masur, and those from the Windy City by Daniel Barenboim. Good as the former were on 15 August in Bruckner's Fourth, they could not compare to the Chicago's magnificent Bruckner Eighth on 9 September, which also celebrated the NCH's fifteenth birthday. Both concerts were uncompromising in their couplings – Ned Rorem's Cor Anglais Concerto with the Philharmonic's principal Thomas Stacey in one and Schoenberg's *Five Pieces* in the other. Charles Rex, the Philharmonic's associate leader, also directed violin master-classes on the day before the concert. There was a live transmission of the concert to an outdoor audience in Meeting House Square in Temple Bar. Writing about the New York Philharmonic in *The Irish Times*, Michael Dervan remarked:

Masur and his players partnered the soloist with admirably balanced transparency and support... Masur's handling of the Bruckner symphony brought long stretches of remarkably quiet playing... the climaxes certainly carried sonic thrills... but which lacked some essential pulse of inner warmth. Good, you might say, but not great.

In his *Sunday Tribune* review of the Chicago Symphony, Ian Fox wrote:

A glowing performance, full of subtlety and power, will go down as one of the great nights at the hall... the range and colour of the orchestra were breathtaking, from the quietest pianissimi from the rich sounding strings to the blazing intensity of the huge brass section. Yet Barenboim... never allowed the shape or structure of the music to be lost... drawing ravishing playing from the orchestra throughout.

Early in the millennium, NCH audiences have enjoyed recitals by such renowned artists as Steven Isserlis, Maxim Vengerov, Evgeny Kissin and Vladimir Ashkenazy. The visits of both the Philharmonia Orchestra, magnificent under Leonard Slatkin and with Frederica von Stade as soloist, and the very fine WDR Symphony Orchestra of Cologne, conducted by Semyon Bychkov and with the Labèque Sisters, were outstanding. Vladimir Ashkenazy returned to the NCH as soloist and conductor of the European Union Youth Orchestra in August. As a special millennium event, the NCH presented a contemporary music series in April featuring the work of seven living Irish composers – John Buckley, Raymond Deane,

Donnacha Dennehy, Benjamin Dwyer, Deirdre Gribbin, Jane O'Leary and James Wilson. Entitled 'Composers' Choice', the series gave each the opportunity to show how their work had been built on the developments of the past. The programmes, which included chamber music by the seven, juxtaposed the works of others who had influenced their compositions.

In August, 'Beo 2000' reflected traditional Irish music in innovative styles. Hosted by the *sean nós* singer, Iarla Ó Lionaird, this exciting evolution included the individual artists Michael McGoldrick and Micheál Ó Súilleabháin, the duo of Martin Hayes and Dennis Cahill, and the groups Altan, Cran, Lia Luachra, Kila with Donal Lunny, and Coolfin.

New music for the millennium brought the premiere of two large-scale works. Philip Martin's cantata for soloists, chorus and orchestra, *Dublin 2000 – a Celebration*, had its first performance with Franzita Whelan, Colette McGahon, Ian Caddy and the RTÉ Concert Orchestra under Proinnsías Ó Duinn in March; Colman Pearce and the NSO introduced Raymond Deane's *Ripieno* on 14 April. The NCH also commissioned a new organ work from Ian Wilson, *History is Vanity*, and this was premiered by Peter Sweeney in June. Another millennium commission – from Dúchas, the Heritage Service – introduced Seóirse Bodley's *Earlsfort Suite*. Bernadette Greevy, with the RTÉ Concert Orchestra under Proinnsías Ó Duinn, gave the September premiere of its settings of three specially-written poems by Micheal O'Siadhail celebrating the National Concert Hall and its surroundings.

Dublin pianist Peter Tuite became RTÉ's 'Musician of the Future' with a young Russian, Alexander Nabioulin, taking first prize in the AXA Dublin International Piano Competition. Their return to the NCH platform is assured while the maturing brilliance of the young artists Finghin

Collins, piano, and Catherine Leonard, violin, makes each of their NCH appearances a special occasion.

This diversity of events in the current year continues and expands the ideals of the first board of 1981. The aspiration to have a universal appeal in both the distinction of the hall's performing artists and the quality of the programmes they offer has not been misplaced over the past two decades.

2000 and Beyond

The desirability of a proper second recital hall must be recognised as a basic essential in the field of performance of small ensembles, chamber music groups, certain solo instrumentalists and singers. In the main auditorium, these can lose much of their intimate appeal and, as audience numbers tend to be more modest in size for some of these events, communication with the performers becomes more remote in the larger venue. The artists themselves will welcome a smaller hall where rapport with their public can be more easily established and readily retained.

A smaller venue would also be an advantageous outlet for the endeavours of the ever-increasing band of young Irish musicians. Opportunities could be afforded for the advancement of their artistic skills in public performance before a discerning audience.

The demand for more experimental programmes, unsuited to the larger auditorium, could also be supplied by the installation of the necessary equipment, while the separate needs of facilitating its use as a venue suitable for some music theatre pieces could, in all possibility, be satisfied.

The NCH now hosts some 400 events each year, with upwards of 300,000 patrons. Those of us who indulge in its pleasures have every reason to be grateful, not only to all involved in its past and current operation but to others who, in 1974 and against much opposition, recognised the potential of the Great Hall of University College, Dublin and who had the wit and wisdom to persevere in their endeavours by giving the state its National Concert Hall.

But what of the future? The planned development of the small recital hall will be a decided asset. Separated from the main auditorium and allowing greater flexibility in rehearsal scheduling will be a boon to artists using it. No longer will they be restricted by schedules in the main hall. Having events in both auditoria on the same evening might even be feasible, while audiences will find a smaller hall an attractive ambience for music-making.

A relocation of those UCD departments still resident in Earlsfort Terrace would certainly assist the NCH in expanding its public and administrative facilities. More spacious restaurant areas would be an advantage, while improved and expanded back-stage space is very necessary. The possibility of reoccupying the entire area originally dedicated to the Exhibition Palace would greatly increase the NCH's potential in answering the growing demands of an eager public seeking diversity and variety in its enjoyment of music.

The ideals of Bartholomew Mosse, Joseph Robinson, Vincent O'Brien, Hamilton Harty, P.J. Little, Olive Smith, Raymond McGrath, Richie Ryan and others have, in many ways, been fulfilled, and in certain instances, surpassed by the blossoming of An Ceoláras Náisiúnta.

NCH Board of Management and Staff

Board of Directors
Dermot Egan
    (Chairman)
Audrey Corbett
William Dowdall
Niall Doyle
Ann Fuller
Pat Heneghan
Joan Hickey
Fergus Johnston
Aiveen Kearney
Peter McEvoy
John McNally
Irene Nolan
Marie-Louise O'Donnell
Joan Parker
Malachy P. Smith

Director
Judith Woodworth

Head of Finance
John T. Nolan

Marketing & PR Manager
Jacqueline Mahon

Contracts Manager
Anne FitzPatrick

IT Manager/PR & Marketing Executive
Michèle Aboud

Sponsorship & Friends Executive
Jenni Barrett

Operations Manager
Barry Walsh

Education & Outreach Manager
Lucy Champion

House Manager
Gavin O'Sullivan

Promoter Services Manager
Mary Lehane

Box Office Manager
Fiona Tully

Box Office Deputy Manager
Colette Grufferty

Box Office Supervisor
Nicola de Bruin

Deputy House Manager
Aidan Quinn

PA to Director
Jane Duggan

Stage Manager
Paul Hunt

Deputy Stage Manager
Kevin Shaw

Stage & Technical Staff
Denis Daly
Paul Kohlmann
Ian Dowdall
Francis Creedon
Jim Tate
Aidan Casserly
Aran Scully

Finance Clerks
Kathy Brogan
Jackie McPhilibin

Box Office Clerks
Niamh Carroll
Honor Hayes
Ruth Ellison
Deborah McHugh

Receptionists
Sheila Dunne
Maura Moore

Security Staff
Ray Doolan
George Hunt
Christie King

PAST STAFF MEMBERS

General Manager
Frank Murphy

Operations Manager
Karan Thompson

House Managers
John Dunne
Brian Raythorn

Marketing & PR Manager
Mari Kennedy

Friends Executive
Emma Conlon

PA to Director
Jacintha Harte

Box Office Deputy Manager
Siobhan Doolan

Box Office Clerks
Nan Walsh
Angela Fox

Finance Clerks
Teresa Clince
Lily Hannaway

Receptionist
Sharon Coade

Visiting Performers at the NCH

INTERNATIONAL CELEBRITIES AT THE NATIONAL CONCERT HALL

From the beginning, the various boards of management of the NCH as well as individual promoters have ensured a continuous flow of international celebrities to grace its platform. Although too many to mention individually, these have included: violinists Joshua Bell, Sarah Chang, Kyung-Wha Chung, Gil Shaham, Nigel Kennedy, Tasmin Little, Midori, Anne Sophie Mutter, Fionnuala Hunt, Isaac Stern and Maxim Vengerov; violists Yuri Bashmet and Tabea Zimmermann; cellists Mstislav Rostropovich, Paul Tortelier, Lynn Harrell, Matt Haimovitz, Steven Isserlis and Julian Lloyd Webber; flautist James Galway; and guitarists Timothy Kane and John Williams.

Among pianists were Dmitri Alexeev, Vladimir Ashkenazy, Alfred Brendel, Philippe Cassard, Barry Douglas, Evgeny Kissin, Zoltan Kocsis, Katia and Marielle Labeque, Radu Lupu, Philip Martin, Pavel Nersessian, John O'Conor, Miceal O'Rourke, Hugh Tinney, Vladimir Ovchinnikov, Mikhail Pletnev, Deszo Ranki, Andras Schiff, Grigory Sokolov, Ivo Pogorelich and Mitsuko Uchida.

Singers have included Victoria de los Angeles, Olaf Baer, Carlo Bergonzi, Grace Bumbry, Monserrat Caballe, Jose Carreras, Jose Cura, Nicolai Gedda, Thomas Hampson, Wolfgang Holzmair, Marilyn Horne, Dmitri Hvorstrovsky, Kiri te Kanawa, Sergei Leiferkus, Suzanne Murphy, Ann Murray, Herman Prey, Elizabeth Soderstrom, Frederica von Stade and Giuseppe di Stefano. Among ensembles have been the Fitzwilliam, Hagan, Panocha, Parisii, Skampa, Takacs and Vogler Quartets.

In a host of other artists have been Joan Baez, Tony Bennett, David Essex, Paddy Glacken, Herbie Handcock, Ute Lemper, Dolores Keane, Nana Mouskouri, Neil Sedaka, Wayne Marshall, Louis Stewart, Niall Tóibín, Dionne Warwick, The Chieftains, Aparis Jazz Trio, John Dankworth and Cleo Laine, Kenny Ball and his Jazzmen, Acker Bilk and his Paramount Jazz Band, McGill Big Band, the Michael Nyman Band and the André Previn Trio.

VISITING ORCHESTRAS

Among the visiting orchestras to the National Concert Hall are the following.

Ulster Orchestra
Bryden Thomson with Bernadette Greevy — 18 October 1981
Mstislav Rostropovich — 28 February 1988
En Shao with Mayumi Fujikawa — 29 November 1991

BBC Philharmonic
Gunter Herbig — 7 January 1983

Edward Downes with Michael Roll & Eugene Sarbu — 15 and 16 November 1984
Sergiu Commissiona with Rivka Golani — 9 and 10 May 1988
Peter Maxwell Davies & Jan Pascal Tortelier — 17 May 1999

Grimethorpe Colliery Band
Ray Farr — 11 January 1983

Royal Liverpool Philharmonic
Marek Janowski with Bernadette Greevy and Philip Fowke — 15 and 16 July 1983

German Bach Soloists
Helmut Winschermann — 4 and 5 November 1983

USSR State Symphony
Arvid Jansons with Valery Klimov — 14 November 1983

Helsinki Symphony
Paavo Berglund with Bernard d'Ascoli — 4 February 1984

BBC Symphony
Mark Elder with Peter Donohoe — 16 February 1985
Marek Janowski — 9 April 1988

Vienna Philharmonic
Lorin Maazel — 28 March 1985

Pittsburgh Symphony
Lorin Maazel — 17 August 1985

National Symphony of Washington
Mstislav Rostropovich — 28 September 1985

Franz Liszt Chamber Orchestra
Janos Rolla with Barry Douglas — 25 February 1986
Janos Rolla with Michael Collins — 2 July 1998

Dresden Philharmonic
Johannes Winkler — 38 April 1986

Toronto Symphony
Andrew Davis with Ivo Pogorelich — 30 August 1986

European Community Youth Orchestra
James Judd with Yehudi Menuhin — 19 April 1987
Vladimir Ashkenazy — 21 August 2000

Berlin Radio Symphony
Heinz Rogner — 27 April 1987

Leningrad Philharmonic
Mariss Yansons with Sergey Stadler — 14 October 1987

Warsaw Philharmonic

Kazimierz Kord with Piotr Paleczny — 2 December 1987

Polish National Radio Symphony

Antoni Wit with Konstanty Kulka — 24 October 1988

Moscow Radio Symphony

Vladimir Fedoseyev with Nikolai Demidenko — 13 November 1988

BBC Scottish Symphony

George Hurst with Christine Cairns — 26 November 1988

Stockholm Philharmonic

Paavo Berglund with James Galway & Marisa Robles — 20 February 1989

Royal Philharmonic

Charles Groves with John O'Conor — 8 May 1989

Vladimir Ashkenazy & Midori — 27 January 1992

Hallé Orchestra

Stanislaw Skrowaczewski — 6 September 1989

Gunther Herbig with Tabea Zimmermann — 29 November 1996

Budapest Philharmonic

Andras Ligeti with Vilmos Szabadi — 14 November 1989

New Jersey Symphony

Hugh Wolff with Karen Williams, Bernadette Greevy, John Garrison, Mark Doss & RTÉ Philharmonic Choir — 16 July 1990

Hugh Wolff with Christopher O'Riley — 15 July 1991

Moscow Bolshoy Theatre Orchestra

Alexander Lazarev with Alexander Rudin — 30 September 1990

Bucharest Philharmonic

Horia Andreescu with Hideko Udagawa — 8 May 1991

Czech Philharmonic

Libor Pesek with Miriam Fried & Garrick Ohlsson — 16 and 17 September 1991

Scottish Chamber Orchestra

Paul Daniel & Peter Maxwell Davies with Evelyn Glennie, Whistlebinkies, John O'Conor, William Conway & George MacIlwham — 18 and 19 September 1991

London Mozart Players

Howard Shelley — 18 November 1991

Howard Shelley — 21 February 1997

North German Radio Symphony (Hamburg)

Michel Tabachnik — 14 December 1991

Prague Symphony

Martin Turnovsky with Rudolf Firkusny — 21 January 1993

St Petersburg State Orchestra

Vladislav Chernouschenko with Vladimir Ovchinnikov — 3 November 1993

Moscow Soloists

Yuri Bashmet — 2 July 1994

Rotterdam Philharmonic

Claus Peter Flor with Lynn Harrell — 6 April 1995

Oslo Philharmonic

Paavo Berglund with Harvard Gimse — 1 December 1995

New York Philharmonic

Kurt Masur with Thomas Stacey — 15 August 1996

Chicago Symphony

Daniel Barenboim — 9 September 1996

European Union Chamber Orchestra

Luigi di Filippi with Emma Jane Murphy — 10 October 1996

Zurich Tonhalle

David Zinman with Radu Lupu — 10 April 1997

Dallas Symphony

Andrew Litton with Joshua Bell — 1 September 1997

Czech National Symphony

Paul Freeman with Jiri Barta — 25 November 1997

Stavanger Symphony

Vassily Sinaisky with Thuls Mork — 30 September 1998

Danish National Radio Symphony

Michael Shonwandt with Emmanuel Ax — 18 October 1998

London Chamber Orchestra

Christopher Warren Greene — 27 November 1998

San Francisco Symphony

Michael Tilson Thomas with Gil Shaham — 20 January 1999

Philharmonia Orchestra

Leonard Slatkin with Frederica von Stade — 20 March 2000

West German Radio Symphony (Cologne)

Semyon Bychkov with Katia & Marielle Labeque — 19 May 2000

Endnotes

CHAPTER 1 — THE SETTING

1. The Rev. C. J. McCready, *Dublin Street Names*, dated and explained. He offers this explanation as being the Rev. W.G. Carroll's work, *The Succession of the Clergy in the parishes of St Bridget, St Michael Le Pole and St Stephen*. Dublin, 1884, p. 7.

2. Calendar of Ancient Records of Dublin in the possession of the Municipal Corporation of the City (CARD). Vol. II, p. 116, Dublin 1891.

3. CARD Vol. IV, p. 256, Dublin 1894.

4. CARD Vol. IV, p. 271, Dublin 1894.

5. The Commissioners for the Advance of the City Revenue appointed by the Easter Assembly of 1663 (CARD IV, p. 256) reported that the seventeen acres should be sold. They consisted of the Mayor, the Sheriffs and the Treasurer, together with five aldermen and twelve members of the Commons.

6. CARD Vol. IV, p. 297, Dublin 1894.

7. Richard Lewis, The Dublin Guide or a description of the City of Dublin, Dublin 1787.

8. *Eighteenth-century Ireland. Inis an dá chultúr,* edited by Andrew Carpenter, Vol. II, pp. 187-95. Dublin 1987. A note on George II and St Stephen's Green, Edward McParland.

9. Born Mary Granville in Coulston, Wiltshire, she was forced into an arranged marriage with Alexander Pendarves, MP for Launceston, Cornwall, 1717. After her husband's death, she married Dr Patrick Delany, friend of Jonathan Swift. Dr Delany was Dean of Down and tutor at TCD. Mrs Delany was considered to be one of the most talented women of the eighteenth century, particularly in the applied arts.

10. The register of baptisms for the parish of Culworth, Northamptonshire, includes the name of a Hugh Leeson entered 1 November 1620. See letter from Rector of Culworth, Northamptonshire, to Francis Leeson dated 14 June 1662.

11. Hugh Leeson's name appears in the Hearth Tax return for the Liberty of Donore, Dublin, as being the owner of eight hearths, including the holder of Lot No. 5 South, St Stephen's Green, Dublin.

12. From Swift Maxim, c1728, Vol. 12, p. 135.

13. A wealthy man, Joseph Leeson, 1st Earl of Milltown (1711–1783) was able to commission a new country house in Wicklow, known today as Russborough, Blessington. Designed by German born architect-engineer, Richard Castle (or Cassels) (c.1690–1751) with possible assistance from Francis Bindon (see Georgian Society records Vol. V, 1913, p. 68), it was begun in 1741. For further information relating to the family and Russborough, see *The Milltowns, A Family Reunion*, National Gallery of Ireland (ed. F. Croke), S. Benedetti, Dublin 1997.

14. *Georgian Society Records*, 1910, Vol. 11, 88.15.

15. The lease between Joseph Leeson, 1st Earl of Milltown, and his son Joseph, 2nd Earl of Milltown, and Patrick Sweetman and his successors was renewed at intervals. Around 1798, P. & J. Sweetman, porter-brewers, moved to Francis Court, and the St Stephen's Green premises were offered for sale. For some time, the government used the site as a commissariat barracks and stores, then a horse bazaar and livery stables. Finally it became the site upon which Wesley Centenary College was built. Today, it is the approximate location of Stokes' Place.

16. Harcourt Street, Dublin, was named after Simon, 1st Earl of Harcourt, Lord Lieutenant, 1772–1776.

17. Dr Maurice Craig, *Dublin*, 1660–1860, p. 228. Dublin 1980.

18. Between 1908–1932, the large section of Clonmell House housed Sir Hugh Lane's Municipal Gallery of Modern Art.

19. Dr Maurice Craig, *Dublin*, 1660–1860, p. 226. Dublin 1980.

20. A.P. Behan, Up Harcourt Street from the Green, Dublin Historical Record, Vol. XLVII, p. 30, Spring 1994,

21. John Scott already had a country estate at Blackrock, Co., Dublin which he christened 'Neptune'.

22. The land was leased by Richard, Archbishop of Dublin, to John Scott for a period of forty years at an annual rent of £22/4/9d.

23. John Scott (1739–1798) was created Baron Earlsfort of Lisson, Co. Tipperary, in 1784, and five years later, Earl of Clonmell. He added an 'L' to his name, making it 'Clonmell', much to the city's mirth and giving rise to the joke — 'Give an inch, and he will take an ell (l)!'

24. Coburg city is situated on the Itz River in the foothills of the Thuringian Forest in N. Bavarian. Neighbourhood castles include Rosenau, the ducal country seat where Prince Albert of Saxe-Coburg-Gotha (1819–1861), Consort of Queen Victoria, was born.

25. Extracts from A. Peter's *Sketches of Old Dublin*, pp. 68–69, Dublin 1865.

26. See W.F. Wakeman, *Tourists' Guide through Dublin and its interesting suburbs*, pp. 6, 7. Dublin 1865.

27. The conveyance of part of the lands of St Sepulchre (the Coburgh Gardens) by the Archbishop of Dublin and the Ecclesiastical Commissioners for Ireland was handed over to Thomas Scott, 2nd Earl of Clonmell, on 4 August 1836. Thomas Scott purchased the fee simple of 9 acres, 3 perches, 25 roods for £1,298/19 /1d for ever at a yearly rent of £78/9/7d.

28. Nos. 62, 63 and 64 St Stephen's Green were small shops. See *Irish Georgian Society Records*, Vol. VI, p. 79.

29. In *The Dublin Directory*, 1840, Earlsfort Terrace first appears with the comment 'unbuilt'.

30. Until the 1870s, the road was to remain relatively underdeveloped in terms of housing.

31. Dr Robert Clayton was consecrated Bishop of Killala in May 1730 and became Bishop of Cork and Ross in 1735.

32. Elizabeth Thomson, *Memoirs of Viscountess Sundon, Mistress of the Robes to Queen Caroline, Consort of George II*, Vol. 11, p. 4. London 1847.

33. Nicholas Sheaff, *Iveagh House: An Historical Description*, Department of Foreign Affairs, p.13. Dublin 1978.

34. Lady Llanover, *The Autobiography and Correspondence of Mary Granville, Mrs Delany*. Vol. 11, p. 394. London 1861.

35. See Chapter 1, p. 18.

36. Due to Lord Clonmell's marriage settlement with Lady Clonmell, there were difficulties in relation to a lease in perpetuity. Clonmell agreed to indemnify Benjamin Lee Guinness against an inheritance charge of £10,000 and other charges on the estate. Clonmell's properties at Bishop's Court (valued at £30,000 in 1839), Oughterard, Co. Kildare and Castle Warden were used as security. See Iveagh Papers.

37. See Registry of Deeds, Dublin, 1862. bk. 13, no. 250.

38. Ada Peter, *Sketches of Old Dublin*, p. 71. Dublin 1865.

39. When the Dublin International Exhibition (1865) closed, Keit went to England. He worked as a gardener at Blyth Hall, Notts (1868) and was appointed propagator, (Royal) Botanic Gardens, Glasnevin, Dublin (1868–1872). He succeeded M. M'Ken as Curator of Durban Botanic Garden (1872–1882) and was appointed curator of Durban's parks and gardens in 1883. He cultivated his own plants from his nursery at Berea Road, Durban and sent South African plants to the (Royal) Botanic Gardens at Glasnevin, Dublin.

40. This device was first used by horticultural writer and editor, John Claudius Loudon, FLS (1738–1843) in his design for the Derby Arboretum (1839–1841). It was Loudon who first conceived a 'gardenesque' style of planting.

41. *The Dublin Builder*, 1 November 1863

42. Edwin Mallins and Patrick Bowe, *Irish Gardens & Demesnes* from 1830, p. 41. London 1980.

43. The archery ground measured 360 feet by 169 feet.

44. John McCullen 'A Victorian Masterpiece', *Irish Garden,* Vol. 4, No. 5, September/October 1995, pp. 28-31.

45. *The Dublin Builder*, 1 November,1863.

46. See Chapter 5.

47. National Archives, Letter dated 4 May 1937 from Dr D.J. Coffey, President UCD to Éamon de Valera, President of the Executive Council, Government Buildings, Dublin.

48. Christopher H. Bland was secretary to Edward Cecil, 1st Earl of Iveagh, until Lord Iveagh's death in 1927. He started life as an apprentice printer and began his employment with the Guinness family assisting Lady Iveagh in furnishing Elveden Hall In 1914, he took over the running of the Elveden estate. A close confidante who investigated, advised and took many decisions on behalf of Lord Iveagh, he became Managing Trustee of Lord Iveagh's will on the 1st Earl's death.

49. National Archives. File S 9885A (Department of the Taoiseach).

50. National Archives. Letter from Lord Rupert Iveagh, 11 St James's Square, London, to Éamon de Valera, dated 4 May 1939. File S 9885A (Department of the Taoiseach).

51. Between 1939 and the official opening of the Iveagh Gardens on 6 October 1941, permission for the use of the gardens was granted only to those institutions allowed by Lord Iveagh before the hand-over. These included the St John's Ambulance Brigade, the Dublin Boy Scouts Association and the Boys' Brigade.

52. National Archives. File S 9885A (Department of An Taoiseach). Letter dated 6 May 1939 from Éamon de Valera to the Right Hon. the Earl of Iveagh.

53. National Archives. File S 9885A (Department of An Taoiseach). Extract from Cabinet Minutes dated 17.5.1939. 'Offer by the Earl of Iveagh of No. 80, St Stephen's Green'. Ref: GC 2/70.

54. Other members of the sub-committee of the Academic Council, UCD, included Professor Eoin MacNeill, Professor J.M. O'Sullivan, Professor J.J. Nolan and Professor M. Tierney.

55. National Archives. File S 9885 (Department of the Taoiseach). Letter from Éamon de Valera to Lord Iveagh dated 23 August 1939.

56. National Archives. File S 9885A. Cabinet Minutes Ref: G.C.2/210 dated 15.10.'40. Item 1. Lord Iveagh's House & Grounds, St Stephen's Green, Dublin.

57. National Archives. File S. 9885 A. Letter to Mr. E. De Valera, An Taoiseach from the President of UCD, Dr A.W. Conway, UCD, dated 24 April 1941.

58. National Archives. File S. 9885 A. See Memo dated 30 Iul, 1941.

59. National Archives. File S 9885 A.

60. The silver key was used by the 2nd Earl of Iveagh and by his father. It was presented by Lord Iveagh to Éamon de Valera, Taoiseach, on 14 December 1939. See National Archives File S.9885 A. Memo dated 18.1.'40. Also see the *Irish Press*, Tuesday, 7 October 1941, 'New Gardens for UCD'.

61. Included among the distinguished gathering were representatives of the academic staff from TCD, Professor A.J. O'Connell and Professor C.H. Rowe.

62. National Archives. File S 138 09A, 2 - 5.

63. John McCulen is also superintendent of the Phoenix Park and Related Heritage Properties, all of which are in the care of the Office of Public Works.

64. The Iveagh Gardens were one of six Irish gardens to receive financial support under the EU's 1993 Preservation of European Architectural Heritage Scheme.

CHAPTER 3 — THE EXHIBITION ERA IN VICTORIAN IRELAND

1. The three Royal Manufactories were the Sèvres porcelain works, the Gobelins tapestry works and the Savonnerie carpet factory.

2. The Marquis d'Avèze arranged an exhibition of goods from the three former Royal Manufactories which was due to take place at the Château de St Cloud. However, on the night before the official opening, Bonaparte, fearing an uprising, ordered him to leave Paris and the exhibition was abandoned.

3. The Paris *Exposition Universelle* of 1855 was regarded as a demonstration of the aspirations of the Second Empire for peace and progress. Napoleon III's cousin, Prince Napoleon, acted as the Chief Administrator.

4. The first exhibition in England, modelled along French lines was 'The National Repository for the Exhibition of New and Improved Productions of the Artisans and Manufacturers of the United Kingdom'. It opened in 1828 on a site now occupied by the National Gallery, Trafalgar Square, London.

5. See Proceedings, RDS, dated 12 February 1829. The following *Notice of a Motion* by Isaac Weld, Esq., Honorary Secretary, one of the principal instigators of the Irish Exhibition Movement states: 'That a Committee be appointed to take into consideration, and to report the practicability of establishing, under the auspices of the Society, an Annual Exhibition of Specimens of the Manufactures and Productions of Ireland, conformable to the plan which has long been adopted in Paris and in other capital cities of the Continent; and to suggest such measures as might facilitate the arrangement, together with the estimates of the probable expenses attendant thereon.'

6. Exhibitions of Arts and Industries were held by the Society on 1835 and triennially from 1838 until 1850.

7. The exhibition of 1841 was more extensive than anything which had preceded it. Due to the effects of the Famine, the Committee of Manufactures were anxious to adjourn the 1847 exhibition but the manufacturers themselves met and insisted that it be held.

8. William Dargan (1799–1867) was born in Carlow and became the prototype of the Railway Kings who were making considerable fortunes in England and abroad. He worked in England with Thomas Telford and on his return, he built the first Irish steam railway from Dublin to Kingstown (Dun Laoghaire). Later, he constructed over 1,000 miles of railways in different parts of Ireland. In 1866, a fall from a horse was the signal for the collapse of his health and his fortunes.

9. The initiative for the Cork Exhibition of 1852, held in the Corn Exchange, came largely from a local businessman, Daniel Corbett. Sir John Benson (1812–1874), architect to Cork Corporation and Cork Harbour Commissioners, added a large gallery to the Exchange which was built of wood. The exhibition was opened on 10 June 1852 by the Viceroy, Lord Eglington, and closed on 11 September. It attracted 138,375 visitors. However, the receipts only amounted to £8,733. Exhibits were arranged in 21 sections and included scientific instruments, poor Law Unions, machinery, and a new innovation in the exhibition arena, a Fine Arts section.

10. *Illustrated London News*, May 1853.

11. 'The Great Exhibition of the Works of Industry of all Nations' was held at the Crystal Palace, London, in 1851 on a 26-acre site. Total attendance: 6,039,195; profit £186,437. Its functions were to celebrate the industrial achievements of Great Britain and the Empire, to raise standards and to promote the sale of existing products. Entries from Ireland included Limerick lace, Belfast linen and Dublin poplin.

12. The site for the Great Industrial Exhibition of 1853 included the area of the forecourt of Leinster Lawn. The front looked out onto Merrion Street and stretched back as far as Kildare Street. Today, part of this area includes the

National Gallery of Ireland and the Natural History Museum.

13. A year later, the London International Exhibition proved to be a demonstration of Victorian design and achievement. It included a Fine Art section. It was built on the site now occupied today by the British Museum (Natural History), Cromwell Road. Advances in the use of steam power, particularly in agriculture, had increased enormously since the Crystal Palace exhibition of 1851. The communications field was well advanced with the use of the electric telegraph, marine cables and the development of printing techniques forging ahead.

14. *The Art Journal*, 1864, p. 211.

15. As a guarantee of his credentials for the post of Company Secretary, Henry Madden Parkinson supplied the Dublin Exhibition Palace and Winter Garden Company with his property, Lota, Coliemore Road, Dalkey, Co. Dublin.

16. Henry Parkinson and Peter Lund Simmonds, *The Illustrated Record and Descriptive Catalogue of the Dublin International Exhibition* of 1865, p.19. London, 1866.

17. Ibid., p. 17.

18. See Chapter 1, 'The Coburg Gardens'.

19. Benjamin Lee Guinness retained 7 acres, 3 roods and 35 perches (Coburgh Gardens).

20. The Draft Assignment of Agreement and covenants drawn up between Benjamin Lee Guinness and the Dublin Exhibition Palace and Winter Garden Company Limited, dated 5 April 1862 for 999 years with an annual rent of £302, was to begin on 1 May 1862 and was to be extensively revised. There were strict conditions for laying out the gardens and pleasure grounds and their maintenance. The agreement specified that certain areas were to be free of buildings in order to safeguard the view from Benjamin Lee Guinness' Iveagh House. A lane was to be made by the company at the rear of St Stephen's Green from Iveagh House to Earlsfort Terrace. Guinness was to make and maintain an entrance gate from his property to the pleasure grounds. He, together with his family, servants and horses, would have uncontrolled access to the lane and entry to the grounds at all times.

21. On 1 February 1863, the Hon. Sophia Hely-Hutchison and her son, John, agreed to let this piece of land to the Dublin Exhibition Palace and Winter Garden Company (Limited) for 250 years at an annual rent of £243.

22. The first premium (prize) amounted to £150 with £75 for the runner-up.

23. *Dublin Builder*, 1 October 1862. Vol. IV, No. 67, pp. 247–251. Apart from A.G. Jones, there were three finalists in the competition. The other two were E.H. Carson (Dublin) and Rawson Carroll (Dublin).

24. An article in the *Dublin Builder*, 1 December 1862, Vol. IV, No. 71, p. 300, mentioned that Alfred Gresham Jones' design was valued at £40,000. This amount, although £5,000 above the specified figure, was guaranteed by Jones as having been procured from an eminent contracting firm in the city.

25. Alfred Gresham Jones Collection, National Library of Ireland, Prints and Drawings' Collection, Cat. No: 2006 (TX).

26. The exhibition entry reads as follows: A.G. Jones 16 Dawson St, Dublin; 10 Grafton Place, Kentishtown, London. 336: Early English Church, West Elevation and Plan. 337. Early English Church, North Elevation. 339. Early English Church, Sections. See Ann M. Stewart, *Royal Hibernian Academy of Arts, Index of Exhibitors 1826-1979*, Vol. 1. Dublin 1986.

27. *Thom's Directory*, 1858. Alfred Gresham Jones is listed as being a partner with Hugh Carmichael in Molesworth Street, Dublin. The listing remains the same until 1863 when Jones appears to go out on his own, aged 41. This is consistent with his winning the International Exhibition Buildings competition in that same year.

28. Merrion Hall (now the Davenport Hotel) was modelled on the Metropolitan Tabernacle, Stoke Newington. Other projects included the Wesleyan Methodist Chapel, Quinsborough Road, Bray, Co. Wicklow (1864); St Paul's, Silchester Road, Glenageary, Co. Dublin (1865); St Kevin's, South Circular Road, Dublin (1889); No. 53 Ailesbury Road, Dublin.

29. Joseph Paxton's famed Crystal Palace was built of iron, glass and wood: 'there are no large pieces of either material employed. The heaviest pieces of cast iron are the girders, which are 24 ft. in length, and none of which weigh more than a ton; the wrought iron consists chiefly of round and flat bars, angle irons, bolts, screws and rivets... Wood is used in the main gutters and Paxton gutters, the arched ribs of the Transept, the sash-bars and ridges, the ground-floor and gallery floors, the lead flats and the external wall, and in some of the girders or trusses. The glass is sheet or cylinder glass, in panes...'. To produce the 34 miles of patent Paxton guttering, 200 miles of sash-bars, together with 3,300 hollow iron columns, specially designed and built machine tools were produced. 300,000 panes of glass were fitted to the structure by glaziers operating from glazing wagons erected high up in the open structure.

30. See Felstead, Franklin J. and Pinfield, L., *Directory of British Architects 1834–1900*. London 1993.

31. From the cover page inscription contained in Alfred Gresham Jones' folio of original drawings in the National Library of Ireland's Prints & Drawings Collection (Cat No: 2006 (TX). (see Note no. 25), it would suggest that he brought this collection to his new home in Australia. In *The Building News*, November 1915, the following extract from an obituary was included: 'In the Dublin Daily papers last week appeared the following notice: "Jones, September 9, 1915, at his residence, 'The Gables', 285 Barkly Street, St Kilda, Melbourne, Alfred Gresham Jones, Architect, late of Dublin and aged 93 years" It recalls the personality, and passing at this advanced age, of a once very well-known Dublin architect, MR Alfred Gresham Jones.'

32. Rowland Mason Ordish was born in Melbourne, Derbyshire (1824) and began his working life in an engineer's office. His designs for an iron bridge spanning the River Thames, Windsor won the approval of Queen Victoria. Ordish was the inventor of the rigid system of suspension, first applying his principles to two bridges over the *River Moldau*, Prague and later to the Albert Bridge, River Thames. He devised and constructed a system of bracing for the dome (Exhibition building, 1862), London which would ensure its stability and safety. He died in London in 1886.

33. See contract drawn up between James Patrick Beardwood & Company and the Dublin Exhibition Palace and Winter Garden Company (Limited). The Iveagh Papers.

34. See Chapter 1.

35. *Dublin Builder*, 15 June 1863.

36. The wrought iron and glass Winter Garden structure employed the same technology as that used for the Crystal Palace exhibition. London 1851. (See Note 29.)

37. For a full technical description of the building, see Alfred Gresham Jones' detailed and comprehensive essay on his architectural design as outlined in the *Illustrated Record and Descriptive Catalogue of the Dublin International Exhibition of 1865*, Parkinson and Simmonds, 1866, Appendix 1, and the *London Builder*, 22 April 1865.

38. *The Dublin Builder*, 20 May 1865.

39. There was also a London committee which included the Victorian educationist, Sir Henry Cole, J.H. Foley, S.C. Hall, S. Redgrave, M. Digby-Wyatt, Owen Jones and the Secretary of the 1853 Dublin Exhibition, Sir C.P. Roney.

40. See letter no: 4044 (RDS.). C.E. Bagot to W.E. Steele dated 9 February 1865.

41. For a more detailed description of the Great Dublin International Exhibition, 1865, see *Dublin Historical Record*, Vol. XLV11, No. 2. Autumn, 1994, *The Dublin International Exhibition, 1865,* Nellie O'Cleirigh, pp. 169-182. (Read to the Old Dublin Society, 16 March 1994.)

42. Parkinson and Simmonds, *The Illustrated Record and Descriptive Catalogue of the Dublin International Exhibition,* p. 92. 1866.

43. *The Freeman's Journal,* 9 May 1865.

44. *Illustrated London News,* 18 March 1865, pp. 252, 256; 13 May 1865, pp. 444, 448 and 452.

45. *Dublin Builder,* No. 126, 15 March 1865.

46. *Dublin Builder,* No. 131, 1 June 1865.

47. *Practical Mechanics Journal,* September 1865, as quoted in the *Dublin Builder,* No. 140, 15 October 1865.

48. *The Freeman's Journal,* 10 May 1865.

49. The number of works of art exhibited in the Dublin International Exhibition, 1853, numbered 1,493 compared with 2,072 in the 1865 Dublin International Exhibition.

50. John Allwood, *The Great Exhibitions,* p. 180. London 1977.

51. Parkinson and Simmonds, *The Illustrated Record and Descriptive Catalogue of the Dublin International Exhibition of 1865,* p. 550. 1866.

CHAPTER 4 — AN ERA COMES TO AN END

1. *The Freeman's Journal,* 7 March, 1868.

2. The total contract was for £70,481/6/7d. By 1865, The Dublin Exhibition Palace and Winter Garden Company (Limited) had paid James Beardwood, builder, £57,292. Beardwood died in October 1865 without having being paid in full. In November 1866, his company brought an action in the Court of Exchequer against the Dublin Exhibition Palace and Winter Garden Company (Limited) for payment of £13,189/1/10d. Beardwood's company owed a supplier, John Martin, timber merchant, £4,584 for materials. The case was referred for arbitration to Frederick Darley, architect to the Dublin Exhibition Palace and Winter Garden Company (Limited), and to Benjamin Lee Guinness. John Martin was awarded his full claims. See Iveagh Papers.

3. See MS NLI 11,200 (2).

4. Ibid.

5. See letter dated 12 October 1867 (copy) from Sir Richard Griffith, Commissioner of Valuation, G. Valuation of Ireland, 6 Ely Place, Dublin to Richard Southwell Bourke, sixth Earl of Mayo, Chief Secretary to the Lord Lieutenant of Ireland. MS NLI 11,200 (2).

6. W.H. Kerr, 3 Walpole Terrace, Clontarf, Dublin.

7. See MS NLI 11,200 (2).

8. See MS 11,200 (3).

9. Professor John Turpin, *A School of Art in Dublin since the Eighteenth Century: A History of the National College of Art and Design.* Quoted from caption illustration no: 34 (between pages 170 and 171). Also see Chapter 9, 'The School's Struggle with Henry Cole's System' and Chapter 10, 'The South Kensington System in Dublin'.

10. See MS NLI 211,200

11. Ibid.

12. Ibid.

13. MS NLI 7,592.

14. *The Freeman's Journal,* 7 March 1868.

15. T.D. Sullivan, A Guide to Dublin and its History, Antiquities and Objects of Public Interest. Dublin [1888]. Quote from the author.

16. *Irish Builder,* 15 April 1868.

17. Edward Hudson, 28 Gardiner Place, Dublin, was officially ordered to proceed to sell all leasehold and other property of the Dublin Exhibition Palace and Winter Garden Company (Limited) on 11 June 1869. His costs for liquidation amounted to £236/17/0d. See Iveagh Papers.

18. The site was described as comprising 14 statute acres between Earlsfort Terrace and Harcourt Street, Dublin. The buildings: 'a magnificent glass transept, Leinster Hall, 2 grand concert rooms (to hold 3,000 and 1,000 persons), fine picture galleries, exhibition rooms, large dining rooms, extensive culinary departments etc.'.

19. By 21 May 1870, debts and liabilities were estimated to be £51,000. See Iveagh Papers.

20. By an order dated 29 May 29 1870, Sir Arthur Guinness, Lord Ardilaun, together with his brother, Edward Cecil, were deemed to be the purchasers of the entire leasehold and other property. They had paid all of the company's outstanding debts and had complied with all financial obligations. See Iveagh Papers.

21. Between 15 April and 24 May 1878, arrangements were made between James Newsome and Sir Arthur Guinness and Edward Cecil Guinness for the hire of Leinster Hall for ten weeks beginning May 27 at £50 per week. See Iveagh Papers.

22. *Art Journal,* 1 July 1872.

23. Patricia Butler, *The Brocas Collection. An illustrated selective catalogue of original watercolours, prints and drawings in the National Library of Ireland with an account of the Brocas family and their contribution to the (Royal) Dublin Society's School of Landscape and Ornament Drawing.* Dublin 1997.

24. The Marezzo Company had its own special cement and a patent for colouring and enamelling this cement. Emden selected a painter for the fountains who would achieve the effect of majolica china. The central fountain had four gas chandeliers upheld by Negress figures and lit around the rims with coloured lights.

25. Jean Nodal, a French stoneworker, was contracted to work on the fountains. He proved troublesome and devious and was dismissed by Sir Arthur Guinness for 'having failed to carry out his work as directed'. He later sued Sir Arthur Guinness. See Iveagh Papers.

26. *Irish Builder,* 15 March 1872.

27. The account for designs and alternative designs for the fountains were executed at a cost of £103/2/0d. This was considered by the Guinness family to be expensive and they were reluctant to pay. This was just one example of the acrimonious exchanges about non-payment of accounts which took place between employers and architect and which resulted in a number of legal actions being brought by Walter Emden against the Guinness family between 1873 and 1874 for non-payment of outstanding accounts for work and materials supplied to the Earlsfort Terrace site. See Iveagh Papers.

28. John Orrell Lever (1824–1897), son of James Lever, a Manchester merchant, was the owner of corn mills at Westport, Co. Mayo. He started a line of steamers from Westport to Liverpool and began running steamers from Galway to America in 1858 which came to be known as the Lever Line. He was elected MP for Galway on 11 February 1859 and was author of *Austria, her position and prospects* (1861).

29. Articles of Agreement between Edward Cecil Guinness and John Orrel Lever, No. 97 St George's Square, Pimlico, London, for sale of the glass Exhibition Buildings, Earlsfort Terrace, Dublin, dated 23 May 1882. See Iveagh Papers.

30. Estimates were received from a Mr Lister of Glasgow and a Mr Donald of Paisley. See Iveagh Papers, 25 March 1880. The estimate for dismantling amounted to £2,000; carriage to steamers, £400; freight to London, £3,000. The cost of erecting the building on its new site in Battersea Park was estimated at £15,000 or less. See Iveagh Papers.

31. The Albert Palace of Science and Art was re-erected in six months on a piece of land between Prince of Wales Drive (then Road) and Lurline Gardens (then part of Warriner Gardens), Battersea. The builders were Braby and Co., working under the direction of the engineers, Bell, Miller & Bell. The Palace, reconstructed from the Winter Garden structure, Earlsfort Terrace, was considerably larger than the original Dublin building and included an Exhibition Palace, Concert Hall (the Connaught Hall), Conservatory, Aviary

and Hippodrome. Distinguished designer and decorative artist, Christopher Resser (1834–1904) was responsible for the decoration of the interior. The gardens were designed by Sir Edward Lee, manager of the Dublin Exhibition, 1872. The building was demolished in 1894.

32. 23 May 1882. Articles of Agreement between Edward Cecil Guinness and John Orrel Lever. See Iveagh Papers.

33. There was provision for renting rooms when required and if available on a daily basis, the cost to vary according to size. The rooms would be serviced. See Iveagh Papers.

34. November 1882. The Board of Works disputed certain points in the draft prepared by Counsel; e.g. they objected to a 12 ft limit on height of walls and were not interested in buying the organ. However, by 16 November 1882, the possibility of purchasing the organ was again under review. They agreed to purchase. See Iveagh Papers.

35. See hand-written note from Edward Cecil Guinness to Commissioners of Board of Public Works dated 24 March 1883. Iveagh Papers.

CHAPTER 5 — THE UNIVERSITY ERA AT EARLSFORT TERRACE

1. The number of students admitted to the Catholic University medical School (Cecilia Street Medical School) up to 1908 was in some years greater than that of the Catholic University of Ireland itself during the same period.

2. National Archives file no: 35752/81.

3. Prior to 1864, projects were approved or designed by the board's architect, James H. Owen (d.1891). It appears that these were transferred to his brother, E.T. Owen, when James H. Owen was promoted to assistant architect in 1864. From then on, his work appears to have been largely administrative. James H. Owen was employed in the late 1850s in designing an extensive coast guard buildings programme around Ireland's coastline. The earliest were constructed in the Dublin area from his designs. He was president of the RIAI 1870–1874 and was also a member of the RHA.

4. National Archives file. Ref: OPW 35752/81.

5. National Archives file. Ref: OPW 35752/81.

6. Edward Kavanagh (1845–1901) was probably the son of a Dublin tradesman and elder brother of landscape artist, Joseph Malachy Kavanagh, RHA (1856–1918). He received his architectural training in the office of John McCurdy (c.1823–1885) and entered the Board of Works as principal draughtsman on 12 July 1881, a position he retained until his death in 1901.

7. A request for separate pricing of this item had already been built into the original tender in case just such a problem might arise.

8. Dr George Moyers was elected Lord Mayor of Dublin in December 1880 and was the first member of the building trade to fill the Civic Chair. Described as a 'thoroughly practical business man and a good employer... who possessed the ability and energy to try to redress the many pressing needs of our working classes', he was a highly respected builder. *Irish Builder*, 1 January 1881.

9. See Specification for Additional Buildings & Royal University Ireland, Dublin, 1884.

10. Nicola Gordon Bowe and Elizabeth Skeoch Cummin, *The Arts & Crafts Movements in Dublin & Edinburgh*, 1885–1925, p. 80. Dublin 1998.

11. Ibid., p. 80. Bookbinders, Sydney Cockerell and T.J. Cobden-Sanderson were contributors.

12. The Arts and Crafts Society of Ireland was responsible for the insurance of the building for the duration of the exhibition, the value of insurance being £14,000. When this was subdivided, it amounted to £13,050 for the building, £800 for the organ, and £150 for furniture.

13. *The Arts & Crafts Movements in Dublin & Edinburgh*, pp. 116, 184.

14. *A Handbook to the Dublin District by the British Association*, p. 346. London 1908.

15. Augustine Birrell (1850–1933), London barrister, wit and liberal politician, became Ireland's longest serving Chief Secretary (1907–1916). His achievements were the Irish Universities Act, 1908, and the Land Act which revised Wyndham's 1903 act in the tenant's favour. His education bill (English) (1906), the Irish Council bill (1914) and the Home Rule Act (1914) all suffered rejection.

16. From an internal UCD report on the state of the college c.1946. An uncatalogued M/S in 'Special Collections', UCD Library, Belfield, Dublin.

17. Edward Cecil Guinness, Earl of Iveagh (1847–1927), was the main force behind the expansion which changed the eponymous brewery from being a small Dublin-based operation when he joined the firm in 1868 to the largest brewery in the world by 1886. During that period, with the help of professional managers, he invested more than £1m in new facilities, all drawn from the brewery's retained profits, and exploited an explosion of growth in the English market. Created an earl in 1919, he devoted his final years to charity, including spending £250,000 on the removal of many of Dublin's slums.

18. The Hatch Street frontage area measured approximately 87 feet by 116 feet.

19. A section of Edward Cecil Guinness' riding school situated on the St Stephen's Green side of the Iveagh Gardens measured approximately 27 feet by 39 feet.

20. Governing Body minutes, 12 June 1911.

21. The inscription on the marble plaque, first floor, UCD, Earlsfort Terrace reads: 'A portion of the ground whereon this college stands was the gift A.D. MDCCCCX1 of Edward Cecil First Earl of Iveagh KP, FRS, LL.D, MA. In accordance with the wish of the donor the gift here commemorated is associated with the name of his old and valued friends — the late Right Revd. Monsignor Gerald Molloy LL.D. Rector of the Catholic University of Ireland and the late Revd. James Healy, Parish Priest of Little Bray.'

22. See Iveagh Papers.

23. Rudolf Maximillian Butler was born in 1872, the only son of John Butler, Barrister-at-law. Educated in private schools in both Dublin and Germany, his architectural career began when he was articled to his future partner, Walter Doolin. Of his many churches, perhaps one of the most appreciated is that at Newport, Co. Mayo, executed in local red sandstone. Churches overseas include St Joseph's, Highgate, London; St Mary's, Glasgow; and the English Roman Catholic church, Avenue Hoche, Paris.

24. R.M. Butler, *The Irish Builder and Engineer*, 17 December 1921. *The Custom House, Dublin, and its Architect* – 1. pp. 798–802.

25. 'Topical Touches', a column which appeared in the *Irish Builder and Engineer*. Butler was appointed editor in that year, a position which he was to hold for the next thirty-five years.

26. From a paper entitled: 'A New Style', R.M. Butler. Butler was president of the AAI between 1907–1908 and his inaugural address to that body appeared later in The Irish Builder.

27. 'A Native Style of Architecture', R.M. Butler, 1925.

28. George James Crampton (1851–1925), builder and contractor, founded the firm in 1879. In 1926, T.A. Crampton was appointed Chairman and Managing Director, a post he held until 1949 when G.H.C. Crampton became chairman (1949–1974). J.S. East was Chairman, 1974–1985. From 1891 to Easter 1965, Cramptons occupied a site at Pembroke Road, Dublin, moving to Shelbourne Road in 1965 and remaining there until 1996 when they moved to Simmonscourt Road, Ballsbridge, Dublin.

29. Richard Turner (c.1798–1881) Ironmaster, Hammersmith Iron Works, Ballsbridge, Dublin was responsible for building some of the earliest glasshouses in Ireland, most notably the Curvilinear Range, Glasnevin and Belfast Botanic Garden (the Palm House). He collaborated with Decimus Burton in erecting the Palm House, Kew, and conservatory in Regent's Park.

30. G.J. Crampton, Builder & Contractor, 1879, G.&T. Crampton, 1907, G.&T. Crampton Ltd., 1923 & G.&T. Crampton Holding Ltd., 1966.

31. Morris & Kavanagh, Quantity Surveyors, 68 Harcourt Street, Dublin.

32. See Bill No. 1. p. 2. Bill of Quantities for Proposed New Buildings, UCD, Section 1 dated 23 April 1914. Messrs Doolin & Butler, Architects, Mansion House Chambers, 27 Dawson Street, Dublin. Measured from the drawings and specification by Morris & Kavanagh, Quantity Surveyors, 68 Harcourt Street, Dublin. Archives, G. & T. Crampton Holdings Ltd.

33. The Aughamadock limestone quarries are situated about a mile from the village of Stradbally, County Laois. They are not in use today.

34. See Agreement dated 31 January 1918 between George J. Crampton and Thomas A. Crampton and UCD Collection: Archives, G.&T. Crampton Holding Ltd.

35. Governing Body minutes, UCD, 17 May 1921.

36. Flann O'Brien, *At Swim-Two-Birds*, pp. 33–34. London, New York 1939. London 1967.

37. Presidents of University College, Dublin: Dr Denis J. Coffey, 1908–40, Dr Arthur W. Conway, 1940–47, Dr Michael Tierney, 1947–64, Dr Jeremiah J. Hogan, 1964—72, Dr Thomas Murphy, 1972–85, Dr Patrick Masterson, 1986–1993, Dr Art Cosgrove, 1994.

38. *National Student* Vol. 4 no. 2 (Dec. 1913), 27.

39. *National Student*. Vol. 4. no.2 (Dec. 1913), 34–35

40. Report of the President 1915/16, 4.

41. *Some memories of Thomas MacDonagh* by 'D.R.' (Desmond Ryan). *National Student*. December 1917.

42. *National Student*. Vol. 8, no. 3. (December 1918), 5–8.

43. F.X. Martin (ed.) *The Easter Rising*, 1916 and *University College, Dublin*. p. 112. Dublin 1966.

44. Report of the President, 1920/21, 30.

45. The Council Chamber at Earlsfort Terrace consisted (and still does today) of a series of three rooms with removable partitions.

46. The vote for the acceptance of the Treaty was 64:57.

47. Governing body minutes, 20 December 1921.

48. On 20 September 1920, Kevin Barry was involved in an ambush of a British Army lorry outside Monks' bakery, Church Street. Three British soldiers were shot and killed. Barry was subsequently charged with murdering one of the soldiers, Private Matthew Whitehead, and sentenced to death. He was hanged on 1 November 1920 in Mountjoy Prison. His execution took place on the Feast of All Saints which only served to enhance the perception of him both as hero and martyr.

49. The Kevin Barry memorial window, 1933. 183 x 86 cm. By 1921, subscriptions for this memorial stained glass window amounted to £100 which had been raised by UCD students. A further £400 was donated by the college in 1923–1924.

50. Illustrations by Richard J. King include *Capuchin Annual*, 1940-69, & 1972–75. *Father Mathew Record*, throughout the 1940s. Also see exhibition catalogue, *Richard King Exhibition*, 1952, Boston College Library. Church commissions included St Mary's Church, Swinford, Co. Mayo, Capuchin Friary, Church Street, Dublin, Our Lady for the Marian Centre at the Church of Our Lady of the Scapular, Manhattan, New York, St Thomas More Jesuit Chapel, University of West Australia, and his last commission for Ireland — *I am the Resurrection and the Life*, 1973 — for St Patrick's Church, Newport, Co. Mayo.

51. The eight panels of the Kevin Barry memorial window read as follows: Cuchulainn and Queen Medb; The Battle of Clontarf; Red Hugh O'Donnell; Patrick Sarsfield; Lord Edward Fitzgerald and Wolfe Tone; Robert Emmet and The 1798 Rebellion; The Easter Rising, 1916.

52. The window bears Richard King's own name shown in the bottom right-hand panel, a rare occurrence for this artist.

53. Report of the President, 1920/21, 30.

54. From uncatalogued material in 'Special Collections', UCD Library, Belfield, Dublin.

55. The Buildings' Committee Minute Book, UCD Archives, Belfield, Dublin.

56. Buildings' Department Archives, UCD, Belfield, Dublin.

57. *Dublin Opinion*, August, 1959.

58. The Department of Agriculture and Food Engineering (UCD), together with the Department of Civil Engineering (UCD), are sited at Earlsfort Terrace, Dublin.

Bibliography

Acton, Charles and Pine, Richard (eds.), *To Talent Alone — The Royal Irish Academy of Music*, Dublin: 1998.

Allwood, John, *The Great Exhibitions*, London: 1977.

Beckett, J.C., *The Making of Modern Ireland, 1603–1923,* London: 1966.

Benedetti, Sergio, *The Milltowns, a family reunion,* [ed. F. Croke], NGI, Dublin: 1997.

Berry, Henry Fitzpatrick, *A History of the Royal Dublin Society,* London, New York: 1915.

Boydell, Brian, *Dublin Music Calendar, 1700–1760,* Dublin: 1988.

Boydell, Brian (ed.), *Four Centuries of Music in Ireland,* BBC, London: 1979, 23.

Boydell, Brian, *Rotunda Music in Eighteenth Century Dublin,* Dublin: 1992.

Boylan, Henry, *A Dictionary of Irish Biography,* Dublin: 1988.

Butler, Patricia, *The Brocas Collection. An Illustrated selective catalogue of original watercolours, prints and drawings in the National Library of Ireland with an account of the Brocas family and their contribution to the (Royal) Dublin Society's School of Landscape and Ornament Drawing,* Dublin: 1997.

Butler, R.M., 'The Custom House, Dublin, and its architect'. 1 & 11 in *Irish Builder.* 1xiii, nos. 27, 28 (28 June, 17, 31 December 1921) pp. 798–802, 833–7.

Catalogue of the Arts and Crafts Society of Ireland (1895).

Catalogue of the Catholic University of Ireland Centenary Celebrations, Newman House, 19–24 July 1954.

Catalogue of the Dublin Exhibition of Arts, Industries and Manufactures, Dublin: 1872.

Catalogue of Dublin International Exhibition of 1865 (Comic Collection), Dublin: 1865.

Colvin, Howard, *A Biographical Dictionary of British Architects 1600–1840* (3rd ed.), London: 1995; New Haven: 1997.

Connolly, S.J,. *Oxford Companion to Irish History,* OUP, Oxford: 1998.

Cox, G.(ed.), *Acton's Music Reviews of Dublin's Musical Life 1955–1985,* Bray: 1996.

Craig, Maurice James, *Dublin, 1660–1860,* Dublin: 1980.

de Courcy, Catherine, *The Foundation of the National Gallery of Ireland,* Dublin: 1985

Dixon, Roger and Muthesius, Stefan, *Victorian Architecture with a short dictionary of architects,* London: 1978.

Doyle, D., 'A Conference Centre in Iveagh Gardens' UCD, B. Arch. Thesis, 1987. Unpublished.

Fleischmann, Aloys (ed.), *Music in Ireland,* Cork: 1951.

Flood, W.H. Grattan, *A History of Irish Music,* Dublin: 1905

Gaine, S., 'Music in the Garden — School of Music, Iveagh Gardens', UCD, B.Arch. Thesis, 1989. Unpublished.

Gilbert, Sir John Thomas, *Calendar of Ancient Records of Dublin in the possession of the Municipal Corporation of that City,* vols. II, IV, Dublin: 1894.

Georgian Society Records of Eighteenth-century Domestic Architecture and Decoration in Dublin, The, Introduction by Desmond Guinness, vols. I, VI, Shannon: 1969.

Gerard, F., *Picturesque Dublin Old and New,* London: 1898.

Gilbert, J.T., Sir, *A History of the City of Dublin,* Dublin (3 vols.): 1861; Shannon: 1972.

Gordon Bowe, Nicola, and Skeoch Cumming, Elizabeth, *The Arts & Crafts Movements in Dublin & Edinburgh 1885–1925,* Dublin: 1998.

Guinness, M., *The Guinness Spirit,* London: 1999.

Hogan, Ita Margaret, *Anglo-Irish Music 1780–1830,* Cork: 1966.

Houghton, Walter E., *The Victorian Frame of Mind 1830–1870,* London: 1968.

Kane, Eileen, 'John Henry Newman's Catholic University Church in Dublin' in *Studies,* Vol. LXV1. No. 262 Summer/Autumn, 1977. pp. 105–120.

Keane, Maureen, *Isabel: Lady Aberdeen in Ireland,* Newtownards, Co. Down: 1999.

Kennedy, Tom, (ed.), *Victorian Dublin,* Dublin: 1980.

Kift, Dagmar, *The Victorian Music Hall — Culture, class and conflict,* Cambridge: 1987.

Lewis, Richard, *The Dublin Guide or A Description of the City of Dublin,* Dublin: 1787.

Lewis, S., *A History and Topography of Dublin City and County (1837),* Dublin: 1980.

Lohan, R., *Guide to the Archives of the Office of Public Works,* Dublin: 1994.

Loeber, Rolf, *A Biographical Dictionary of Architects in Ireland, 1600–1720,* London, 1981.

Lyons, F.S.L., *Ireland Since the Famine,* London: 1973

McCartney, Donal, *The National University of Ireland and Éamon de Valera,* Dublin: 1983.

McCartney, Donal, *UCD: A National Idea, The History of University College,* Dublin: 1999.

M'Cready, C.T., *Dublin Street Names, Dated and Explained,* Blackrock, Co. Dublin: 1975.

McCullen, John and Mary Davies 'A Victorian Masterpiece', *Irish Garden,* Vol. 4, No. 5. Sept/Oct 1995, pp 28–31.

McDermot, M.J., *Dublin Architectural Development,* Edited and Illustrated by A. Brioscu, Dublin: 1988.

MacDonnell, Hercules, *A Book of Dates, Operatic, Dramatic and Musical,* privately printed, Dublin: 1878.

McParland, Edward, 'A note on George II and St Stephen's Green' in *Eighteenth-Century Ireland. Inis an dá chultúr* edited by Andrew Carpenter. Vol. 11; Dublin: 1987. pp. 187–195.

Mallins, E. and Bowe, P., *Irish Gardens and Demesnes from 1830,* London: 1980.

Martin, F.X. (ed.), *The Easter Rising 1916, and University College, Dublin,* Dublin: 1966.

Meenan, F.O.C., *Cecilia St: The Catholic University School of Medicine 1855–1931,* Dublin: 1987. *National Student, The* 1910–1921; new series 1923; 1930–35; continued irregularly as *National Student/Comhthrom Feinne* 1935–52; then as *National Student* 1952-53.

National University of Ireland Handbook 1908–1932, NUI, Dublin: 1932.

O'Brien, Flann, *At Swim-Two-Birds,* London, New York: 1939. London: 1967.

Ó Broin, Léon, *The Chief Secretary: Augustine Birrell in Ireland,* London: 1969.

Ó Cléirigh, Nellie 'Dublin International Exhibition, 1865' (Read to The Old Dublin Society, 16 March 1994). Vol. XL V11, No. 2. Autumn 1994. pp. 169–182.

O'Connor, Anne, and Parkes, Susan, *Gladly Learn and Gladly Teach: A History of Alexandra College and School,* Dublin 1866–1966, Dublin: 1983.

O'Connor, C. and O'Regan, J. (eds.), *Public Works: The Architecture of the Office of Public Works 1831–1987*, Architectural Association of Ireland, Dublin: c.1987.

O'Kelly, Pat, *The National Symphony Orchestra of Ireland 1948–1998 — A Selected History*, Dublin: 1998.

Ó Maitiú, Séamas, and O'Reilly, Barry, *Ballyknockan, A Wicklow Stonecutters' Village*, Dublin: 1997.

Parkinson, Henry, and Peter Lund Simmonds, *The Illustrated Record and Descriptive Catalogue of the Dublin International Exhibition of 1865*, London: 1866.

Pearsall, Ronald, *Victorian Popular Music*, Newton Abbott: 1973.

Peter, Ada, *Sketches of Old Dublin*, Dublin: 1907.

Peters, Tom F., *Building the Nineteenth Century*, Cambridge, Mass., and London: 1996.

Pine, Richard and Acton, Charles (eds.), *To Talent Alone — The Royal Irish Academy of Music 1848–1998*, Dublin: 1998.

Reynolds, M., 'The Work of Alfred Gresham Jones', Thesis, School of Architecture, UCD, 1996. Unpublished.

Richardson, Ruth and Thorne, Robert, *The Builder: Illustrations Index, 1843–1883*, London: 1994.

Sacerdos [Finlay SJ, Peter], 'Mr Birrell's University Bill', in *New Ireland Review*, (June 1908), 210–20.

Scholes, Percy, *The Oxford Companion to Music*, London. (Many editions).

Sheaff, Nicholas, *Iveagh House: An Historical Description*, Department of Foreign Affairs, Dublin: 1978.

Sheehy, J., *The Rediscovery of Ireland's Past: The Celtic Revival, 1830–1930*, London, 1980.

Sproule, John, (ed.), *The Irish Industrial Exhibition of 1853, A detailed catalogue of its Contents etc.*, Dublin, London: 1854.

Stewart, Ann M., *Royal Hibernian Academy of Arts: Index of exhibitors 1826–1979*, Dublin, 1986.

Stockwell, La Tourette, *Dublin Theatre and Theatre Customs 1637–1829*, Kingsport, Tennessee: 1966.

Sullivan, T.D., *A Guide to Dublin: its history, antiquities and objects of public interest*, Dublin: 1888.

Tierney, Michael (ed.), *Struggle with Fortune: a miscellany for the centenary of the Catholic University of Ireland 1854–1954*, Dublin: 1954.

Tierney, Michael, 'The New College, 1908–1954', in *Struggle with Fortune*, op. cit. pp. 230–37.

Turpin, John, *A School of Art in Dublin since the Eighteenth Century: A History of the National College of Art and Design*, Dublin, 1995.

University College, Dublin : The past, the present, the plans, Dublin: 1976 (no author or ed. given); Dublin, 1959.

Vale, Mary, 'The Origins of the Catholic University of Ireland', in *Irish Ecclesiastical Record*, lxxxii (1954), 1–16; 152–64; 226–41.

Wakeman, W.F., *Old Dublin*, Second series, 1887.

Walsh, Tom, *Opera in Old Dublin 1819–1838*, Wexford: 1952.

Warburton, J., Whitelaw, the Rev. J., and R. Walsh, the Rev., *History of the City of Dublin*, London: 1818.

Williams, Jeremy, *A Companion Guide to Architecture in Ireland, 1837–1921*, Foreword, Mark Girouard, Blackrock, Co. Dublin: 1994.

Williams, Raymond, *Culture and Society 1780–1950*, London: 1958.

Woodham-Smith, Cecil, *Queen Victoria — Her life and times, vol. 1, 1819–1861*, London: 1972.

Archival Sources

Battersea Library, Central Library, Battersea, London SW11.

British Architectural Library. Royal Institute of British Architects, 66 Portland Place, London W1N 4AD.

Board of Works (Files of John F. Kennedy Memorial Hall; Files of the National Concert Hall)

Crampton Archive (G. & T. Crampton Ltd, Simmonscourt Rd, Dublin 4).

Gilbert Library (Records of the Dublin Historical Society; *Freeman's Journal* files; *The Irish Times* files)

Irish Architectural Archive.

Iveagh Papers (Farmleigh, Chapelizod, Dublin). Papers relating to: Arthur Guinness; Sir Benjamin Lee Guinness; Sir Arthur Edward Guinness, Baron Ardilaun; Edward Cecil Guinness, 1st Earl of Iveagh; Rupert Edward Cecil Lee Guinness, 2nd Lord Iveagh.

The Library of the Institution of Civil Engineers, 1 Great George Street, Westminster, London SW1P 3AA.

National Archives, Dublin. (Including: Files of the Department of the Taoiseach (Concert Hall & State Opera House); Files of the Department of Finance (Concert Hall)

National Library of Ireland.

NUI Archives.

Royal Dublin Society Library.

RIAM Library (Minutes of the Dublin Orchestral Society)

Trinity College Library, Dublin.

UCD, Archives Department, Main Library, Special Collections, Buildings Department.

Newspapers and Periodicals

Art Journal (nineteenth century)

Building News and Engineering Journal

Capuchin Annual

Cork Examiner

Dublin Historical Record

Dublin Opinion

Dublin University Magazine

The Engineer

Father Mathew Record

Freeman's Journal

The Illustrated London News

Irish Architect: The bulletin of the Royal Institute of Architects in Ireland

The Irish Builder (formerly *The Dublin Builder*)

The Irish Builder and Engineer

Irish Independent

The Irish Times

Journal of the Proceedings of the Arts and Crafts Society of Ireland

Journal of the Royal Institute of British Architects, London

The London Builder

Royal Dublin Society Proceedings (from 1740 onwards)

Sunday Tribune

Official Government Publications

Dáil Éireann Debates.

Irish Universities Act, 1908, Dublin Commission, University College, Dublin.

Royal Commission on University Education in Ireland, First Report (1901); Final Report; and Appendix to the Final Report (1903).

Seanad Éireann Debates.

University College, Dublin Act, 1960.

Works of Reference

Annals of the Theatre Royal Dublin.

Dictionary of National Biography, London: 1908.

Dublin Builder.

Dublin Directory.

Grove Dictionary of Music and Musicians, The, London: 1925.

Thom's Directories.

Acknowledgements

The National Concert Hall and the authors are most grateful to the following who have supported and contributed to this publication: Michael O'Doherty, Principal Project Architect; Allen Smith, Site Architect; Angela Rolfe, Senior Architect; and in particular to Caroline Pegum, OPW, for her report on the NCH and the Iveagh Gardens. Also Margaret Gormley, David Griffin, Norma Jessop, Rena Lohan, Dr D. Craig, Dr Bill Simpson, David Crampton, Nóirín Moynihan, the Dowager Marchioness of Normanby, Mary Lynch, Viscount Boyd of Merton, Brendan O'Donoghue, Dónal Ó Luanaigh, the Countess of Iveagh, the Earl of Iveagh, Ian Fox, Meredith Davis, Mary Kelleher, Charles and Vanessa Butler, Tom O'Conor, Bernadette Chambers, Michael Chrimes, Dr Jane Oldfield, Dr M. Kennedy, Mark Hely-Hutchinson, Ken Hannigan, Catriona Crowe, Ian Roberts, Gráinne MacLochlainn, R. Nulty, F. Packenham-Walsh, Dr Gerard Long, Dr Maurice Craig.

The authors also wish to acknowledge the assistance of Air Consult International, Lindsay Armstrong, Paddy Brennan, Lewis Clohessy, Veronica Dunne, Dermot Egan, Philip Gavin, Gerard Gillen, Anthony Hughes, Síle Larchet-Cuthbert, Máirtín McCullough, Gerry Moriarty, Frank Murphy, Eimear Ó Broin, Annroaí Ó Beolláin, the staff at the Board of Works, Fred O'Donovan, Angela Roche, Richie Ryan, Betty Searson, Philip Shields, Richard Stokes and Annemarie Stynes.

The authors would also like to thank the staff of the institutions who have been so helpful when consulted in the course of this research: the Director and staff of the National Concert Hall, the Irish Architectural Archive, National Archives, National Library of Ireland, University College, Dublin, Trinity College Dublin Library, National Photographic Archive, National University of Ireland, Dublin City Archives, Royal Dublin Society, Máire Kennedy and the staff of the Gilbert Library, Battersea Public Library, London, the British Architectural Library, Royal Institute of British Architects, London, the Library of the Institution of Civil Engineers, London, Dublin Civic Museum, Department of Foreign Affairs Archives and the Royal Irish Academy of Music.

Finally, a special word of thanks to Wolfhound Press Publisher, Seamus Cashman, Editor Roberta Reeners and Illustrations Editor Peter Costello, together with the staff whose help, patience and sense of humour all contributed to making this publication possible.

Index